Shapeshifting Subjects

TRANSFORMATIONS: WOMANIST,
FEMINIST, AND INDIGENOUS STUDIES

Edited by AnaLouise Keating

*A list of books in the series appears
at the end of this book.*

Shapeshifting Subjects

Gloria Anzaldúa's Naguala and Border Arte

KELLI D. ZAYTOUN

UNIVERSITY OF
ILLINOIS PRESS
Urbana, Chicago, and Springfield

ISBN 9780252044434 (hardcover)
ISBN 9780252086519 (paperback)
ISBN 9780252053436 (ebook)

todos juntos—
luciérnagas
de la noche
soñando
el cosmos

we all together—
fireflies
in the night
dreaming up
the cosmos

nehhuantin tocepan—
tixoxotlameh
yohuatzinco
tictemiquih
in cemanahuactli

—Francisco X. Alarcón
"Flor y canto / Flower and Song / In xochitl in cuicatl"

Contents

Series Editor's Foreword   ix

Preface   xiii

Acknowledgments   xvii

INTRODUCTION: Toward a Radically
Relational Consciousness   1

CHAPTER ONE. La Naguala in Theory and Practice   9

CHAPTER TWO. "An Artist in the Sense of a Shaman":
Border Arte as Decolonial Practice   41

CHAPTER THREE. Connections with Arab American Feminism   65

CHAPTER FOUR. "Reaching Through the Wound to Connect":
Trauma and Healing as Shapeshifting   95

CONCLUSION: Toward New Potentials of Imagination   121

Notes   131

Works Cited   151

Subject Index   165

Gloria Anzaldúa Works Index   171

Series Editor's Foreword

ANALOUISE KEATING

What does transformation look like? What's the relationship among language, reading, writing, and progressive social-justice work? How can we use words, ideas, theories, and stories to develop inclusive, life-affirming communities? How can we enact transformation in our daily practices and other areas of our lives? The series Transformations: Womanist, Feminist, and Indigenous Studies has its origins in these and related questions. Grounded in the belief that radical, progressive change—on individual, collective, national, transnational, and planetary levels—is urgently needed and, in fact, possible (although typically not easy to achieve), this book series exists to offer new venues for transdisciplinary scholarship informed by women-of-colors theories and post-oppositional approaches to knowledge production and social change. The series Transformations invites authors to take risks (thematically, theoretically, methodologically, and/or stylistically) in their work—to build on while moving beyond disciplinary- or interdisciplinary-specific academic rules, and through these risks to invent new (transdisciplinary) perspectives, methods, and knowledge.

Books in this series foreground women-of-colors theorizing because these theories offer innovative, though too often overlooked, perspectives on transformation. Women-of-colors theories give us the intellectual grounding and visionary yet pragmatic tools to understand, challenge, and alter the existing frameworks and paradigms that structure (and constrain) our lives. These tools are riskier, more innovative and imaginative . . . rich with the potential to transform. Take, for example, post-oppositionality as an alternative approach to social-justice work (including progressive academic scholarship). Post-oppositionality invites us to think differently, to step beyond our conventional rules, and to learn from, build on, and liberate ourselves from the oppositionally based theories and practices we generally employ. I describe these alternatives as "post-oppositional" to underscore both their relationship to oppositional thought and their visionary invitation to move (at least) partially through it. Post-oppositionality enacts relational approaches to knowledge production, identity formation, and social change that borrow from but don't become trapped within oppositional thought and action. Post-oppositionality neither completely rejects nor entirely moves beyond oppositionality but, instead, enacts a complex dance with it, creating new perspectives as it does so. Although post-oppositionality can take many forms, these forms typically share several traits: belief in people's interconnectedness with all that exists, acceptance of paradox and contradiction, and the desire to be radically inclusive—to seek and create complex commonalities and broad-based alliances for social change.

Kelli D. Zaytoun's *Shapeshifting Subjects: Gloria Anzaldúa's Naguala and Border Arte* brilliantly illustrates these post-oppositional traits and others, as well. Indeed, the entire book is grounded in a radically relational approach. Look, for instance, at her insightful analysis of Anzaldúa's complicated relationship to Indigeneity. Zaytoun thoughtfully sorts through the various scholarly critiques; looks carefully at Anzaldúa's research, experience, and discussions on the topic; and offers a remarkable, powerful interpretation. She models a post-oppositional approach to scholarship that we can learn from and enact in our own work, thus fulfilling her aspiration to create "a theoretical project with practical aims." (*I love this connection between theory and practicality, this reminder that theorizing can be profoundly practical.*) I attribute Zaytoun's skillful post-oppositionality, at least in part, to her deep understanding of relationality and relational selfhood.

Zaytoun's profound understanding of relationality is evident throughout the book: in the connections she draws between Anzaldúa and Arab American women's writing; in her innovative approach to Anzaldúa's theories of la naguala and border arte; in her analysis and engagement with Nahua metaphysics, new materialist theory, and posthumanist thought; and in her interpretation of la naguala as "a practice of consciousness"—to mention only a few of the most striking examples.

Shapeshifting Subjects embodies the book series' aspirations in other ways, as well. Guided by some of Anzaldúa's most innovative, provocative work, *Shapeshifting Subjects* is transdisciplinary, boldly inclusive, risky, and accessible to read. I want to linger over this last item. (*Well, if space allowed I would linger over all of the points packed into that sentence.*) All too often, we confuse elite language with intellectual prowess and elevated thought, but by so doing we restrict ourselves to a narrow, exclusive audience. Zaytoun does not take this route to knowledge creation. She works carefully and intentionally to communicate effectively with a wide audience, aspiring to dissolve "disciplinary boundaries and the barriers between the academy and everyday life and community." With this aspiration and intentionality, Zaytoun (like Anzaldúa herself) bridges academic fields and contemporary worlds, offering new perspectives with important implications for us all.

Preface

I could imagine her feeling her wings growing wide,
her feathers soft and glimmering, her ears little
feather tufts, eyes golden yellow, she's perched
high in a tree. The sky behind her is indigo. She is
able to see far into the distant night. She listens to
the gentle breezes against her face.
—Gloria Anzaldúa

As a child I had a vivid, recurring dream in which I could fly at night. In that threshold between wakefulness and sleep, I would leave my body and float to the ceiling and drift around the house. Someone or something seemed to be keeping me afloat, and weightless and wide-eyed, I would glide, sometimes swoosh around from room to room. In my dreams and imagination at that early age, my experience of the world was much more vast and intimate than it is today. With vigor I stretched my arms to feel the sky; pumped my bike pedals till I soared; touched and talked to plants, bugs, and birds; and all the while felt either carried by, or one with, something with wings. As I grew older, I lost touch with those dreams and forms of play, but I remember the sensation to this day, a sensation that I, in the process of writing about the naguala, have come to identify as a shamanic journey, my participation in an experience and a realm beyond the concrete, yet so visceral that it serves as my first memory. When I first wrote about the dream, I had conjured the memory as I was reflecting on how I connected, in terms of "border" identities, with Gloria Anzaldúa. At the time I linked the unexpected image to a passage in *Borderlands / La Frontera: The New Mestiza* about reconciling a Christian upbringing with pagan interests,[1] but I didn't realize until now that I shared this with Anzaldúa, too: an encounter with—and as—la naguala, the "shapeshifter."

Perhaps part of why Anzaldúa's work first appealed to me—maybe to you, too—is because she reminds us that we can change shape, that we have a "dreaming body,"[2] one that, if we are paying attention, feels as real as flesh and bones. La naguala makes the senses more alive, delivers us to imaginal worlds and to each other, by way of the will or by chance. We inhabit those images and stories; we inhabit each other's feelings and the dynamic worlds around us; we become the owl, ocean, tree, maybe even the enemy, for a little while. Then we shift again, transformed. We share a story, a lesson, a song, a meal, a contribution to change, the only constant.[3] We offer or witness a performance, give ourselves over to the energy of the moment, feeling it move through the air, our bodies, animating the room, the space outdoors. La naguala is a creative process and practice, and "the creative process is an agency of transformation."[4]

My vision for this book is to provide an opportunity to think deeply and radically with Anzaldúa about relationships among subjectivity, imagination, and transformation. I want us to consider that Anzaldúa's use of metaphor, of story, is not to represent reality but to create it and to encourage us to do the same. I want us to consider that the imaginary is real and important because, at the very least, if we must make a distinction between them, the imaginary fashions the physical world,[5] the conditions in which we live, how others see us and how we see ourselves, how we are treated by and treat others and our environment. In a world of violence, pain, and oppression so powerful we learn to inflict it upon our very selves, how do we make pathways to authentic creative desires, to new and ever-shifting embodiments, to ways of becoming, relating, and working together for the good of all? Anzaldúa borrows the Indigenous concept of the shapeshifter and reworks it amidst her present cultural moment, painstakingly blending stories and rituals from her heritage with those of the times and places in which she lived her life. As I argue in the book, rather than reviving or romanticizing the past, Anzaldúa is acting as border artist, a concept she defines, to decolonize our very senses and orientation and our ideas of time, space, and the cosmos.

Like many people reading feminist literature in the 1990s, I came to know Anzaldúa by way of *Borderlands / La Frontera*. Studying psychology and literature in graduate school, I surprised myself, an Arab American who grew up in the Midwest United States, by my interest in Anzaldúa. I discovered, however, that although the "actual physical borderland" Anzaldúa described was unfamiliar to me, the psychic borderlands were not. Borderlands: "Wherever two or more cultures edge each other."[6] These borderlands felt like my own shifting sense of home. Meeting Anzaldúa and experiencing her lead a classroom and lecture (in the engaging, collaborative way that I found out later she did lots of things) left me committed to thinking more about and studying her writing. That commitment led me to many years of discovering and following the path of la naguala, the shapeshifter, in Anzaldúa's work.

This book sustains a focus on Anzaldúa and the published conversation on her oeuvre, especially that which engages with her Indigeneity. This discussion includes criticisms of her use of Aztec mythology; these important critiques pushed my thinking, and I am grateful for them. As the scholarship on Anzaldúa has continued to expand across disciplines as each year passes, I seek to bring many of these lines of thought together in this book. Although Anzaldúa's work is included and cited in most literary anthologies, and scholars have found useful and fleshed out her concepts in book-length projects, to my knowledge this is the second of only two single-authored monographs on her.[7] I dedicate this work to Anzaldúa and my Anzaldúa-inspired writing comadres, without whom this project would not exist. Shifting the shape of subjectivity and reality, we and (or as) our owl-eyed and slithering nagualas journey toward interconnection, creativity, hope, and loving transformation.

Acknowledgments

Books are projects that involve an enormous amount of commitment and sacrifice, not only from the author but also those around them. Yet, these projects lead to exciting discoveries, connections, growth, and joy, too. Thinking and writing about la naguala and experiencing shapeshifting in myself, my work with others, and the creation of this text have brought me many rewards and pleasures. Many people have contributed, in large and small ways, to my vision for this book and efforts to complete it.

I am especially indebted to AnaLouise Keating, who has encouraged my thinking and writing about Anzaldúa over many years and has generously shared with me her invaluable insight, feedback, and wisdom. Her efforts to make Anzaldúa's writing available to us, before and after Anzaldúa's death, and her own scholarship on Anzaldúa and beyond are truly a unique gift. AnaLouise's vision for this series served as a big part of the foundation from which I imagined this project, and I am thrilled the book has a home here. I am profoundly grateful to Mariana Ortega, whose support, advice, deep questions, and evaluation of my work pushed my thinking in important directions. Her scholarship and the Latina/x Feminist Philosophy Roundtable, which she founded, have been immense sources of inspiration for me. I am tremendously grateful for the opportunities to have interacted at the Roundtable with those who gave me feedback, in various ways and at various stages, on my work on Anzaldúa's naguala, including Linda Martín Alcoff, Theresa Delgadillo, PJ DiPietro, María Lugones, Jennifer McWeeny, Cynthia Paccacerqua, Laura E. Pérez, Andrea J. Pitts, Shireen Roshanravan, Elena Ruíz, Chela Sandoval, and Gabriela Veronelli. I thank Pedro, Jen, and María, especially, for offering substantial commentary and encouragement. No longer with us at this writing, María leaves a significant legacy, and her passing is a loss that is felt deeply by many, including me. I am also greatly appreciative of Suzanne Bost for her extensive assessment of my work and her backing. Her scholarship on Chicana feminist literature and posthumanism and on Anzaldúa's work, particularly, helped me to expand my theorizing. Norma Cantú has also given me support for which I am humbly grateful. Her scholarship and tireless work to ensure that Anzaldúa's legacy is kept alive are exceptional.

I appreciate the opportunities I've had to present with talented scholars who are also moved by Anzaldúa's work. Thank you to AnaLouise, Betsy Dahms, Gabrielle Hartley, Robyn Henderson-Espinoza, and Martina Koegeler-Abdi. I am also fortunate to have presented with Martina, Deniz Durmus, and Zeinab McHeimech in my early efforts to link Anzaldúa with Arab American feminism. I am grateful for their encouragement and inspired by their own pursuits. The Society for the Study of Gloria Anzaldúa also provided occasions for me to present in spaces with those who appreciate Anzaldúa and continue her legacy. I am thankful for the support of those I've met and interacted with there, especially Robert Gutierrez-Perez, Larissa Mercado-López, Sonia Saldivar-Hull, and, of course, Norma, SSGA's founder.

A research grant from the Wright State University College of Liberal Arts helped to fund my travel to the Nettie Lee Benson Latin American Collection at the University of Texas at Austin to study the Anzaldúa Papers. I am indebted to Christian Kelleher and the other excellent librarians past and present at the Benson and to the Anzaldúa Literary Trust. Of my many fortuitous experiences at the archives, spending a week with Amelia Montes sharing ideas and conversation was the most memorable and enriching. May our paths keep crossing.

To the students in my, so far, only Anzaldúa graduate seminar, who celebrated with me when I received this book contract and who far exceeded my expectations, thank you for engaging fully and fiercely in the course. Those students were Sarah Bostic, Dylan Colvin, Reilly Dixon, Winona Doubrava, Jillian Edwards, Erika Graver, MacKenzie Hamilton Emrick, Megan Helderbrand, Andrew Hurst, Tina Puntasecca, Greyson Sanders, Daniel Schack, Erin Sherrets, and Jaclyn Tusing. Thank you to Tina and Dylan, especially, for taking Anzaldúa from classroom to community. Tina, with her project on a collective "hacienda caras" as gentrification resistance in Chicago's Pilsen District, and Dylan, who organized an open-to-the-public, Anzaldúa-inspired interactive art show with East Dayton, Ohio, artist Andy "Feo" Espino, at his space, El Rincón Arts Studio, in which our class participated. Dylan and Tina, your unwavering commitment to activism and sense of ethics truly give me hope for how future generations of Anzaldúa scholars will "do work that matters" and make a difference to higher education and beyond. Of the many rewards I gained from the art show, Andy's designing of the cover art for this book was one for which I am forever grateful. The Dayton community is very fortunate to benefit from his talent and contributions as a border artist. Tina's continued friendship is another unexpected gift that grew during her time as a student at Wright State University from many conversations and writing together about Anzaldúa.

I am thankful for my brilliant colleagues at Wright State and friends in academies across the United States and beyond for helping me bring this book to fruition. Such help came in a variety of forms, from ideas offered in writing groups to insights gleaned in conversations and gestures of encouragement, in general. I have learned much from my colleagues and have appreciated their support immensely. Thank you to Jessica Penwell Barnett, Nicole Carter, Deborah Crusan, Heather Crystal, Chris DeWeese, Judith Ezekiel, Erin Flanagan, Geneva Gano, Nancy Garner, Ashley Hall, Kirsten Halling, Romena Holbert, Barbara Hopkins, Hope Jennings, Sharon Lynette Jones, Crystal Lake, Sally Lamping, Laura Luehrmann, Carol Loranger, Noeleen McIlvenna, Carol Mejia-LaPerle, Barry Milligan, Sirisha Naidu, Z Nicolazzo, Paulette Olson, Annette Oxindine, Juli Parker, Nimisha Patel, David Seitz, Alpana Sharma, Valerie Stoker, Andrew Strombeck, Marie Thompson, Cindy Vanzant, Amber Vlasnik, and Michele Welkner. Annette, especially, you were always there, my dear friend. Additionally, without my longtime mentors Marcia Baxter-Magolda, Lillie P. Howard, Mary Beth Pringle, and Anne Sisson-Runyan and their belief in my potential, this book would not have been possible. I am also grateful to Wright State University's chapter of the American Association of University Professors for tirelessly defending our faculty's rights and benefits.

The staff at the University of Illinois Press has been a pleasure to work with, particularly Jennifer Argo, Kevin Cunningham, Alison Syring Bassford, Ellie Hinton, Dustin Hubbart, and Dominique Moore. I owe a big thank you to freelancer Mary Lou Kowaleski for her patience and careful copyediting eye! I am grateful to Dawn Durante, now editor in chief of the University of Texas Press, who believed in my project and helped me secure my contract when she was an acquisitions editor at University of Illinois Press at the time I proposed the book. Judy Lyon Davis's superb job on the index is also much appreciated.

Lastly, I thank other friends and my family for their constant love and support. Sarah Amin, Karen Crist, and Jamie Sharp, our weekly gatherings in the time during which I wrote the bulk of this book sustained me. Jamie, I hold dear our friendship, your insights, and always sound assessment and advice. Thank you to "wise women" Catherine Queener and Pamela Wallace-Stroble for the decades-long, cherished friendship and feminist camaraderie. Susan Allen, Melissa Benton, and Rebecca Kuder, your friendship and support of my writing have meant the world to me. Ellen Adkins, your wisdom and guidance, as always, moved me to all the best places. My dear family, David J. Byrne and Chris, Collin, and Mike Goebel, thank you for reminding me to be in the moment and not lose sight of what matters most. My greatest gift in life has been watching my three children, David, Chris, and Collin, lean into creativity and sow the seeds of their imaginations. Thank you to Ann Goebel, Lou Zaytoun, Katherine Cox, and last but never least, my beloved sister, Jennifer Zaytoun. Jen, you have taught me that the lines between self and other and dependence and independence are always, necessarily, and joyfully blurred. You, above all, are why I do this work.

Shapeshifting Subjects

Toward a Radically Relational Consciousness

In addition to community building we can transform
our world by imagining it differently, dreaming it
passionately via all our senses, and willing it into
creation. As we think inspiring, positive, life-generating
thoughts and embody these thoughts in every act we
perform, we can gradually change the mood of our
days, the habits of years, and the beliefs of a lifetime.

—Gloria Anzaldúa

Shapeshifting Subjects: Gloria Anzaldúa's Naguala and Border Arte is a
transdisciplinary, women and queer of colors, feminist-focused study that
proposes a radically inclusive and expansive approach to selfhood, creativity, knowledge production, healing, and coalitional activism informed by
the work of Gloria Anzaldúa.[1] A theoretical project with practical aims,
Shapeshifting is, above all, invested in exploring new theories and practices of relational selfhoods that are simultaneously personally rich and
socially accountable. The book finds in Gloria Anzaldúa's shapeshifter, or
naguala, a term she draws from nagualismo,[2] a groundbreaking theory of
subjectivity that describes in detail a relationship between "inner work"
and "public acts" that can serve to strengthen discussions of the role of individual persons and their creative acts in social and transformative justice
work ("now let us shift"). Anzaldúa's focus on the untapped potential of a
complex and radically relational consciousness provides a way to consider
the metaphysics of selfhood, in general, without sacrificing the specific
contexts or social realities within which individual selves are created.

Deeply embodied, rooted in its surroundings, and invested in the
potential of the imagination, Anzaldúa's la naguala is a practice of consciousness that leads a person to transform self and subjectivity[3]; part of
the practice includes a sense of merger with others and one's surround-

ings without being appropriated by them. This crucial characteristic of la naguala offers scholars and activists alike a way of thinking through how the self can be both one and multiple. This book, in part, seeks to add to recent philosophical discussions of self that complicate the argument that the self is either singular or plural and, instead, sees selfhood as both. Although scholars have turned to Anzaldúa to make or support claims about selfhood, most have focused on Anzaldúa's concepts of borderland and mestiza consciousness, and, more recently, nepantla, mestizaje, la facultad, and nos/otras.[4] Shapeshifting's detailed emphasis on la naguala and Nahua metaphysics, specifically,[5] brings much-needed attention to an overlooked, cutting-edge contribution of her work to the study of subjectivity and is of interest to a number of fields and a topic that often brings them together; those fields include, for example, philosophy, psychology, sociology, literary studies, and social-justice, gender, queer, trans, decolonial, and Indigenous studies. The language and concepts in this book are meant to be accessible to a broad audience in hopes of breaking disciplinary boundaries and the barriers between the academy and everyday life and community.

Shapeshifting moves theorizing on subjectivity toward an understanding of selfhood that takes seriously an individual human's expansiveness, embeddedness, and agency in an ever-changing, radically relational existence. In the spirit of what AnaLouise Keating calls "threshold theorizing," which begins "with the presupposition that we are intimately, inextricably linked with all human and nonhuman existence," and by way of Anzaldúa's nagualan consciousness, Shapeshifting introduces an approach to selfhood and subjectivity that pushes the meaning of relationality in new directions, beyond not only Enlightenment worldviews but beyond contemporary theorizing as well, including the postmodern, feminist, phenomenological, and new materialist foundations appreciated and engaged in the text (Transformation Now! 11). Shapeshifting insists on a method of inquiry that prioritizes women and queer of colors critiques and Indigenous worldviews and seeks to create cross-discipline and genre conversations.[6] Indeed, Shapeshifting suggests that theorizing on selfhood and subjectivity is limited and inefficient in the academy to date precisely because of lack of attention to women and queer of colors critique and Indigenous thought and the integrating of academic fields and theoretical bases. Of the contemporary Western feminist theories taken up in the text, new materialisms, particularly posthumanism, are explored in most detail, given posthumanism's critique of Enlightenment-based humanism's anthropocentric bias and privileging of reason and transcendence over other forms of knowing and being, such as those associated with the body and among the human body, nonhuman life forms, and other matter. These aspects of posthumanism are a present in Anzaldúa's theorizing as well, but *Shapeshifting* points out important distinctions between posthumanism and Anzaldúan thought, emphasizing Anzaldúa's unique position as a theorist who does not rely on one philosophical, particularly Western philosophical, foundation. This exploration is the focus of chapter 1.

Shapeshifting takes seriously the possibilities of post-oppositional politics, one predicated on what Keating has termed "post-oppositional consciousness"—on individual and collective levels—and sees Anzaldúa's nagualan consciousness as a way into transformational justice work in the twenty-first century (*Transformation Now!*). As scholars like Keating and M. Jacqui Alexander argue, dependence on oppositional categories in forming individual and collective identities, although historically useful and necessary for resistance, is not enough to bring about the type of radical change needed to dismantle contemporary, systemic oppression.[7] To be clear, in my view, post-oppositionality is not against the notion of identity, even oppositional identities, when the social context calls for an oppositional perspective or stance as a temporary strategy, for instance, in articulating individual or collective experience as different from another. However, as Keating warns, acknowledging differences, even intersectional ones, without doing the hard work of forging interrelationships, "leads to restrictive understandings of personhood, narrow identity politics, and binary oppositional tactics" (*Transformation Now!* 37). A postoppositional consciousness does not react against but reacts *with* its context and understands identities, personhoods, and relationships *as always incomplete and permeable.* In highlighting Anzaldúa's work on naguala, this volume offers a way of thinking about postoppositional consciousness that transforms the limited understandings of subjects understood within oppositional frameworks. Chapter 3 addresses the possibilities of postoppositional consciousness most directly.

Lastly, *Shapeshifting* seeks to honor the work and potential of the artist, including writers, in relationship to their audiences. Following Anzaldúa, *Shapeshifting* argues that creative acts are transformative, including in metaphysical ways, and that Indigenous artistic rituals and practices can contribute to revealing, re-forming, and healing the wounds of coloniality, including those of internalized oppression. In other words, writing through the wound is decolonial work that is constantly evolving as readers engage with the writing, as the process reshapes selfhoods, agencies, and realities, outside coloniality's hold on not only aesthetics but also sensibilities.

Shapeshifting begins by tracing the development of Anzaldúa's theory of la naguala and explores it within the late twentieth- and early twenty-first centuries' trajectory of feminist thought, particularly theorizing on self and subjectivity. Because Anzaldúa engages substantially with shamanism and Nahua mythology and metaphysics, the issue of appropriation and primitivism is addressed with respect to Anzaldúa's own responses to her critics and also in her concept of "border arte." Border arte offers an intricate description of how border artists consciously work with past and present to generate new creative forms that avoid the pitfalls and violence of appropriation. Next, the text brings the concept of la naguala into conversation with Arab American feminist writers, building on Anzaldúa's interest in working across differences but within the unique specificities of experience and by exploring nagualan consciousness with relationship to practical strategies for coalition building. The final chapters explore woundings and trauma, including transgenerational trauma, in mobilizing subjectivity and artistic expression, and how la naguala initiates decolonial, healing responses to trauma. La nagualan consciousness is explored within its place in shamanic journeying, which suggests that art forms, including writing, and their audience enact a practice of transformation that functions outside modern epistemologies, aesthetics, and ontologies.

Chapter 1, "La Naguala in Theory and Practice," introduces readers to the shapeshifter trope in contemporary American fiction and Anzaldúa's use of the term in her published and unpublished works. The chapter offers an exploration of how Anzaldúa's theory of la naguala contributes to late twentieth- and early twenty-first centuries' feminist theorizing, particularly feminism's turn toward the embodied subject, and is considered in conversation with new materialisms, particularly posthumanism. Importantly, Anzaldúa's work on la naguala is considered within Indigenous feminism, philosophy, and ritual and its potential links to decolonial subjectivity. Although Anzaldúa's attention to shapeshifting is largely overlooked by scholars, this chapter demonstrates that la naguala inspired and played a major role in Anzaldúa's theorizing on subjectivity and the prevalent use of the language of "shifting" throughout her writing, particularly in one of her last published essays, "now let us shift . . . the path of conocimiento . . . inner work, public acts" (2002, 2015). Anzaldúa's naguala offers a notable vision of subjectivity in which subjects are strengthened in creative connection to other humans and nonhuman matter. However, given Anzaldúa's investment in her Indigenous ancestry and nagualismo, la naguala points her theorizing in the direction of understanding subjectivity as participating in what the Nahua refer to as "teotl," a self-generating life force or energy that is neither material nor spiritual in a Western sense but its own substance of which everything in the cosmos is a part. The posthumanist dimensions of Anzaldúa's work are investigated in the chapter as they connect to her radical skepticism of Western ontology, rational epistemology, and the Enlightenment-based humanist subject. In Anzaldúa's theory of naguala, she expands and simultaneously decenters human experience, rendering the subject contextualized and pervious, yet undiminished. This argument is placed in conversation with analysis of Anzaldúa's shift from a focus on mestiza to nepantleran consciousness, noting the critical role of the naguala in conocimiento, meaning knowledge, or, as Anzaldúa uses the term, a transformative journey toward a complex and expansive subjectivity. Although Anzaldúa's naguala shapeshifter can be read as a trope for what is required of individuals and collectives in their quest for a more just world, this chapter complicates the idea of la naguala as a trope and positions it as a creative, decolonial practice that participates in the refashioning of subjectivity, personally and collectivity.

Chapter 2, "'An Artist in the Sense of a Shaman': Border Arte as Decolonial Practice," responds to the major critiques of Anzaldúa's work as too metaphorical, utopian, essentialist, and primitivist, as well as dehistoricizing and obscuring a diversity of contemporary Indigenous peoples on both sides of the US-Mexican border. These concerns relate to Anzaldúa's claims to Indigenous heritage and her use of Mesoamerican mythology. This chapter considers Anzaldúa's replies to the critiques published in her lifetime as well as other scholars' responses and proposes that Anzaldúa's Indigeneity, informed by her mestizaje heritage and study of shamanism, contribute to her practice of what she calls "border arte," or the unique, creative expression of artists who straddle two or several cultural borders. Aware of their positionality in colonized spaces, border artists work not to preserve a past but to create new assemblages informed by their heritage but also the sources, materials, sociality, and politics of the artists' particular cultural moment. I argue that Anzaldúa's refashioning of Mesoamerican mythology and summoning of la naguala and nagualismo is a conscious, carefully considered, and successful personal and political decolonial move for Anzaldúa, not a naïve, nostalgic, nativist, or primitivist approach. Anzaldúa's writings and rituals were not representations of Indigenous experience but an art form that engages with her influences and audience and operates outside colonialist logic. I suggest that we read her work as the decolonial practice she intends it to be, a shamanic ritual of which la naguala plays a major role. Lastly, the chapter traces the seeds of Anzaldúa's early thinking about la naguala and its decolonizing potential in *Borderlands / La Frontera: The New Mestiza*. I also identify in the structures of *Borderlands / La Frontera* and Anzaldúa's posthumously published *Light in the Dark / Luz en lo Oscuro: Rewriting Identity, Spirituality, Reality* a parallel pattern of conocimiento and shapeshifting in the texts themselves, each beginning with chapters featuring events that mark arrebato, or rupture or fragmentation, and ending with chapters that reassemble hope, possibility, and reality. The middle chapters, too, correspond with the stages of conocimiento, featuring nepantla, Coatlicue, and Coyolxauhqui states, respectively.

Chapter 3, "Connections with Arab American Feminism," forges links between Anzaldúa's work and the work of Arab American feminists, who have historically been overlooked in mainstream US feminist scholarship and social-justice work. Bringing together writings by women inspired by two seemingly disparate cultures in America (Arab American and Chicana), this chapter explores the expression of shapeshifting, or nagualan consciousness, in the acts of writing and activism. My analysis is careful not to find sameness in experiences described by writers; instead, this chapter highlights patterns in writers' practices of self-identity and formation while honoring writers' specificities in their cultural and social contexts. This chapter analyzes how the contributors of the pioneering collection *Food for Our Grandmothers: Writings by Arab-American and Arab-Canadian Feminists*, edited by Joanna Kadi (Joe Kadi), as well as Evelyn Shakir, author of *Bint Arab: Arab and Arab American Women in the United States* and *Teaching Arabs, Writing Self: Memoirs of an Arab-American Woman*, and other contemporary writers and theorists describe experiences of identities and relationships that resonate with Anzaldúa's descriptions of nagualan consciousness. Positioned at not only multiple intersections of identity but also in identity locations that shift and are difficult to define, even temporally and spatially, Arab American women write of experiences that are rich with complexity and fluidity. Themes are discussed in connection with the features of la naguala as well as Keating's three lessons for the development of post-oppositional consciousness: making connections through differences, positing radical interrelatedness, and listening with raw openness. Highlighted in the chapter are examples of how critics have drawn from Arab American women writers in constructing theories and strategies for activism and coalition work.

Chapter 4, "'Reaching Through the Wound to Connect': Trauma and Healing as Shapeshifting," builds on the idea of the transgenerational, relational, shifting subject introduced in chapter 3 and explores how trauma, including "generation after" (Marianne Hirsch) and "susto pasado," or "past trauma" (Patrisia Gonzales), informs subject formation and how shamanic artistic expression initiates decolonial agency, transformation, and healing that is place and time specific. The chapter examines how, for Anzaldúa, the site of trauma, directly and indirectly connected to the colonial wound, is the place from which most of her writing projects begin, and la naguala shows up to facilitate recovery and transformation. I argue that the text itself, given its status in participation with teotl, is engaging with its readers in shapeshifting at the time of the writing and in the process of being read or witnessed. I situate this process in Walter Mignolo and Rolando Vazquez's understanding of "decolonial aestheSis," or the decolonizing of the senses and expression. Writing like Anzaldúa's is aware of the trauma of coloniality and enacts a practice outside of modern ways of knowing, expression, and being. The chapter considers a breadth of Anzaldúa's work, published and unpublished, as "writing from the wound" and a shamanic refashioning of the cosmos. La víbora, or the nagual snake or serpent, is discussed for its specific role in Anzaldúa's creative practice, the linking of personal and collective unconsciousness to consciousness. She refers to this practice as "flights of imagination." Underscored in this chapter is how the naguala serves as Anzaldúa's vehicle to "el cenote" (well), or the "unconscious reservoir of meaning" where shamanic images reside, the source of creativity, and the well from which transformation stems (55). Her "Flights of the Imagination," chapter 2 of *Light in the Dark / Luz en lo Oscuro*, adds to la naguala's role in the imaginal work that is critical to the Anzaldúan subject of experience, a subject that is multiplicitous and at the same time singular, integrated and individuated, ever shifting, and expansive.

The book concludes in "Toward New Potentials of Imagination" with a reflection on how imaginative endeavors determine realities, from violent to liberating. Eli Clare's work in *Brilliant Imperfection: Grappling with Cure* reveals the nuances in imagining and pursuing futures for a diversity of bodies and ecosystems. As humans engage with scientific, medical, environmental, and other technologies, they enact visions of transformation that need to carefully consider the most silenced and so-called imperfect among us. The work of adrienne maree brown with the science-fiction novels of Octavia Butler also gives a nod to the boundless potential of visionary fiction to shaping radically transformed realities. This section considers Clare's and brown's storytelling as a shapeshifting activity. These writers remind us that imagining liberating futures is very much reliant on the tools of the times and their ever-present connection to ideology. With respect to Anzaldúa, the chapter highlights Anzaldúa's aim to work with metaphors as a "poet-shaman."

I invite readers to imagine with me and this text possibilities for subjectivities that are always in relation and in motion, subjectivities that cultivate and honor difference and creative expression. As subjectivity is understood as constantly evolving and as including not only persons but also contexts beyond humans, our affiliative groups, also always shifting, can become wider and more diverse in resistance to oppressions in their multiple forms. Anzaldúa asks her readers to consider the naguala, the shapeshifter, as a process and practice of selfhood and agency, a self that seeks a full awareness of its ever-changing context and understands its inextricable link to it. The shapeshifter blurs lines between the material and the spiritual, self and other, and the imaginative and the concrete. Deeply aware of the impact of coloniality on individual lives, the planet, and the cosmos, la nagualan consciousness offers not only a metaphor for transformation but also a vehicle for it. The invitation is always open. Thank you, dear reader, for joining the journey.

CHAPTER ONE

La Naguala in Theory and Practice

Creativity is a liberation impulse, an activity that
transforms materials and energy.
—Gloria Anzaldúa

Can we think of ourselves in cosmologies that
affirm interconnection, communality, ambiguity?
I think of Gloria Anzaldúa as enacting and
expressing a cosmology for the new mestiza.
—María Lugones

This chapter explores the significance of la naguala/the shapeshifter across Gloria Anzaldúa's published and unpublished writings and places la naguala in conversation with contemporary feminist approaches to subjectivity. Inspired by a variety of influences but most notably her own Indigenous ancestry,[1] Anzaldúa's conception of la naguala, considered within feminism's move from late twentieth-century identity politics and poststructuralism toward today's new materialisms and decolonialism, offers a complex example of a radically relational subjectivity that resonates with yet departs from and complicates more recent theories of subjects and selfhood. Anzaldúa's la naguala as a theory and a practice presents an account of subjectivity that deconstructs the traditional Western dualisms of mind/body, matter/nonmatter, matter/spirit, and self/other. Importantly, as Anzaldúa engages with Indigenous philosophies and rituals, principally nagualismo, her theories attempt a decoloniality of subject formation.[2] Anzaldúa's use of Indigeneity is not without its critics, which chapter 2 discusses in detail; however, my analysis suggests that Anzaldúa's theories and artistic expressions, informed by postcolonial and feminist awareness and political purpose, avoid romanticizing or reinstating the past. By way of a specific transcultural practice of what she refers to as "border arte," Anzaldúa works to avoid the pitfalls of cultural appropriation and primitivism. An invoking of nagualan consciousness is a critical part of this process. Before examining the politics of Anzaldúa's borrowing from Indigenous culture and practice of border arte, this chapter explains her terms and theories, her influences, and how her work can enhance discussions among other scholars and activists with similar investments in social and environmental justice.

La naguala, the feminine form of "nagual" (also spelled nahual and na-hualli), is a Nahuatl concept associated with Pre-Classic Olmec–inspired depictions of shapeshifting humans or of animal guardians or companions or spirit guides. In the Nahuatl language, words containing the root "na" (such as Nahuatl itself) are associated with knowledge or creative power.[3] Anzaldúa was keen to each of these definitions, for in addition to using naguala in its more well-known shapeshifting human/animal expression, she employed the term more broadly to refer to a powerful intuitive sense that serves to enhance relationality, a "a creative dreamlike consciousness able to make broader associations and connections than waking consciousness" and a "hyperempathetic perception [that] fuses you with your surroundings" ("now let us shift" 577; "Putting Coyolxauhqui Together" 250).[4] Attention to the latter use of la naguala, particularly, complicates contemporary critical conversations that focus on borderland, mestiza, and nepantleran subjectivity in the context of identity politics and justice work. Although Anzaldúa's naguala shapeshifter can be read as a trope for transformation, I argue that naguala is more than a trope in the conventional sense; it is a designation for a literal capacity of subjectivity that, among other contributions, resists understandings of subjects rooted in Enlightenment-based humanisms.[5] More specifically, nagualan subjectivity is negotiated in contexts within which human interaction and rational epistemology are just a part. Contrary to the self-determined, self-sufficient humanist subject, Anzaldúan subjects are strengthened, not undone, in creative connection to humans and nonhuman matter.[6] La naguala is not merely a trope because, according to Anzaldúa, the transformation that naguala invokes extends purpose into the physical world by way of the imagination,[7] which she viewed as energy-producing and as "real" as matter. La naguala, situated both in and beyond the body, shifts the shape and the boundaries of the subject, beyond strictly intellectual, humanist frameworks.

The claim that naguala is more than a trope is situated in Anzaldúa's na-gualismo-informed beliefs with respect to conceptions of subjectivity and reality. In addition to investigating the sources that influenced Anzaldúa directly, those related to her upbringing as well as the academic and non-academic texts she read, this chapter examines Anzaldúa's understanding of naguala in light of academic sources on Mesoamerican metaphysics, including those published since her death in 2004. Exploring Anzaldúa's grounding in Indigenous ontology with theories of posthumanism and, more generally, new materialisms serves as the foundation from which the book engages throughout in critical conversations with scholars' recent work on Anzaldúa's theories of subjectivity. First is a brief overview of the character of the shapeshifter in Anzaldúa's work, followed by theoretical and critical considerations.

The Path of La Naguala in Anzaldúa's Work

Anzaldúa is one of countless storytellers and writers who continue to invoke the long-standing image of the shapeshifter in their work. Transcending limits of all types, shapeshifters today are employed to represent changes in identities, circumstances, life stages, and paths—transformation and flexibility, in general, as Kimberley McMahon-Coleman and Roslyn Weaver point out in their substantial study on the topic. The most popular contemporary American depictions of shapeshifters are of werewolves, a phenomenon likely connected to their prominence in Greek and Roman mythology. However, shapeshifters have a long presence in cultures across the globe, and many have influenced American popular literature from Japanese to Norse history and culture (6–7). McMahon-Coleman and Weaver also report that the appearance of shapeshifters in contemporary literature and film is on the rise; however, they found little critical work on the subject, especially when compared to the research on vampires and other monsters that, for the most part, maintain human-like consciousness and form whereas shapeshifters transgress them. As shapeshifters are often associated with Indigenous groups, McMahon-Coleman and Weaver recognize the postcolonial politics that show up in narratives like *The Vampire Diaries*, *Underworld*, and *Twilight*, where, with troubling implications, werewolves are dependent on and dominated by white vampires (104).[8] Scholarship on the *nagual* shaman in literature is especially inadequate and is "limited to discussion of one or two authors" (9). Why the rise in public interest in shapeshifters in fiction and film but lack of scholarly interest in the topic?

While the experience of shapeshifters as always-in-flux outcasts appears to resonate with many readers, perhaps the shapeshifter's seemingly distant relationship to the enlightened, rational human is responsible for its lack of exploration by academics. Like humans acutely aware of their lack of belonging any one place, shapeshifters are outsiders, "marked as different," beings that "cannot reconcile their multiple identities and are forced to inhabit life on the edges of society" (McMahon-Coleman and Weaver 184). Shapeshifters as popular figures, therefore, reflect the real-life experience of navigating the rigid expectations of the contemporary world while they appeal to our intrigue with animals and the supernatural.

Perhaps, in light of its posthumanist features that emphasize extreme human transformation and the deep links among humans, animals, and the spirit world, part of the shapeshifter's lack of *academic* attention is not surprising given the humanist roots of scholarly work. Maybe shapeshifters, as conduits to our sensorial, animalistic intuition and deportment, take us too far from humanity, even the dark side represented by vampires and monsters, for our rational consideration. Academics elevate our human potential for logical analysis and emotional restraint. However, shapeshifters remind us of the lack of reason and individual control that permeate human life, a reality that is experienced daily but not well explained by secular, rational approaches. Read with the Indigenous philosophy (discussed later in the chapter), though, shapeshifting can be understood as allowing for *more* subjective control when control is viewed not as an individual power *over* something but as a power *in conjunction with* the other people and contexts within which individuals participate.

Attending to the shapeshifter is long overdue and offers much potential for rethinking the boundaries of subjective experience. McMahon-Coleman and Weaver make the case: "As uniquely fluid characters, shapeshifters are deployed in myriad ways to explore contemporary society and how it affects us" and their place in literature has "becom[e] particularly relevant in times of social upheaval" (184). Anzaldúa's work on the naguala is, among many other things, a contribution to how the shapeshifter is summoned in order to call for a transformation in how we relate to each other and our environment in times of conflict and turmoil as subjects of a newly defined, relational humanity. An outline of her use of the concept follows.

Anzaldúa employs the term "la naguala" in several of her published writings, including the ones discussed in this chapter: "The New Mestiza Nation: A Multicultural Movement," "Putting Coyolxauhqui Together: A Creative Process," "now let us shift . . . the path of conocimiento . . . inner work, public acts," "Speaking Across the Divide," and *Light in the Dark / Luz en lo Oscuro: Rewriting Identity, Spirituality, Reality.* Although written in the order listed above, the first and last selections were published after her death; "Putting Coyolxauhqui Together" and "now let us shift" were published as book chapters in the final five years of Anzaldúa's life but were also a part of her dissertation, which was posthumously published as *Light in the Dark / Luz en lo Oscuro*. Nagual/naguala is also present in Anzaldúa's poetry and her unpublished papers, notes, and short fiction, notably in her unfinished and unpublished short stories "Lechuza," "My Nagual," "Vigil of the Lizard," and "Werejaguar." For the purposes of this chapter, my analysis is focused on her published essays, particularly "now let us shift," where her parting vision of transformational self-work, coalition-work, and social-justice activism is clearly outlined. However, the idea of shapeshifting fascinated Anzaldúa even in childhood and is mentioned in her unpublished writing notes as far back as the 1970s.

Although Anzaldúa's emphasis on la naguala in her publications appears in the last years of her life, published evidence for her interest in shapeshifting shows up years before that in her interviews with Linda Smuckler in 1982 and Christine Weiland in 1983, where she refers to shamanism and extending the body's physical limitations.[9] In the introduction to Weiland's interview, which is in the form of a conversation between Anzaldúa and AnaLouise Keating, Anzaldúa mentions her story "Puddles," in progress at the time,[10] which involves the character of la Prieta changing into a shapeshifting "lizard-woman" ("Within the Crossroads" 72). Whereas Anzaldúa's early publications, *Borderlands / La Frontera: The New Mestiza* (1987), in particular, are often read as being concerned with primarily the US-Mexican border and Chicana lesbians, Anzaldúa states she was also addressing broad borders and identities—the "psychological," "sexual," and "spiritual" borders that were "not particular to the Southwest" and the idea that identities are always "shifting and multiple" (*Borderlands / La Frontera*, preface). In the 1990s and beyond, the latter points became important to scholars seeking to address the problems posed by the identity politics of the late twentieth century, particularly, the idea of identity as a singular, representative, set point of reference. From *Borderlands / La Frontera* and her other works, scholars take up a number of Anzaldúa's concepts that help express the indeterminacy of identity: borderlands, mestiza consciousness, mestizaje, nepantla, queer, and nos/otras, to name a few. La naguala comes later, as Anzaldúa's definitions of identity and subjectivity become more expansive.

After *Borderlands / La Frontera*, Anzaldúa's work focuses on the challenge but necessity of what she called "alliance-coalition work," and the ways in which she describes herself and identities, in general, become more complex and inclusive ("Bridge, Drawbridge" 143). Keating helps make this point in her citation of a 2002 excerpt from Anzaldúa's journal: "Shortest bio GEA [Anzaldúa]: Feministvisionaryspiritualactivistpoet-philosopher fiction writer" (*Gloria Anzaldúa Reader* 3). The running together of labels here suggests a seamless fluidity, as if even these wide designations were not broad enough. Her work takes a turn later in her life in what Keating calls Anzaldúa's "desire to go beyond description and representation by using words, images, and theories which stimulate, create, and in other ways facilitate radical physical-psychic change in herself, her readers, and the various worlds in which we exist and to which we aspire" ("Editor's Introduction," xxiii). La naguala is an expression of the aforementioned desire, an image, theory, and practice of subjectivity. For Anzaldúa the naguala serves as a vehicle that deconstructs and decolonizes embodiment and being. More specifically, Anzaldúa takes up and develops the term "naguala" as a means for communicating her insistence on the fluidity of identity, the work of the imagination, and what Keating refers to as Anzaldúa's "metaphysics of interconnectedness," which become critical to her later writings ("Risking the Personal" 9).

Anzaldúa's initial public mentions of the term "nagual" appear in talks and interviews in the 1990s.[11] She uses "nagual" in 1992 in one of those talks, "The New Mestiza Nation," and then the term begins to appear more consistently in her work, including in one of her last writings, a 2003 e-mail interview with Inés Hernández-Ávila, published as "Speaking Across the Divide" shortly before her death.[12] Reading these two pieces together helps to reveal the development of her theorizing with the concept.

Later published in *The Gloria Anzaldúa Reader*, "The New Mestiza Nation" reflects Anzaldúa's early thinking about the nagual as a reference to "a person who is changing identity" (211). She says, "We shift around to do the work we have to do, to create the identities we need to live up to our potential" (211). Her claim "Identity is shape-shifting activity" foreshadows her focus on naguala and nepantla in the 2002 "now let us shift" (discussed further into the chapter) (211). In "Speaking Across the Divide," Anzaldúa uses the feminine version "naguala" and explains the naguala in another way, as assisting with creative activity, as "mysterious forces that guide" her "from the inner world" (293). This form of naguala, the "daimon" (meaning shapeshifter in this context), is described in much more detail in her 1999 "Putting Coyolxauhqui Together," which is the first time Anzaldúa's use of the term appears in print, twelve years after the publication of *Borderlands / La Frontera* ("Speaking" 293). This understanding of la naguala, fleshed out in "Putting Coyolxauhqui Together" and discussed in the interview with Hernández-Ávila, becomes important to Anzaldúa's final writings.

Besides "now let us shift," Anzaldúa's most extensive treatment of la naguala in her essays (prior to her posthumously published "Flights of the Imagination") is in "Putting Coyolxauhqui Together." In this substantial essay on the writing process, to which "now let us shift" was a "sister" piece, she refers to naguala as an "imaginal consciousness," "the dreaming body . . . that's emotionally complex, diverse, dense, deep, violent, and rich, one with a love of physicality and the ability to switch bodies and their expressive codes instantly" ("Putting Coyolxauhqui Together" 253, 250). Anzaldúa describes how she "invokes this [naguala] sentience" to assist her in becoming in an intentionally physical way the subject about which she writes (250): "You become an internal experience, a particular emotional state or mood; you give life to tumultuous feelings, to raging anger. You become the crashing waves, the lighthouse with its beacon" (250). For Anzaldúa, an image induces physiological shifts in the body, and producing images (the function of naguala), more specifically, embodying them, is a prerequisite to writing about them.[13] Later in her work, she extends the function of naguala to connecting with other people and surroundings, more generally, as a precondition for social-justice work.

In "now let us shift" Anzaldúa clarifies, for the first time, the position of la naguala in conocimiento or naguala as a specific practice of subjectivity in transformation, as the initiator of the inner work required for action in the outer world.[14] For Anzaldúa, conocimiento comes from "multileveled" attention to "your surroundings, bodily sensations and responses, intuitive takes, emotional reactions to other people and theirs to you, and most important, the images your imagination create" ("now let us shift" 542). Identifying conocimiento as a path to "counterknowledge," or "the unaccepted or illegitimate knowledges and ways of knowing used outside the inner circle of dominate ways," she suggests that conocimiento provides an alternative to oppressive, socially constructed ways of knowing and being. Additionally, conocimiento, aided by the image of the naguala, encourages a change in how experiences of subjectivity and identities are created, with more flexibility and perviousness, a change that will facilitate more harmony, personally and collectively, more potential for coalitional work across differences ("Quincentennial" 178).

In "now let us shift" Anzaldúa describes the seven nonlinear stages of a subject's journey back and forth between "inner work" and "public acts"; she offers a detailed look at a subject's struggle for a rich experience of selfhood while becoming more radically interconnected (540). The stages begin with "el arrebato," or an abrupt upheaval in one's former ways of knowing, a physical or emotional crisis that forces the consideration of change. Stage 2, "nepantla" is when a subject internally negotiates old ways with new ways of thinking. Stage 3, "Coatlicue" (or "Serpent Skirt," the Nahua earth goddess of life and death and mother of the gods) or stagnation, represents a resistance to change, until stage 4, a call to go out of stasis into stage 5, "Coyolxauhqui" (Nahua moon goddess),[15] where the subject begins remaking itself. Stage 6, "the blow up . . . a clash of realities," is a process of confrontation and conflict with others that ultimately facilitates deeper, radical connection. In the seventh and final stage of conocimiento, Anzaldúa suggests that subjects act from the position of what she calls "the knower," which has several functions. One of these functions, that of naguala, "arouses the awareness that beneath individual separateness lies a deeper interrelatedness," and this reveals the aspect of Anzaldúa's work that resonates with not only the Indigenous ontologies from which she draws but also the posthumanism and new materialisms (discussed in the next section) (569). A close reading of the function of la naguala in "now let us shift" ends the chapter, but first a range of theoretical implications related to the concept is brought into relief.

La Naguala: Theoretical Considerations in Academic Feminism

Because a major feature of my interpretation of la naguala is its resistance to Enlightenment-based humanisms, I engage most substantially in this chapter with posthumanism and new materialisms, theoretical approaches that are largely motivated by this feature, as well, or with those that operate outside of Western humanisms altogether, for example, Indigenous metaphysics. Before moving into those approaches, however, I recognize the significant work of Latina/x feminist phenomenology in exploring Anzaldúan thought and subjectivity.[16]

Latina/x Feminist Phenomenology

Numerous Latina/x feminist philosophers have employed Anzaldúa's theories in conjunction with Western and Mexican philosophies and postcolonial theory, most notably Linda Martín Alcoff, Mariana Alessandri, Natalie Cisneros, María Lugones, Mariana Ortega, Cynthia Paccacerqua, Andrea Pitts, and Ofelia Schutte, to name a few. These scholars have paved the way for Anzaldúa to be taken seriously in academic philosophy and have transformed feminist philosophy in significant ways by considering Anzaldúa as an important theorist.

Anzaldúa has been read alongside and has complicated Western philosophers, such as Martin Heidegger (Ortega), Friedrich Nietzsche (Cisneros and Schutte), and Soren Kierkegaard (Alessandri); postcolonial theorists, such as Walter Mignolo and Alfred Arteaga (Lugones); and Mexican philosophers, such as José Vasconcelos (Pitts). Ortega draws from Anzaldúa throughout her work, most recently Anzaldúa's theories of mestiza and nepantla in her account of multiplicitous selfhood that considers the lived experience of "being-between-worlds, being-in-worlds, and becoming-with" (*In-Between* 3). These are just a few examples of how Latina/x feminist philosophy, mostly grounded in phenomenology, incorporates Anzaldúa into discussions of subjectivity and selfhood. (I make reference throughout the book to some of their theories and the important critical conversations they have initiated.) Because Ortega works with Anzaldúa in substantial ways, including commentary on la naguala, more about her theorizing will close this section.

Within the last decade, some Latina/x scholars outside philosophy use an eclectic approach to highlight Anzaldúa's concept of spirituality, moving how we read her outside Western, humanist frameworks. For example, Theresa Delgadillo's *Spiritual Mestizaje* (2011) explores Chicana narratives that serve as examples of Anzaldúa's spiritual mestizaje put forth in *Borderlands / La Frontera*, a process that, as Delgadillo emphasizes, is about the development of one's relationship to the sacred, or "a recognition of worlds or realities beyond those immediately visible and respect for the sacred knowledge that these bring" (4). I agree with Delgadillo, who says that "to imagine spiritual mestizaje is in some ways to enact it," and I find in la naguala—developed after *Borderlands / La Frontera*—another similar but more specific type of spiritual praxis in Anzaldúa taking place (2). Laura E. Pérez brings attention to how Anzaldúa blends religions and spiritual practices and refers to Anzaldúa as a "spiritual teacher" whose work is notable in a time of "neocolonizing secularism that privatizes spirituality to cage it and denies spirituality or the scope of its nature" (142, 141). Pérez's powerful tribute to Anzaldúa highlights and elevates the often-overlooked spiritual and subsequent decolonial aspects of Anzaldúa's writing. Felicity Amaya Schaeffer follows Delgadillo's definition of spirituality, plus other features of Anzaldúa's theorizing to argue for "spirit matters," or "stored energy latent in all forms," bringing together new materialisms and Indigenous thought (1025). (I mention Schaeffer again later, as Schaeffer takes up the concept of naguala, and her reading is much in line with mine.) These scholars, who use a mix of sources outside Western philosophy as well as traditional Western theories, are opening up new directions for interpreting Anzaldúa. Returning to phenomenology, the chapter looks in more detail at Ortega's account of subjectivity and la naguala in Anzaldúa.

Working with Anzaldúa and the Heideggerian concept of Dasein and Lugones's "world-traveling," Ortega calls for an account of selfhood that is both multiple and singular, what she calls a "multiplicitous selfhood." Ortega says that the multiplicitous self is always in process, situated in present "material circumstances" but circumstances that simultaneously include "particular histories" and "multiple positionalities" (being in and being-between-worlds) ("Latina Feminism" 250). The multiplicitous self also operates in a "deep coalition" achieved in relating and communicating with others across differences, that is, "becoming-with" (*In-Between* 168). Her carefully crafted theory, explained in the language of Latina/x feminism, existentialism, phenomenology, critical race theory, and personal narrative in the vein of Anzaldúa, articulates an original, decolonial approach to selfhood and being. Ortega's account of self is groundbreaking in its bridging of tensions between Western and postcolonial approaches, such as those relating to the singularity versus plurality of self. Unlike many scholars', Ortega's explanations and analyses of Anzaldúa include not only *Borderlands / La Frontera* but some of Anzaldúa's later works as well.

Ortega understands Anzaldúa's complex self as an inner/separate yet expansive sense of being when she claims that Anzaldúa "appeals to a sense of oneness and totality of self while at the same time recognizing its plurality or multiplicity" (*In-Between* 43). She acknowledges that Anzaldúa referred to identity as "shape-shifting activity" and then concludes, "Shape-shifting of identities can be considered tactical or strategic" (*In-Between* 45). Earlier in the chapter Ortega also refers to la naguala/shapeshifting as a strategy, one associated with Anzaldúa's conception of la facultad, an intense sense of awareness of one's surroundings, a "survival tactic" she introduces in *Borderlands / La Frontera*: "This notion of la facultad becomes more complex in the account of the naguala as la nepantlera is capable of having this sense and awareness as she shifts from one perspective to the other" (37). I also see la naguala as deepening the complexity of la facultad and the shifting of perception but emphasize that naguala shifts the boundaries of subjectivity itself, including in bodily ways (discussed later in the chapter). In other words, I seek to complicate Ortega's idea of "becoming-with" by thinking about connection on metaphysical levels. Additionally, la naguala is connected not only to facultad but also to other activities and practices of selfhood, such as the work of the imagination in its contribution to creative acts like writing, as well as a deep sense of connectedness with not only other persons but also with objects and environmental forces, and a sense of transition into other states of experience (e.g., nepantla, dreaming, and even death).

One important detail to add to Ortega's discussion of naguala as a strategy is that naguala includes not only the "acute awareness" of facultad but also a sense of merger with someone or something else ("You become what you observe") *and* the capacity to undo that merger (*Borderlands / La Frontera* 60; "Putting Coyolxauhqui Together" 250). In other words, naguala allows for a movement from connection to isolation. Importantly, by way of naguala, the subject is not "hijacked" by their own emotions or the emotions of others ("now let us shift" 569). This capacity or practice of consciousness demonstrates how the subject, always in motion, experiences a sense of separateness and connectedness and, certainly, an experience of a consistent selfhood—a tie that binds, so to speak. Ortega argues that Anzaldúa's account of self "has a sense of being an 'I' existentially and spiritually, the possibility of being a whole, of healing and 'integration'—a self that remains multiple and one" (*In-Between* 46). I complicate Ortega's theory by suggesting that Anzaldúa's concept of la naguala can be read as not only a phenomenological strategy that supports a sense of singularity *and* multipleness of self but also, when understood within the Indigenous metaphysics from which she borrows the term, a creative expression of the self's animistic participation with the self-generation of the cosmos, what the Nahua people referred to as "teotl." I make the case that Anzaldúa's take on self, particularly la naguala, needs to be understood in terms of Nahua metaphysics in order to fully appreciate Anzaldúa's work and its potential to inform the social-justice movements in which she was invested.

In addition to Anzaldúa's late works themselves, posthumanism, new materialisms, and, ultimately, Nahua metaphysics help to explain, beyond the realm of phenomenology, the animistic foundations in the practice of nagualan subjectivity. An interest in radical interconnection between human and nonhuman agents links them all, but there are important differences. Posthumanism and new materialisms seek to destabilize, yet still work with, Western approaches to agency, relationality, and subjectivity. Posthumanism interrogates human supremacy and autonomy, a project related to the broader field of new materialisms that questions the passivity of matter and the metaphysics of agency. The Nahua philosophy discussed here is a subset of Indigenous Mexican studies that offers interpretations of the worldview and accompanying practices of the Nahua. A distinction between matter and nonmatter is not consistent with Nahua philosophy, which is described as being concerned with process rather than substance metaphysics.

Comparing the metaphysics of the Nahua and other Indigenous peoples, therefore, with Western theories like posthumanism and new materialisms is complicated given the radical differences between them in how reality is constituted; bringing them together, however, is critically important. Chinese-Métis scholar of Indigenous philosophy Sebastian De Line sums up a persistent concern of Indigenous academics in pointing to a "negligence concerning Indigenous contributions to scientific and philosophical knowledge [that] needs to be addressed within academic institutions in the Americas" (8). The appropriating of Indigenous concepts in Western theories and labeling them as "new" is of particular concern. Métis anthropologist Zoe Todd, for instance, in "An Indigenous Feminist's Take on the Ontological Turn: 'Ontology' Is Just Another Word for Colonialism," poignantly addresses how recent interest in the complex and inextricable relationships among the environment, humans, and cosmologies, in the Euro-Western academy in her field and beyond, is eliding the work of Indigenous scholars and teachers who have been discussing these concepts for decades. Such concepts are not only an integral part of many Indigenous philosophies but, as Todd points out, also important to the legal orders that are at the foundation of struggles for sovereignty by Indigenous peoples worldwide (18). Making reference to Todd's work, critical heritage–studies scholar Colin Sterling takes seriously the "appropriative dimensions of many posthumanist concepts," which, he points out, "seem to co-opt Indigenous knowledge systems in a dangerous extension of Euro-American exceptionalism" (1030). Said another way, Jerry Lee Rosiek, Jimmy Snyder, and Scott L. Pratt assert that scholars "risk becoming colonialist caricatures by reinscribing long-standing patterns of erasure of Indigenous peoples and thought when they disregard Indigenous studies literature on agent ontologies" (12). These and other critiques by Indigenous and postcolonial studies of the Western academy, and of posthumanism and new materialisms particularly, are considered in the following discussion.

Posthumanism

A few critical works have linked Anzaldúa with theories of posthumanism,[17] and some of these are unpublished, but such conversations have been useful in advancing a better appreciation for Anzaldúa's radical skepticism of Western ontology and the individuated subject of humanism, her often-overlooked interest in nagualismo, and her place in broader contemporary theoretical discussions. As Suzanne Bost states, "[m]ost fundamentally, for understanding the work of Anzaldúa, we need a worldview that is no longer centered around the human or those epistemologies that privilege human reason and human transcendence over the nonhuman world" ("Diabetes, Culture, and Food" 28). Broadly defined, posthumanism is critical of human exceptionalism, more specifically, the assumptions that place the human as autonomous from and superior to nature and other animals given the human's intellectual and speech capacities. Posthumanism asserts that human agency and intention, indeed, even the constitution of the human itself, are enmeshed in and dependent upon environmental systems.

Emerging in the late twentieth century in the humanities and expanding across the academy, posthumanism took up a notable presence in academic feminism with the publication of Donna J. Haraway's "Cyborg Manifesto," in which she argues that humans are a blend of organism and machine—the social, biological, and technological—resisting the dualism and essentialism associated with humanism.[18] Within the varied approaches, Anzaldúa's work connects with a posthumanism that is distinct from transhumanism, which, according to Carey Wolfe, is in a sense "an intensification of humanism" in its attempts to use technology to transcend embodiment and privilege human autonomy and immortality (xv). The posthumanism that parallels Anzaldúan thought does not repress its animality nor its embodiment and interdependence; posthumanism does not reject technology necessarily but asks that all forms of existence, not just human, be carefully respected when considering technology's uses and implications.

This first characteristic is displayed in Anzaldúa's work as a rejection of what Etienne Balibar has called the humanity/animality dichotomy, or the idea "that 'the human' is achieved by escaping or repressing not just its animal origins in nature, the biological, and the evolutionary, but more generally by transcending the bonds of materiality and embodiment altogether" (qtd. in Wolfe, xv). Reminding us of the "animal in you and your animal-companion, yourself and other," Anzaldúa places the naguala on both ends of the Western animal/human dichotomy ("Putting Coyolxauhqui Together" 249). In an interview with Smuckler, Anzaldúa states, "We are afraid of the parts of us . . . that are like animals. . . . We only know the consciousness part of ourselves because we don't want to think that there's this alien being in the middle of our psyche. For my whole life,

I have felt like there's this alien being inside myself" ("Turning Points" 40). Anzaldúa made a continuous effort not to lose sight of this part, the animality, the *alien*ated aspect of ourselves as human. Anzaldúa invokes the naguala, in part, as a reminder that the embodied, lived experience of the human is also animal, suggesting that the naguala, "animal-in-you," is, indeed, not just a metaphor.

Other characteristics of Anzaldúa's work, such as a subject's acute awareness of deep relationality and physical embodiment, coalesce with posthumanism and can be seen, for example, in her essay "Let Us Be the Healing of the Wound: The Coyolxauhqui Imperative—la Sombra y el Sueño" in *Light in the Dark / Luz en lo Oscuro*. This essay is a commentary on the September 11th terrorist attacks, a time during which Anzaldúa says she "couldn't detach from the victims and survivors and their pain," describing her reaction in intense corporeal images, as taking her breath away, wounding and "[a]rresting every vital organ" in her (9).[19] However, to Anzaldúa, defensiveness and retribution were not appropriate ways to respond to this complex tragedy. She says of the US government's "hasty handling" of the event, "Our actions have ripple effects on all people and the planet's environment" (10, 21). In the editor's introduction, Keating says that the essay expounds on Anzaldúa's "ethics of interconnectivity" and "can be read as Anzaldúa's invitation to move through and beyond trauma and rage, transforming it into social-justice work" (xxiii). Informed by this insight and others, the relationship between pain, trauma, including transgenerational trauma, and the mobilizing of a radically relational subjectivity is further explored in chapter 4. I mention it here to speak to the breadth and depth of possibility when thinking about posthumanist capacity and Anzaldúa's works together.

Keating brings Anzaldúa into conversation with posthumanism by describing what she sees as Anzaldúa's posthumanist mythos or animist-inflected ontology, which emphasizes Anzaldúa's "radical interconnectedness with the more-than-human world" ("Gloria Anzaldúa's Posthumanist Mythos" 2). Keating says that Anzaldúa's posthumanism has at least four layers: her view of self as having "porous boundaries"; her identifying of herself "with and *as* the nonhuman—the alien other"; her broad definition of "life" that "blur[s] the boundaries between human and nonhuman life"; and her animist-inflected ontology (5). Anzaldúa's use of the naguala is evidence of all four of these categories and one more related category: her view of consciousness as existing within *and* outside of the body. For Anzaldúa, the means to achieving expansive consciousness, and the radical interconnectedness emphasized by Keating, are la naguala: a practice of transforming the boundaries of subjectivity by way of the imagination. Such imagination and openness, what she identifies as prerequisites for coalition work, require a resistance to anthropocentrism, a rejection of the enclosed and elevated human subject.

Similarities can be seen between Anzaldúa's theories and the vitalist foundations of and ethics related to Rosi Braidotti's posthuman condition, which focuses on rethinking human experience as radically and inextricably linked with all living matter and scientific and technological advancements. Rereading Baruch Spinoza's vitalism through Gilles Deleuze and Pierre-Félix Guattari, Braidotti's monistic philosophy includes an account of *zoe*, a self-organizing, dynamic life force that persists within, outside, and beyond the human. Braidotti's take on the human's radically relational status gives way to an ethics that is more communal and ecological than Enlightenment-based humanism's individually oriented focus. Similar to Braidotti, Anzaldúa speaks of "the spark" that's "in everything," saying that some prefer to call it "God" and others "creative force" ("Within the Crossroads" 102). But Anzaldúa's approach relates, perhaps, even more closely with Jane Bennett's "vital materiality," which takes as its emphasis the agency of nonliving matter, or "thing power," and, borrowing from Deleuze and Guattari, "assemblages," or "ad hoc groupings of diverse elements, of vibrant materials . . . living, throbbing confederations that are able to function despite the persistent presence of energies that confound them from within" (24). The spark for Anzaldúa is found not only in living beings but also "in the tree, in the rock," and she goes on to say, "It's the same substance; it's universal" ("Within the Crossroads" 102). Her intense awareness of objects and nonhuman energy is clear across her writing, as in the essay about September 11th, when Anzaldúa seeks out "medicine" by watching ocean waves and imagining a distant storm and its effects, listening to what the environment might contribute to the vastly healing testimonio she seeks to create ("Let Us Be" 21).[20]

Importantly, however, Anzaldúa departs from Braidotti and Bennett in her emphasis on consciousness and spiritual practice; for her the spark *is* "consciousness" ("Within the Crossroads" 102). Braidotti is wary of the language of consciousness, which she discusses and critiques in its uses by humanists as transcendental, universal reason and logic, fueling the imperialism of nineteenth-century Germany, France, and Great Britain (15). Anzaldúa's understanding of consciousness, however, is informed by her practice of shamanism, or what she refers to in her late works as "chamanería," the Spanish equivalent of shamanism ("Flights of the Imagination" 223n2). She says, "To chamanas, consciousness refers to that part of our being called 'spirit'; rocks, rivers, and animals have consciousness," and "the universe is conscious," again emphasizing that the spark is a part of everything. Indeed, awareness is available "to those who pay attention," even by way of "ancestors inhabiting other world" ("Flights of the Imagination" 24). This belief is a significant guiding principle for Anzaldúa, whose inspirations for her storytelling and writing—her life's calling—come to her by way of la naguala from "el cenote," or an "underground well of memories and shamanic images" ("Flights of the Imagination" 24). Undeniably, her lifework is rooted in this shamanic spiritual practice. She says in her introduction to *Light in the Dark / Luz en lo Oscuro*:

> Shamanic imaginings happen while reading or writing a book. The controlled "flights" that reading and writing send us on are a kind of "ensueños" similar to the dream or fantasy process, resembling the magical flights of the journeying shamans. My image for ensueños is of la Llorona astride a wild horse taking flight. In one of her aspects she is pictured as a woman with a horse's head. I "appropriate" Mexican Indigenous cultural figures, such as Coyolxauhqui, symbols, and practices. I use imaginal figures (archetypes) of the inner world. I dwell on the imagination's role in journeying to "non-ordinary" realities, on the use of the imaginal in nagualismo and its connection to nature spirituality. This text is about acts of imaginative flights in reality and identity constructions and reconstructions. (6–7)

The above is a clear example of the importance of spiritual inspiration and practice to not only Anzaldúa's writing but also to her ways of knowing and being. To fully and responsibly understand Anzaldúa's ontology means crediting and appreciating the Mesoamerican shamanism that guided her. This is one of the major tasks of this book and one I begin to bring into relief in the next section. Although Anzaldúa's theorizing by way of Indigenous practice deviates from posthumanist thinkers like Braidotti and Bennett, it is still certainly aligned with them. Indeed, Anzaldúa's work can be seen as evidence for what Braidotti calls a rise in the postsecular condition that follows Enlightenment-based humanism, one that is motivated by "non-western sources of moral and intellectual inspiration" as much as Western ones (46). She notes, "Black and postcolonial theories have never been loudly secular," and identifies examples of writers, such as Patricia Hill Collins, Audre Lorde, Maria Mies, Adrienne Rich, Vandana Shiva, and Alice Walker, who recognize the significance of spiritual practices in women's struggles (33). Indigenous Mexican thinkers like Patrisia Gonzales and scholar of Mesoamerican women's intellectual traditions

Paloma Martinez-Cruz, who are discussed in this text, can be added to this list, as well. They are two of a growing number of scholars studying Indigenous Mexican worldviews and rituals with relationship to gender. Their work, like Anzaldúa's, is situated in calling out the violence and oppression of colonial experience and Enlightenment principles as it also calls for better understanding of the deep interconnections of humans to each other and the environment.

New Materialisms

An important aspect of the relationship between posthumanism and Anzaldúa's work is its place in a broader context of contemporary feminism's new materialist turn. By the end of the twentieth century, feminist theorists in addition to Haraway begin to take up a response to poststructuralism's linguistic/discursive approach to sex and gender differences, particularly what they describe as its lack of attention to materiality. This new, multidisciplinary "embodied and embedded brand of materialism," as Braidotti calls it, of which posthumanism is a part, attempts to move beyond the debate that places essentialism and constructionism in opposition to each other, a debate that has been troubling feminism for decades (Dolphijn and van der Tuin 21). This new materialism calls for a focus on the relationship between our corporeality and a broadly defined material world—taking on a new, expansive metaphysics of matter and materializing—and argues for the inextricability of nature/culture, human/ nonhuman, and other binaries, which produce not only epistemological and philosophical considerations but also ethical and ontological ones.[21] Some of the most prominent feminist scholars today, such as Sara Ahmed, Karen Barad, Jane Bennett, Braidotti, Claire Colebrook, Elizabeth Grosz, and Nancy Tuana, to name only a few, are engaging with new materialist ontologies. Keating reminds us that women of colors, including Anzaldúa, were creating "intensely embodied, materialist theory for decades" before this materialist turn ("Editor's Introduction" 217n72). However, Anzaldúa and other women of colors, including Indigenous scholars, are often underread and assumed to be focused on strictly identity politics and critiques of white privilege instead of sought after as sources whose work might provide a basis for new epistemologies and ontologies.

Additional critiques of some of the arguments of new materialisms come from Ahmed, who questions that feminism ever turned away from the material and biology, or was antibiological, and points to the rich feminist scholarship that has consistently engaged with biological data, such as Haraway's 1989 *Primate Visions* and Sarah Franklin's 2003 "Rethinking Nature-Culture: An Anthropology and the New Genetics" (Ahmed 35). Ahmed comments that the entry point of new materialism is not an engagement with historical materialism but, instead, is a critique of feminism for "reduc[ing] matter to culture," which she finds problematic. She suggests, implicating Barad's work (discussed in the next paragraph), "that the very claim that matter is missing can actually work to reify matter as if it could be an object that is absent or present," holding up the matter/culture binary it seeks to dissolve (33, 35). Ahmed also critiques scholars borrowing from and building upon Western thinkers like Darwin while not engaging with feminists on the topic. Other critiques are highlighted in editor Victoria Pitts Taylor's book *Mattering: Feminism, Science, and Materialism* (2016). Lisa H. Weasel, in her essay on opportunities in epigenetics, recognizes that not enough attention has been given to the material manifestations of intersectionality in new materialism and seeks to "reconfigure the relationship between the social and material in the analysis of power and oppression, transforming the relationship between social and material from one of binary opposition to one of mutual co-construction and interstitial enactment" (105). These questions of the Western foundations from which new materialism emerges and on which it relies and its lack of attention to historical materialism, including scholarship and testimonies by women of colors, are important considerations for scholars and activists as the field develops.

Although Anzaldúa is allied with new materialists in her emphasis on embodiment and critique of the self-enclosed subject of Enlightenment humanism, her grounding in Indigenous and women-of-colors' critiques, compared with the Western foundations of others associated with new materialisms (such as Elizabeth Grosz's reliance on Charles Darwin, Deleuze, and Henri Bergson, Braidotti's on Spinoza and Deleuze, and Claire Colebrook's on Karl Marx, G. W. F. Hegel, and Bergson), reveals important additions to and departures from them. Anzaldúa's theories, for example, do not reject or downplay the linguistic emphasis of poststructuralism as some materialisms do. While Karen Barad, in her notable critique of poststructuralism's lack of attention to the dynamism of the biological world, says, "Language has been granted too much power," in determining reality; Anzaldúa, in her focus on treating language as equal to matter and not representation, sees words and stories as playing an integral role in the composition and transformation of reality (*Meeting the Universe* 132, 133). Keating acknowledges and honors this perspective in what she calls

Anzaldúa's poet-shaman aesthetics, "a synergistic combination of artistry, healing, and transformation grounded in relational, indigenous-inflected worldviews" ("Speculative Realism" 51). In poet-shaman aesthetics, "words are not simply representational"; they "have causal force" ("Speculative Realism" 52). Keating points to Anzaldúa's sole reference to the "poet-shaman," the healer, or one who uses imagery, song, and words (creative ability, in general) to make change. Providing extensive textual evidence for Anzaldúa's sense of poet-shaman aesthetics, Keating demonstrates that in Anzaldúa's belief, "linguistic images, when internalized, can trigger the imagination, which then affects our embodied state—our physical *bodies*—at the cellular level" ("Speculative Realism" 53). In other words, imagining, writing, and reading are not only bodily acts to Anzaldúa but they are also bodily acts with vast transformative power.

Barad would not deny that language shapes reality; indeed, she sees its agential qualities and seeks to break down the distinction between cultural forces, such as language, and matter. However, as a theoretical physicist situated in Western science studies, Barad is responding to and working with Western metaphysical principles, unlike Anzaldúa and postcolonial and Indigenous writers who turn to metaphysics outside of and predating the Western world. Barad elaborates on Danish physicist Niels Bohr's quantum mechanics, revising theoretical and methodological approaches to phenomena using a framework she calls "agential realism." Her important contributions to new materialisms include the idea that agency is not a property of subjects but, instead, is the result of what she calls "intra-action," or the interdependent relations or "entanglement" among co-constitutive agents or what she calls "'things'-in-phenomena." Ahmed, though, finds Barad's starting assumption that "language [has] come to be more trustworthy than matter" to be problematic and reminds us that to poststructuralism, "words are far from trustworthy" ("Posthumanist Performativity" 801; Ahmed, "Some Preliminary Remarks" 34). Braidotti, too, takes on a critique of poststructuralism as part of her project, saying that although she has "great respect for deconstruction," she also has "impatience with the limitations of its linguistic frame of reference" and "prefer[s] to take a more materialist route to deal with the complexities of the posthuman" (30). Although Barad and Braidotti ultimately seek to resist binary distinctions and the existence of any "individually determinate entities with inherent properties," their treatment of language is focused on its representational usage and is therefore limited and skeptical rather than fully pursuant of possibilities (Barad, *Meeting* 137).

As mentioned earlier, unlike most scholars working with new materialisms, Anzaldúa is not focused on engaging with Western theories of philosophy, although she does draw from them (as Alessandri recently traced), or on moving from a linguistic turn to a new take on the constitution of matter. Her theorizing is best described as guided by an Indigenous or, more specifically, a Nahua metaphysics that says reality is neither material nor immaterial but ambiguously both, understood as teotl in the Nahuatl language, or "dynamic, vivifying, eternally self-generating and self-regenerating sacred power, force, or energy" (Maffie 12).[23] Gonzales refers to this "animating energy" or "Great Mystery" as "a communicative being" with which humans interact; it is "life and [that which] creates life [and] is honored, sacred, and powerful, giving order and manifesting throughout the universe" (xix). Other Indigenous groups of the Americas speak of a similar concept. Lakota scholar and activist Vine Deloria Jr. explains that the Sioux and other Native American tribes "experienced life in everything" and that in a "living universe . . . [n]ot only is everything related, but it also participates in the moral content of events" (49, 52). Such approaches to reality, therefore, see agency as multiplicitous, mutual, constantly shifting movements in a living universe. In Nahua worldview and in Anzaldúa's work, agency is always already pervasive and, in part, nonhuman; indeed, the line between human and nonhuman is blurred as well (all is a part of energy, or teotl), and Anzaldúa does not dwell on proving these points but, instead, demonstrates them in her writing.

Since nonhuman agency is frequently assumed in Indigenous ontologies, the focus of the scholarship is on process and principles rather than on justification of the idea. Rosiek, Snyder, and Pratt explain that in Indigenous-studies literature, there is "less need to argue for agent ontologies against more mechanistic ontologies that have characterized Western thought for centuries," and, instead, there is an emphasis on "working out specific performative and ethical implications of agent ontologies on their own terms" (6). Citing a wide range of Indigenous scholars—Snyder a member of the Indigenous Mexican and Native American Kickapoo Tribe himself—they clarify that one feature does seem to be consistent across variations of Indigenous worldviews: that agency is relational and specific to the moment; more precisely, they say that agency "emerges out of *particular circumstances* in such a way that its most salient features are missed if it is dealt with primarily as a general abstraction" (6, emphasis mine). Agency, therefore, always involves a radically inclusive context and process.

Reading Anzaldúa's writing with this take on agency in mind, the breadth of all involved, human and nonhuman, in the production of the work becomes clearer. For example, each chapter of *Light in Dark / Luz en lo Oscuro* begins with her situating herself in her surroundings and her awareness of them: the moon over her house, haunting images on the television screen, tree roots, foghorns, winds, grasses, and her sense of her body in deep, penetrable connection with these elements. Anzaldúa introduces her readers to what inspires her thinking in the moment of the writing or in the memory that prompts it. Anzaldúa's narrators of her fictional work as well, from Prieta to Andrea to LP, are steeped, sometimes for pages, in their immediate environment. For instance, LP in "Reading LP" is introduced to readers as she engages in an intense series of interactions with her surroundings, "thrashing" in water and drying herself in the sun. LP then "studies the landscape as she would a painting but she can't maintain the distance necessary to be merely an observer." LP is "embedded in it," and "[t]o look at it is to look at herself." As she ponders how she fell into a canal, the event that begins the story, she believes "[s]he could solve the mystery of what's just happened to her if only she could read the landscape, as if the land could give her a message through its feel, sounds, and smells" (251). Anzaldúa's "metaphysics of interconnectedness," as Keating calls it, can be linked to feminist new materialisms and agent ontologies, but its approach, given her processes, concepts, and ethics, is more accurately described as Indigenous.

Bringing Anzaldúa into conversation with not only Western-based feminist theorists but also Indigenous scholars and Native feminist theories not only broadens our understanding of her but also critically serves as a corrective to the marginalization of Indigenous scholars and their work. Highlighting feminist Indigenous thought on agent ontologies brings into relief how settler colonialism and its inseparable links with heteropatriarchy continue to damage and extinguish Indigenous peoples, their sexualities, practices, philosophies, and metaphysics. Pointing out the spiritual and sacred dimensions of Indigenous agent ontologies is a necessary but challenging part of this corrective work. Feminist Indigenous scholar and methodologies expert Linda Tuhiwai Smith explains that "concepts of spirituality" and "arguments of different indigenous peoples based on spiritual relationships" stand in stark contrast to and are hard to accept by Western knowledge and religious systems (78).[24] Anzaldúa's metaphysics of interconnectedness, including her unapologetic references to the spiritual, therefore, is not just personal; it is also a deeply resistant, political, and decolonial move.

North American Indigenous ontologies consistently include a spiritual dimension and take on power, which is viewed as "not [an] instrumental means of acting on other beings, but [as] emerg[ing] in relation with other beings like animals, rivers, places, and stories" (Rosiek, Snyder, and Pratt 12). Human connection to place, and agency generated in human-place interaction, are critical to many Indigenous ways of knowing and being. Mohawk and Anishinaabe scholar Vanessa Watts says the "animate nature of land" is "beyond being alive or acting," as it is "full of thought, desire, contemplation and will" (23). She describes what she calls "Place-Thought," the Indigenous understanding that thought, physical embodiment, and place are always intertwined. She explains, "Place-Thought is based upon the premise that land is alive and thinking and that humans and non-humans derive agency *through the extensions of these thoughts*" (21, my emphasis).[25] LP's experience mentioned earlier, for instance, can be read as a process of Place-Thought. Place speaks, inspires, educates, and humbles; place teaches us that we only survive by way of interdependence.

Native feminist theories connect the denial and silencing of this embedded way of knowing to oppression and eradication of Indigenous peoples. "Land is knowing and knowledge" and "not property," explain Indigenous feminist scholars Maile Arvin, Eve Tuck, and Angie Morrill. "Conceptualizations of land and place that rely upon latent notions of property are tangled in the ideologies of settler colonialism, dependent on constructions of land as extractable capital, the denial of Indigenous sovereignty, the myth of discovery, and the inevitability of the nation-state" (21). Similarly, to claim that land has agency, using theoretical grounding that doesn't include Indigenous worldviews, risks participating in the settler colonialism that continues to obscure and oppress Indigenous peoples. My discussion follows throughout the book of Anzaldúa's take on the relationships among land, persons, knowledge, and spirit and looks carefully at her use of Indigenous references and shamanism, in general, and its political implications.

This book seeks to bring attention to Anzaldúa's theorizing on agency that specifically names Indigenous practices, nagualismo/chamanería, as significant to how she understood subjectivity and relationality. Indigenous studies has burgeoned since Anzaldúa's death; I attempt to bring some of that scholarship, including critiques of Anzaldúa, into conversation with her work. Given the multiple ways in which Anzaldúa works with Mexican Indigenous mythology and ideas, I see much potential for other scholars to add to this effort. This book works most specifically with Nahua theories of subjectivity and agency. The chapter now turns to the Indigenous beliefs and principles that informed Anzaldúa's work.

La Naguala and Indigenous Metaphysics and Practice

Anzaldúa's major influence, from which she draws her concept of la nagual, is nagualismo, a Mesoamerican form of shamanism. Anzaldúa did not follow one particular author or forms of nagualismo; her influences and sources are academic and nonacademic and are multiple and varied. Anzaldúa respected and blended a variety of Western and Indigenous epistemologies and ontologies, as well. As the concept naguala itself suggests, flexibility and change were important to Anzaldúa. According to Keating, "[Anzaldúa] believed that Native philosophies offer crucial alternatives to conventional western thought," but also important is that she "did not seek to 'recover' 'authentic' ancient teachings and simply insert them into twenty-first-century life" ("Speculative Realism" 58). Keating refers to this practice of revisionist Mesoamerican mythmaking by Anzaldúa and other Chicanas as a "go[ing] 'back' to go forward—mixing discovery with invention, developing new (although sometimes presented as ancient) narratives in which prehistorical, historical, and contemporary issues of gender, culture, sex, nationality, class, and worldview converge" ("Mesoamerican Mythmaking" 530). The next chapter, which explores Anzaldúa's theory and practice of border arte, is congruent with this point made by Keating. The following is a consideration of Anzaldúa's revisionist use of nagualismo and the naguala in conjunction with the sources she read and cited and of new scholarship on the concept and the Indigenous philosophy from which the term "naguala" emerges.

Despite the very public controversies surrounding his work and legacy, Anzaldúa found inspiration in the writings of Carlos Castaneda, a Peruvian-born, University of California Los Angeles–trained anthropologist-turned-nagual, known for his popular series of books chronicling his encounters with an Indigenous Mexican Yaqui shaman named don Juan Matus. Whether or not Juan Matus and Castaneda's tales are "true" is still a controversy; regardless, his insights and lessons remain of interest to many. Anzaldúa was aware of Castaneda's critics. Even she refers to Castaneda's books as "novels (which he passed off as anthropological field notes)"; however, her frequent references to his writing demonstrate that she found in his explanations of concepts a means for describing her thinking on the naguala, particularly ("Flights of the Imagination" 225n13). Keating offers an account for why Anzaldúa continued to work with Castaneda's ideas even if his stories were fiction: Anzaldúa's "respect for the imagination's epistemological and ontological functions prevents her from entirely rejecting Castaneda's work (because imagination, according to Anzaldúa, gives us access to important truths—valid and useful information about reality)" ("Editor's Introduction" 218–219n80). In other words, Anzaldúa appreciated and perhaps found validity (her library included a number of sources on shamanism) in Castaneda's teachings, even if his interactions with Matus were drug-induced hallucinations, fictional stories, or both. To Anzaldúa the line between the real and the imagined was blurry. As she said in "Putting Coyolxauhqui Together," "[t]he unconscious and the physical body do not distinguish between what is really happening and what is imagined or envisioned—both are equally real" (250). Anzaldúa's perspective here is supported by contemporary interpretations of reality in Mesoamerican philosophy.

Two major features of Anzaldúa's naguala—imagination and trans-formation, or more broadly, creativity and movement—are in line with the foundational principles of Mesoamerican metaphysics. According to James Maffie's extensive review of the literature on and analysis of Aztec philosophy,[26] the Aztec/Nahua people hold to what Western philosophers call a "process metaphysics" in contrast to a substance metaphysics, mean-ing that "processes rather than perduring objects, entities, or substances are ontologically fundamental" (12). These processes are all a part of one thing—teotl, or a self-generating energy-in-motion—a tertium quid that is neither solely material nor immaterial but an "actualizing energy" (47). This energy is sacred as well, in immanence and in movement with the cosmos. For these reasons, Maffie says, the Aztecs were constitutional monists and pantheistic. Aztec constitutional monism, however, does not insist that reality is made up of one of two distinct kinds of substances (i.e., mind/matter, matter/spirit) like some monisms do. "Unlike materialism," says Maffie, referring to materialist monism, "it [Aztec constitutional mo-nism] does not claim that reality consists exclusively of matter and does not aim to reduce mind to matter" (47). Matter isn't reduced to mind, either. Importantly, what counts as "real" is movement and transformation, which is the nature of teotl. "Realness" as "becoming" is different from the Platonic or Aristotelian "be-ing" or "is-ness," which implies permanence. Even the sacred in Aztec metaphysics is dynamic.

Maffie goes on to identify three types of motion-change, the dynamics of reality, in teotl: *ollin* (oscillating, pulsating, like a beating heart or an earthquake), *malinalli* (twisting, whirling, spiraling, like in the digestion of food or the spinning of thread), and nepantla (weaving, intermixing, comingling, like in the mixing and shaking of things together, and sexual activity). Nepantla is most important, as it encompasses the other two;

it explains the self-generating aspects of teotl. A thorough explanation of each of these motions and how they are enacted in teotl is beyond the scope of this chapter. Nepantla will be discussed later, however, as Anzaldúa makes extensive reference to this concept, sometimes in conflict but sometimes consistent with Maffie's take on the idea. The focus here is the fundamental role of the artist and shamanic transformation, the nagual particularly, in the regenerative movement of teotl. Understanding Aztec metaphysics also helps us to grasp the very complicated question of the essence of nagual/shapeshifting.

The continuous regeneration and refashioning of the cosmos is characterized in Aztec metaphysics in two ways: artistic creation and shamanic shapeshifting (Maffie 38). For example, music and stories and using new and old materials to make fabrics and jewelry all characterize and participate in the regeneration of the cosmos; this point is often the subject of Nahual poetry and storytelling, including in the "song-poems" known as "xochitl in cuicatl" ("flower and song") of the Nahuas. In addition to being associated with transformation and the animal into which a shaman transforms, the concept of shamanic shapeshifting has been linked to the idea of "guise" or "double" or "mask," and researchers have noted the use of masks in shamanic traditions across Indigenous groups (Maffie 40). Historically, scholars have assumed that masking was used as a deception or disguise; however, Maffie argues, given the monistic nature of teotl, shamans do not assume a disguise when wearing a mask but become one with and animate the spirit of the animal depicted by the mask: "It is a mistake to think the jaguar [for example] does not really exist because it is merely illusion (or illusory). . . . So likewise it is a mistake to think that the cosmos does not really exist because it is merely illusion (or illusory). Both jaguar and cosmos are real; both exist" (41). All are of the same tertium quid, all participate equally in the creative movement of the ritual. Shamans use figures (like paper cutouts in more contemporary times), masks, and other artistic creations and include writings like Anzaldúa's to communicate their visions, including out-of-body ones, of the cosmos. The nagual, shapeshifting, therefore, is a creative process in which the shaman presents an expression of and becomes one with the self-generating force that is teotl.

In Anzaldúa's first few pages of notes on what became her essay "now let us shift," she pulls from Hans Peter Duerr's reference to Castaneda's *Tales of Power* as she works through her own definition of naguala ("'now let us shift,' writing notes"). She mentions don Juan's description of naguala to Castaneda: "The nagual is the part of us for which there is no description—no words, no names, no feelings, no knowledge" (Castaneda 125). In nagualismo, a critical distinction is made between the *tonal* and the *nagual*. Chroniclers of Mesoamerican cosmology have understood the tonal to refer to a lifelong animal-guardian spirit and the nagual, an animal into which shamans could transform;[27] however, undergirding these definitions are also larger ontological principles that, with respect to the Yaqui peoples, Castaneda attempts to explain to Western readers in his texts. The tonal refers to "everything we think the world is composed of" and the nagual to "the part of us which we do not deal with at all," or that which is beyond the socially imposed understanding of the limits of human experience and potential (Castaneda 126, 125).[28] The tonal *is* a guardian, albeit a "narrow-minded" one, more of a "guard," as Castaneda's character/spiritual guide Matus says, that leads one through the social world of rules and mores, reason, right and wrong (121). The nagual, on the other hand, is difficult to describe, because when we do so, we pull it into the tonal. However, according to nagualismo, the nagual accounts for creativity, or sabiduría mística, or mystical wisdom, a means for human expression of and expansion into the unknown (Bayardo).

Other chroniclers of Nahua thought found in Anzaldúa's library and citations, such as preeminent twentieth-century Mexican philosopher and historian Miguel León-Portilla, also describe the nahual as adviser and guide to understanding the unknown.[29] Nagualismo honors the realms of the unreasonable or impossible, that which is beyond human(ist) vision and other conventional senses, while nagualismo holds that humans can access the realm of the nagual, if proper attention is paid to how it surfaces: by way of dreams, hallucinations, physical sensations, illnesses, creative expression, and other conditions and practices of the body. In other words, in nagualismo, there are multiple forms of living in and knowing the world as humans, and not all can be seen or explained rationally, but all involve the body. Read in light of Maffie's more recent analysis, the realms of the tonal and nagual are metaphysically one.

In her interviews with Keating, Smuckler, and Weiland, Anzaldúa reveals the influence of the tonal/nagual concept in her reference to the body as having both visible/physical and invisible/energetic properties. She believed that awareness of the physical and energetic body as one entity occurs through various states like dreams, trances, and others. Although this idea has been discussed so far as a characteristic of the Indigenous traditions of interest to Anzaldúa, the line between what is and is not "real" varies more broadly across time periods, regions, and worldviews. Although contemporary Western thought dictates that dreams and hallucinations should be held suspect as forms of knowledge, literary critic Jacqueline Rose reminds us that "the boundaries between reality and hallucination are culturally specific and historically (as well as psychically) mobile" (407). In other words, what might seem to be imagination or even madness in some cultures, time periods, and personal experiences might be perceived as real and highly regarded in others, and the line between the real and the imaginary is socially constructed.

Anzaldúa's regard for the role of the imagination in lived experience, what she also calls "the work of the naguala," is demonstrated, for example, when she says, "Once fed blood, once fleshed, the bones of inert and abstract ideas become embodied, become mental and emotional realities living inside your skin" ("Putting Coyolxauhqui Together" 250). In her use of the image of naguala, Anzaldúa suggests that the experience of subjectivity on emotional, cognitive, spiritual, and physical levels expands beyond a logical realm yet maintains an embodied state. To Anzaldúa the image of naguala functioned to facilitate a person's metamorphosis into a fictional character, a deeper relationship, another feeling or mood, or some other state of being, even death. And to her, the image and its effects were as real as matter. With the above in mind, we can see why Anzaldúa took her writing so seriously; she understood its potential ability to inspire deep transformation. As Jane Caputi states, "Anzaldúa herself is a sort of shapeshifter.... Once you encounter her words and images you may never experience self/world/other in quite the same way again" (186). The idea that Anzaldúa "is a sort of shapeshifter" suggests that she considered her writing a shamanic practice. Betsy Dahms develops this idea by proposing that Anzaldúa, through her use of imagery and metaphor, engages in the "initiation," "quest," and "healing" practices of the shaman, practices that affect writer and reader alike ("Shamanic Urgency" 10). Ultimately, Dahms puts forth that the "poet narrator" of Anzaldúa's work invites the reader into self-work and healing, which precipitates collective healing and positive societal transformation ("Shamanic Urgency" 21). Perhaps, Anzaldúa, intentionally and creatively, set out to unleash la naguala, the shapeshifter, into our individual and collective imaginations as the vehicle through which the boundaries of selfhood and other—other selves, other beings, and contexts, in general—blur. This use of naguala becomes clearest in "now let us shift" (discussed later).

For Anzaldúa, la naguala is not only a metaphor or even a word or image saddled with the power to inspire a change in one's thoughts but is also an energetic process, a practice of consciousness that triggers a change in the body's "expressive codes" in order "to become what you observe" ("Putting Coyolxauhqui Together" 250). Although the type of "becoming" mentioned in the previous quote might be interpreted as simply an intensity of feeling of interconnectedness, a spiritual sense of oneness but not a concrete one, Anzaldúa insisted that the body and the spirit were tightly linked, or two different aspects of the same vital force ("Within the Crossroads" 99). Evidence suggests her worldview of reality, agency, and subjectivity is consistent with the Aztec metaphysics and concept of teotl put forth by Maffie. She says in "Geographies of Selves," "We are all strands of energy connected to each other in the web of existence. Our thoughts, feelings, experiences affect others via this energy web" (83). Instead of relating to the boundless potential of the cognitive, the imaginative, or the spiritual as out-of-body entities, Anzaldúa saw them as part of the body, which also had the potential to expand in ways yet unknown to humans. Regarding shapeshifting, particularly, Anzaldúa said that present-day humans do not have the skills to literally shift their bodies into another form of matter as we define it today, such as an animal or a tree, but she believed that our understanding of human potential was stifled by our lack of commitment to creative potential. Anzaldúa's case for shapeshifting today is that it occurs on the level of the imagination, and the imagination has vast power to transform our bodies and worlds.

By invoking the naguala, Anzaldúa honors the long tradition of nagualismo as an invaluable, embodied source of knowing and being in the world. She uses the image of the naguala to incite possibilities that resist and extend beyond Enlightenment-based humanism's conceptions of relationship, subjects, and identities. By taking up the image and concept of la naguala in her discussion of self-transformation, Anzaldúa calls for a way of thinking about the individual human body that is more expansive yet also more decentralized with relationship to its surroundings than traditional humanist conceptions. La naguala facilitates the movement toward "a connectionist view," one that is empathetic and compassionate, one that fuses the self with its surroundings—people, animals, objects, even activities like writing ("now let us shift" 569).[30] Although Anzaldúa is discussed here as resistant to humanist principles, I note, like Keating and Kimberly Merenda do, that Anzaldúa does not dismiss the category of human, she "transforms" and expands it ("Decentring the Human" 8). As Keating and Merenda describe, "Anzaldúa does not only insist—in the face of racism, sexism, and other forms of relentless dehumanization—on her humanity. She is not content to simply self-define as 'human'" ("Decentring the Human" 8). Naguala is an important example of Anzaldúa's thinking about the human transformed beyond current conceptions. A closer look at Anzaldúa's most extensive discussion of la naguala in such a transformation, put forth in "now let us shift," follows.

La Naguala as Subjective Practice

In "now let us shift," Anzaldúa describes in most detail how la naguala functions to move one's awareness from "the ego" or "customary point of view" to a "connectionist view" in the larger course of conocimiento (569).[31] This process also includes another concept that becomes important to Anzaldúa's later work, nepantla.[32] The details of this progression are most specific in the following paragraph:

> When you shift attention from your customary point of view (the ego) to that of la naguala, and from there move your awareness to an inner held representation of an experience, person, thing, or world, la naguala and the object merge. When you include the complexity of feeling two or more ways about a person/issue, when you empathize and try to see her circumstances from her position, you accommodate the other's perspective, achieving un conocimiento that allows you to shift toward a less defensive, more inclusive identity. When you relate to others, not as parts, problems, or useful commodities, but from a connectionist view, compassion triggers transformation. . . . Moving back and forth from the situation to la naguala's view, you glean a new description of the world (reality)—a Toltec interpretation. When you are in a place between worldviews (nepantla), you're able to slip between realities to a neutral perception. A decision made in the in-between place becomes a turning point initiating psychological and spiritual transformations. (569)

Anzaldúa's focus in the above is on the transition, the cyclical movement of consciousness from the egoistic (individualistic) to the compassionate (naguala) and then to the "neutral" place (nepantla). In other words, in conocimiento, one experiences a merger of self-other ("accommodat[ing] the other's perspective"), or shapeshifts, in the process of moving to the location of nepantla, where one radically breaks from the categories that defined the old self (569). As Martina Koegeler-Abdi suggests of Anzaldúa's move from discussions of mestiza to nepantleran consciousness, the mestiza consciousness maintains "hybrid inclusivity," embracing many categories of identities at once, while for the nepantlera, categories are no longer viable. My analysis adds to Koegeler-Abdi's revelation by pointing out that nepantleran consciousness is achieved by a practice in which a subject experiences others with empathy and compassion, a shapeshifting movement, in order to sever itself from the need to cling to narrowly defined frames of reference with respect to identity. Resisting stagnation, naguala allows the subject to move from self to other and to the middle, so to speak. As Anzaldúa states, by way of naguala, the subject takes on "the flexibility to swing from your intense feelings to those of the other without being hijacked by either" (569). To Anzaldúa, the shift in consciousness has physical effects and creates a change in the way the body communicates, feels and expresses emotions, and takes action, effects that, in turn, create change outside the body as well. A couple of paragraphs after the one excerpted above, Anzaldúa again refers to "shifting to the neutral place" as naguala. Discussing it here begins to answer Koegeler-Abdi's call in her conclusion to examine "other overlooked implications of Anzaldúa's legacy" associated with "becoming nepantleras" (85).

The shifts in consciousness facilitated by la naguala are worthy of critical attention by Anzaldúa scholars as we consider the theoretical and practical move to nepantleran subjectivity, particularly when viewed in light of new perspectives on nepantla in Mesoamerican philosophy. Additionally, a focus on the naguala provides a more accurate and thicker description of Anzaldúan subjectivity. A closer look at naguala's appearance in "now let us shift" provides an explanation of the experience of subjectivity in stage 7 of conocimiento as having multiple parts. Anzaldúa states: "When a change occurs[,] your consciousness (awareness of your sense of self and your response to self, others, and surroundings) becomes cognizant that it has a point of view and the ability to act from choice. This knowing/knower is always with you, but it is displaced by the ego and its perspective. This knower has several functions. You call the function that arouses the awareness that beneath individual separateness lies a deeper interrelatedness 'la naguala'" (568–569). The "knower" to which Anzaldúa refers here represents a complex consciousness and subjectivity, one that is not closed or complete but flexible and fluid. La naguala is the mediator, the aspect or practice of consciousness that shifts one from an ego state to interconnectedness or oneness with its surroundings, and then to a state of transition or openness—nepantla. Naguala is the movement and a merger, a practice, a gerund—"shapeshifting"—a noun with verbal features.[33] In order to imagine and enact a fluid subjectivity, in order to imagine and enact movement on individual and collective levels, exploring la naguala—as a theoretical and concrete project—is necessary. Attention to shifts—in thinking, feeling, acting, and becoming—allows for opportunities to create spaces where more of such transitions can occur.

As described above, la naguala plays the pivotal role in the movement between the subject's "inner work" and their participation in coalitional efforts, a goal of stage 7 conocimiento. That said, naguala shows up for the significant transition in two other stages of conocimiento, stages 2 and 4. In stage 2, "nepantla . . . torn between ways," naguala "connects you to . . . (your dream or energetic bodies) and to unconscious and invisible forces" that shift you into new ways of knowing (549). In stage 4, "the call," Anzaldúa gives specific instructions for invoking la naguala: "To learn what to transform into[,] you ask, 'How can I contribute?' You . . . listen to la naguala and the images, sensations, and dreams she presents. . . . (Naguala) prompts you to take responsibility for consciously creating your life. . . . Holding these realizations in mind, you stand at the brink and reconsider the crossing" (557).

The above quote demonstrates how la naguala is a purposeful practice of subjectivity. Also in stage 4, Anzaldúa fleetingly reveals her relationship to one of her nagualas, the jaguar, which recurrently appeared to her in dream-states and near-death experiences. She mentions the "lechuza eyes" (owl eyes) of naguala here, too, which she says "rous(e) you from the trance of hyper-rationality induced by higher education" (556). With each stage that involves a movement from inner stagnation, including nepantla, the call (el compromiso), and shifting realities, naguala is there, guiding the subject through new transitions. Perhaps, to Anzaldua, naguala is always present, sitting unseen and patient, at every way station of conocimiento,[34] waiting for the moment to stealthfully make her move. Sometimes the movement toward knowledge or conocimiento involves desconocimiento, or isolation, and Coatlicue; sometimes it involves coming to harmony and connection, because, according to Anzaldúa, "the knowledge that exposes your fears can also remove them," and "detours are always part of the path" (553, 554). Critically, the "shift," she says, "must be more than intellectual," more than humanistic (554).

Naguala entered and exited Anzaldúa's essay in various ways throughout her dozens of drafts of "now let us shift." Its final appearance and performance are fairly consistent and transparent throughout the essay but so far also fairly ignored by critics. This chapter honors la naguala and the relationship between this character-concept and Anzaldúa's theory of subjectivity, most developed in "now let us shift." Given the number of times—47—that she uses the language of "shift" in this carefully crafted essay, we do Anzaldúa a disservice by ignoring the shapeshifter's presence. Attending to the significance of la naguala, however, requires a nod to posthumanism, a more-than-human context, a more-than-rational epistemology, and, importantly, the Indigenous influences and philosophy that inspired her use of the term and concept. Understood in these terms, Anzaldúa's naguala has not only posthumanist but decolonial potential. This latter claim is the focus of chapter 2.

CHAPTER TWO

"An Artist in the Sense of a Shaman"

Border Arte as Decolonial Practice

I felt a calling to be an artist in the sense of a shaman—
healing through words, using words as a medium for
expressing the flights of the soul, community with the
spirit, having access to these other realities or worlds.

—Gloria Anzaldúa

Gloria Anzaldúa's significant engagement with an Indigenous past remains one of the most celebrated yet controversial features of her work. *Borderlands / La Frontera*, particularly, is praised for its feminist-centered rewriting of the Aztecan pantheon, explained in part as a challenge to the sexism and homophobia in twentieth-century Chicano nationalism. However, some critics also express concerns about Anzaldúa's use of Indigenous knowledges, reading her, for example, as too metaphorical (Debra Castillo, María Socorro Tabuenca Córdoba), utopian (Benjamin Alire Saenz, Pablo Vila), and essentialist (David Rieff, Domino Perez). More-substantial critiques relate to the prospect that Anzaldúa is participating in modern literary primitivism (Rieff, Shiela Contreras), as well as dehistoricizing and obscuring a diversity of contemporary Native peoples on both sides of the US-Mexican border (Perez, Contreras, Nicole M. Guidotti-Hernández, María Josefina Saldaña-Portillo). This chapter engages with and complicates these critiques, explores Anzaldúa's and other critics' responses to them, and asserts a call to take seriously, albeit vigilantly, Anzaldúa's employment of a Nahua mythology and metaphysics as a decolonizing act. The chapter emphasizes that Anzaldúa's Indigeneity, informed by her mestizaje ancestry and study of shamanism, serves as the primary source of not just her poetics but also a strategic practice that she refers to as "border arte" and looks at the relationship between border arte and conocimiento with Sarah Soanirina Ohmer's reading of conocimiento as a shamanic exercise and "decolonizing ritual" ("Gloria" 142). I deepen this claim by focusing on la naguala as an aspect of conocimiento that Anzaldúa had been developing since *Borderlands / La Frontera*, strengthening its importance in her entire body of work. The chapter begins with an exploration of the study of shamanism in the academy and in Anzaldúa, particularly, as this complicated topic informs how scholars have come to their concerns and criticisms about Anzaldúa's use of Indigenous references. Anzaldúa uses the language of shamanism substantially throughout her work, which calls for a brief foray into this complex term.

Mesoamerican Shamanism in the Western Academy and Anzaldúa

As the previous chapter establishes, the concept of Anzaldúa's la naguala is a radically thick description of a practice of subjectivity influenced by Mesoamerican shamanism and expanded in her post–*Borderlands / La Frontera* work. Few scholars have taken up a study of Mesoamerican shamanism as means for gleaning new insights into Anzaldúa's work and its applications.[1] As Leisa Kauffman points out:

> Although shamanism plays an explicit role in Anzaldúa's world, few critics have made the connection between this aspect of her spiritual/ religious world view and the theoretical and political content of her writings. Few critics, in other words, have recognized that her use of Nahua mythical and literary tradition plays a deeper role in her writing than mere metaphor. Although Anzaldúa herself explicitly says this, the trend nevertheless has been to regard her as an exoticizing writer using the indigenous as a literary vehicle for her thematic concerns. This concern becomes even more acute in an academic context in which she is tokenized as the Chicana writer everyone reads. (66)

I underscore Kauffman's assertion that the lack of deep discussion on shamanism in relationship to Anzaldúa has significant implications, including misinterpretations of and missed opportunities to engage with the nuances of her work. Several reasons are likely for the lack of attention to Anzaldúa's shamanism including the academy's lack of studies on shamanism and the problems inherent in applying Western lenses to Indigenous worldviews and practices. Also, to study Anzaldúa's Indigeneity means sitting, likely uncomfortably, with the potential problems of cultural appropriation.

While Western awareness of shamanic traditions is found in writings as far back as the Middle Ages, archeological evidence indicates that shamanic activity existed many centuries before that, perhaps even as far back as the earliest-known human groups (DuBois 26). Europeans first used the term "shamanism" to describe the ancient religious practices of the Siberian Tungus tribe and others of northeast and central Asia (Stutley 3).[2] Later, the term was extended by anthropologists to include Indigenous beliefs and traditions in North and South America that appeared to Westerners to be similar to those in Eurasia (a result of the widespread diffusionist approach). Researchers reported that shamanism in its broadest sense adheres to an animistic worldview and practices that include healing powers; human interactions with spirits,[3] particularly those in animal forms; and "trance"-like activities during which the human spirit travels outside the body (Stutley 2). Pre–twenty-first-century academic study of shamanism, however, is sparse and largely fraught with problems, deeply steeped in Enlightenment principles and, simultaneously, approached and understood as a worldview from Christian perspective and with Christian concepts, such as good and evil and other binaries. The most recent scholarship, including the work on Nahua metaphysics, exposes the inadequacies, inaccuracies, and colonialist implications of Western readings of shamanism.

Until the 1960s, research on shamanism was primarily situated in early to mid-twentieth-century formalism and primitivism. Christianity was hailed as "the pinnacle of all the world's various religious traditions," and shamanic beliefs were viewed as "defective, overly mysticized, or even altogether outside of the province of religion itself" (DuBois 8). Animism was believed to be a part of the primitive mind. Because diffusionism—or the belief that cultural traits and change arise by imitation, not inventiveness—influenced the social sciences for much of the twentieth century, researchers tended to flatten differences between groups in their exploration of Indigenous imagery found in artifacts around the world. In their call for more-scholarly rigor in research on the historical origins and concepts of the Mesoamerican shaman and shamanism, art historians Cecelia F. Klein, Eulogio Guzmán, Elisa C. Mandell, and Maya Stanfield-Mazzi argue, "There is a pressing need to create a more refined, more nuanced terminology that would distinguish, cross-culturally, among the many different kinds of roles currently lumped together under the vague and homogenizing rubric of 'shaman,'" and that the study of shamanism contributes to an "ahistorical, apolitical, irrational 'Other' that was initially constructed during the conquest and colonization of the Americas"

(383–384). Addressing this concern, for instance, contemporary Mexican anthropologist Saúl Millán explores in his fieldwork how nagualism shifted after the colonial introduction of livestock farming in the Nahua, Huave, and Tzotzil Maya given the differences in their understandings of the animal world (64–65). Because the Nahua people saw humans and animals as equivalent, what is referred to as horizontal nagualism,[4] the introduction of animal husbandry changed this ancient relationship.

Other twenty-first-century researchers are also taking a long-needed, skeptical, and deconstructive look at early classifications of shamanism and the effects of primitivism—literary and otherwise—that pervade Western scholarship. Furthermore, now that more scholars of Indigenous heritage are contributing to these conversations, they are also offering radically new ways of understanding and explaining the nuances in Mesoamerican thought and tradition. Paloma Martinez-Cruz, for instance, makes a distinction between what she terms centripetal and centrifugal knowledges, the former associated with the individuated being and thinking of Enlightenment humanism and the latter with collaborative performance-based, nontextual ways of knowing rooted in Nahua women's traditions. Martinez-Cruz's interdisciplinary work, which is personal and historical in approach, explores medicines and rituals from the Olmecs to contemporary Mazatec shamans, documenting for the first time formerly excluded wisdom of Mesoamerican women healers and their influence today. Importantly, her work is decolonial in approach, deconstructing the intellectual authority of Western humanism.

In addition to the problems concerning Eurocentric bias and the placement of Indigenous practices around the globe under one vague umbrella term, what we understand in the academy about shamanism is troubled by tensions related to what counts as scholarly evidence (traditionally, the rational and observable), and, due to the immense differences between Western and Indigenous reality, what counts as reliable interpretation. For example, what Western researchers describe as a "trance" is unintelligible to those, such as the Mixe shamans in southern Mexico, who do not distinguish between waking and dreaming states (qtd. in Klein et al. 388). Additionally, Christian missionaries wrote the earliest accounts of shamanic cosmologies, interpreting Native views through the lens of their own belief system. As Thomas A. DuBois asserts, "Missionaries thus often made nearly automatic use of concepts from their own religions— e.g., heaven, hell, demons, God—to characterize the beliefs of the people whom they were proselytizing, in the process harmonizing belief systems which in fact may have evinced essential differences in key concepts and understandings" (51). Their accounts today are highly suspect; however, one exception to the harshest critiques is sixteenth-century Franciscan friar Bernardino de Sahagún's *Primeros Memoriales (First Memorials)* and *Historia General (General History)*, also known as *The Florentine Codex*, which still serves as a major reference for scholars seeking to understand Mesoamerican cosmology.

Sahagún spent more than a half-century with the Nahua people, learned their language, and—in Nahuatl—interviewed and attempted to record the perspectives of a diversity of informants, including the shamans. He is known as one of the first to develop what centuries later became the anthropological method of ethnography and is described as "indigenist" or pro-Indigenous (Anderson 17). Miguel León-Portilla says of Sahagún's writings, "The original Nahuatl texts, it must be stressed, are not the work of Sahagún, but of his elderly native informants from Tepepulco and Tlatelolco. They are describing what they saw and learned as young men in the Calmécac, the institutions of higher learning, before the arrival of the Spaniards, and they speak with authority on these matters" (9–10). Mexican American historian Davíd Carrasco refers to Sahagún's writings as "the single most valuable source of information concerning the native culture of the Basin of Mexico and adjacent territory at Contact" ("Sahagún"). However, Sahagún was, indeed, an evangelist and brought a Christian message to the Natives with whom he interacted. As DuBois emphasizes, "Most of the ethnographic descriptions of shamanic cosmologies left to us by scholars of the past describe shamanic traditions among peoples already experiencing concerted missionization" (51). An active missionary effort had been in place for half a decade when Sahagún arrived in La Villa Rica de la Vera Cruz from Old Spain in 1529. Despite his efforts to accurately represent the Nahua from their own perspective, even the highly praised Sahagún was not immune from error.[5]

Scholarship concerned with primitivism in images of Mesoamerican religions and the Western art forms it purportedly influenced began to burgeon at the end of the twentieth century. As Klein et al. argued, such primitivist interpretations appealed to "self-serving nationalist and commercial interests both within and outside of Latin America" and served and continue to serve as an "Othering" process (383–384).[6] Klein et al. also assert that the historical move in the 1950s and 1960s of Douglas Fraser, Peter Furst, and Mircea Eliade from diffusionism to idealist or religious explanations of Mesoamerican artistic choices dismissed secular, materialist explanations and were flawed in their reliance on ethnographies of Westerners.

This focus on what were thought to be the cosmological beliefs of shamanism, which were highly subjective and in some ways suspiciously parallel to Christianity to begin with, and the tendency to assume these beliefs of shamanism were universal across groups worldwide, were problematic to those like Klein et al. in the materialist camp at the turn of the twenty-first century. However, even Klein et al. as critics of studies on shamanism emphasize the importance of conducting research but with careful attention to specificity and the pitfalls of ethnocentric assumptions. Klein et al. saw value in, for instance, comparing shamans to priests, doctors, and political actors. In other words, removing the emphasis on and exoticization of what are seen as the magico-spiritual components of shamanism also help to remove the tendency to "other" pre-Columbian societies. However, Klein et al.'s work generated a substantial response. Furst vigorously refuted Klein et al.'s arguments,[7] citing errors in the claims; others say that Klein et al. were too severe in reinforcing a division between materialists and idealists.

Today, the new materialist turn and Indigenous studies present an opportunity to complicate both approaches, interrogating the divisions between the spiritual/material and other binaries. Maffie's study (2014) on Aztec metaphysics is the most substantial review of the scholarship and analysis on the topic to date. As we go through the third decade of the twenty-first century and beyond, more and much-needed research in Indigenous studies by Indigenous people will inform how we read Anzaldúa for years to come. Concerns about primitivism remain appropriately strong, including concerns about Anzaldúa's work.

Before wading into the critiques, some themes are identified that have recently emerged as scholars make links, despite the challenges in doing so, between Indigenous cosmology and Anzaldúa's writing from her children's books to her interviews.

Regarding the importance of shamanism to Anzaldúa, some scholars point out her Nahua-inspired logics and poetics while others focus on Anzaldúa, the author/narrator, as shaman, and her writing a shamanic practice. Most do both to some degree. Leisa Kauffman, for instance, claims that Anzaldúa's fourth of seven essays in *Borderlands / La Frontera* serves a particular thematic and narrative purpose associated with Mesoamerican nahualism and mythology. Highlighting Anzaldúa's reference to the "godwoman," Coatlicue, within herself, Kauffman links the concept of teotl to what Anzaldúa is expressing here: the oneness of gods and humans, albeit a female god-man, subverting the dominance of patriarchal male deities of the Aztecs (58). Kauffman also points out how Anzaldúa, as narrator, enacts a shamanistic performance of sorts midtext, becoming the earth deity, or Cihuacoatl/"Snake Woman," and passing through the "vagina dentata" (devouring mouth) motif—or caves of origins—to give voice to herself as decolonial poet, writer, and activist (60). Others, too, such as Jane Caputi, Carrasco and Roberto Lint Sagarena, Betsy Dahms, Keating, and Ohmer, liken Anzaldúa to a shaman and her writing a healing practice that remakes the world, from *Borderlands / La Frontera* to "now let us shift." Similarly, George Hartley refers to Anzaldúa as "the curandera of conquest" or "healer of la herida abierta (the open wound)" imposed by the physical and psychological borders created by neocolonialism ("Curandera" 135).

Reading Anzaldúa, most specifically *Prietita and the Ghost Woman / Prietita y la Llorona*, with the works of Indigenous scholars and theoreticians Linda Tuhiwai Smith, Waziyatawin Angela Wilson, and Gerald Taiaiake Alfred, Hartley emphasizes that calling Anzaldúa a curandera is "no metaphor" and that her work as a healer has "decolonizing impact" (140, 149). He makes a substantial argument for how she participates in the elements of curanderismo (healing practice), including ceremonial ritual, the practice of soul retrieval ("making face"), and the transmission of cultural knowledge. Hartley says that although the work of Smith, Wilson, Alfred, and Anzaldúa did not directly influence each other, there is much symmetry between contemporary Indigenous decolonizing projects and Anzaldúa's spiritual activism. Felicity Amaya Schaeffer turns our attention to Anzaldúa's Indigeneity, too, when Schaeffer takes up the term "spirit matters" to explore what she calls "a greater identity category" at work in Anzaldúa's writing (1005–1006). She says, "I use the term 'spirit' in conjunction with the active verb tense 'matters' to foreground the ways spirit materializes worlds, privileges Mesoamerican Indigenous knowledges, and matters to feminist theorizations of fleshy cosmologies" (1006). These scholars take on the double responsibility of legitimating links between Anzaldúa and what is not usually deemed rational and academic—the spiritual and religious ritual—while also addressing the charges that these references are essentialist and primitivist.

More recently, PJ DiPietro brings together theories of posthumanism, new materialisms, and Indigenous, postcolonial, disability, and trans studies and employs what PJ calls Anzaldúa's "teoría del materialismo *nagualista*" (theory of nagualist materialism) in arguing for "la materialidad *espiritual*" (the spiritual materiality) of queer, travesti, and trans corporalities in past and present Indigenous communities in Abya Yala (280).[8] DiPietro says that Anzaldúa's theorizing resists the subject/object, human/nonhuman, matter/spirit binaries by her "práctica chamánica de transmutación" (shamanic practice of transformation), or nagualismo (281). Seeing similarities among the Indigenous practices of the Cuareca, Kuna, Koya, Aymara, and Toba highlighted in PJ's study and Anzaldua's work with Nahua cosmologies, DiPietro says that not just as myth but also as "una modalidad intersubjetiva" (intersubjective modality), Anzaldúa's naguala interrupts settler colonial logics and transfigures the limits and forms of subjectivity (283). DiPietro sees this work as "pluralismo poshumanista" (posthumanist pluralism) and a decolonizing of the transgender body (283).[9]

DiPietro's efforts move Anzaldúa scholarship in important directions by bringing together many threads of contemporary feminist theorizing and taking seriously the decolonizing potential of Anzaldúa's work with Nahua cosmology and shamanism. Although my argument says that Anzaldúa's writing supports the idea of a constitutional monism in line with Maffie's description of Nahua metaphysics, I don't see DiPietro's pluralism as necessarily inconsistent with my view. DiPietro is seeking to trouble material monism and, more generally, humanist traditions by arguing for a pluralism that exposes the material and metaphysical imposition of gender and (Western) "humanity," more specifically the coloniality of transgender subjectivities, onto Abya Yala. Part of DiPietro's project includes the important work of unpacking and resisting the violence wielded at gender nonconforming bodies in the service of the human/nonhuman, subject/object binaries introduced by coloniality. Asserting that such subjectivities are not, at the level of substance, singular but multiple and mobile does not necessarily mean that those subjectivities are not a part of a process that is neither strictly matter nor spirit but something different, part of a metaphysics beyond Western conception. Indeed, DiPietro says that trans modalities, including nagualism, bring to bear possibilities that are not quite human or animal but are part sacred (285). Perhaps, the tertium quid—the not-matter, not-spirit but something else—of Nahua metaphysics encompasses such a modality.

Adding to these and other conversations on Anzaldúa's work as shamanistic practice, the chapter will argue that Anzaldúa's concept of border arte, of which the naguala is a part, stands up to the critiques of her use of Indigenous theories and practice. The next section outlines some of those concerns. Others are taken up in the section that follows on border arte.

Addressing the Critics

Anzaldúa herself confidently engaged with the critiques that circulated in her lifetime, even adopting and repurposing the term "new tribalism" that David Rieff used, in a derogatory way, to describe her work in a 1991 article. Rieff referred to Anzaldúa as a "professional Aztec," claiming that she and others like Luis Valdez held "monolithic views of consciousness" and focus too much on race over class and economics (44). Anzaldúa self-assuredly took up Rieff's term as an opportunity to correct his misreading of her and to clarify that, to her, race was a colonial construct; she was committed to honoring cultural heritage and the reality of experience informed by colonialism and patriarchy and simultaneously dismantling it ("Speaking Across the Divide"). Although her choice of term was tricky, perhaps ill-advised, Anzaldúa begins referring to a "new tribalism" as this next step—"a more inclusive identity" that interrupts the "imposition" of racialization enacted by "dominant culture" in the service of its privilege ("Speaking Across the Divide" 283). Her idea of a new tribalism "is a social identity that could motivate subordinated communities to work together" (283). It can be read as an opportunity to expose what Walter D. Mignolo refers to as "the colonial difference" or the categories, logics, and mechanisms of coloniality articulated from the perspective and in the voice of the subaltern (*Local Histories* 13).[10]

Anzaldúa's focus on the "social" aspect of new tribalism and other forms of identity like her often-cited mestiza is critical: consciousness and subjectivity for Anzaldúa were relational, communicative, not static. As Linda Alcoff importantly observes in "The Unassimilated Theorist," "[f]or Anzaldúa the positive articulation of mestiza identity is a project to be undertaken, rather than something that already exists" (257). Alcoff also recognizes that Anzaldúa's concept of hybridity and mestiza identity includes a sense of rootedness and coherence; without it a sense of insecurity and even forms of violence (stemming from machismo, for instance) can result. New tribalism was one way in which Anzaldúa articulated this positive effort. What was "new" about new tribalism was that rootedness was to be intentionally constructed outside the categories of culture imposed by coloniality, and coherence was accomplished by way of collective strategy and work among diversely oppressed groups ("Speaking Across the Divide" 283). A mechanism that not only resists modern, colonial logics but also allows a repressed border imaginary to flourish,[11] the new tribalism was Anzaldúa's attempt to transgress monolithic views of consciousness, not perpetuate them as Rieff accused.

Domino Perez offers a nuanced perspective on new tribalism, reinforcing the above point made by Alcoff when she states, "Mestizaje is a dynamic process . . . constantly evolving, and it serves as a precursor to Anzaldúa's emerging theory of new tribalism" ("New Tribalism" 490). Perez, however, while commenting on "the potential application" of new tribalism, also notes what she saw as flaws. Relying on the little that Anzaldúa said about it, Perez sees as problematic Anzaldúa's explanatory metaphor of new tribalism as "an orange tree made strong through grafting" (495).[12] In addition to critiquing this metaphor for its connection to a biological rather than a social process, Perez says, "The metaphor of the tree is ultimately lacking because the kind of transformation Anzaldúa is talking about is being imposed on a living entity: the tree did not choose to have its strength or productivity altered" (496). We understand and see as effective Perez's reading of the metaphor because of a Western understanding of the relationship between humans and trees. But the tree-of-life metaphor, which Anzaldúa expands on extensively in her posthumously published "Flights of the Imagination," offers another way of thinking about the tree informed by Anzaldúa's practice of nagualismo. She says, "I've been developing an ongoing relationship with the spirit of trees and nature sites since I was a child. . . . I can alter consciousness in order to communicate with them. . . . We have a body awareness of trees and they of us" (24). This statement suggests that Anzaldúa's interactions with a tree wouldn't be imposed and also complicates the idea that the development of a tree is strictly biological.

I make this point to show that Anzaldúa consistently relied on a shamanic ontology and metaphysics that profoundly affected her thinking about binaries, identity, subjectivity, and activism; by not reading her full body of work and by undervaluing her attempts to move away from Western constructions of subjects by way of her Nahua imaginary, we risk misreading her. In fairness to Perez, her critique was written before the publication of "Flights of the Imagination," where Anzaldúa's reference to Nahua ontology and metaphysics is most developed. Aside from the tree metaphor, Perez's additional concern that Anzaldúa's appropriations of an Indigenous past and inventions of new identity categories can affect conceptions of tribal peoples does warrant important consideration.

The potential for erasure of those Indigenous peoples who are not mestizo or mestiza is a significant worry, one that Anzaldúa expressed and critics expand on. Perez, for example, asks, "How does one acknowledge or even begin to claim or account for Indigenous heritage without erasing or disenfranchising living tribal communities?" ("New Tribalism" 499). Perez, like a number of other critics, is looking specifically at, again, Anzaldúa's new tribalism and the concept of mestizaje put forth in *Borderlands / La Frontera*. The critique is related to implications for tribal communities who are content with their guiding mythologies and, indeed, must struggle to protect and maintain them and even their very lives. On this point, Perez cites María Josefina Saldaña-Portillo, who asserts that Anzaldúa's reviving of myth mimics Mexico's Institutional Revolutionary Party's state-sponsored promotion of mestizaje at the expense of contemporary tribes. Since, according to Nicole M. Guidotti-Hernándéz, Anzaldúa limits her source of Indigeneity to ancient times, she obscures and subsequently denies the violence against those Indians who are not read as mestizo/a today, including violence against Indians by Chicanos in the nineteenth century in Arizona.[13] Perez recognizes Anzaldúa's wish not to "inadvertently contribute to the cultural erasure . . . of people who live in real Indian bodies," but Perez also says "the possibility of . . . doing so is high" (500). Perez argues that Anzaldúa's "romantic fictions" further establish "Aztec hegemony" and "narrative of empire" and recommends that Chicanos and Chicanas today focus on, for example, the past and current links among Mexicans, Indians, and labor instead of the reviving of myth (500).

Although Anzaldúa might have seen this look at labor as important, she was a storyteller, poet, and visual artist. Images and narrative inspired her creative expression. That expression, in part, was aimed at imagining new identities rather than comparing those imposed by colonialism. Also, as Suzanne Bost argues, instead of making romantic truth claims about or declaring "unmediated access" to an Indigenous past, Anzaldúa's "claim to pre-Columbian 'memory' is deliberately ahistorical and ideological," because it is informed and transformed by contemporary feminist and postcolonial sensitivity and discernment (*Encarnación* 41). In other words, Anzaldúa works within and counter to Aztec tradition in a new articulation, not reinstatement, of Aztec myth in her revising of colonial and patriarchal appropriations of Mexican Indigenous figures. I connect this process to her description of border arte (expanded on in the next section).

Part of Perez's criticism is that Anzaldúa "does not engage with the fact that the Aztec empire was an oppressive entity that forced other tribes to pay tribute and/or submit to its power" ("New Tribalism" 494); however, Anzaldúa does describe this specific history in *Borderlands / La Frontera*. She documents the mid-fifteenth-century wars-of-flowers decade during which the Aztecs became "a militaristic state" and explains how the three-centuries-long fall of the Aztec empire was, in part, due to erosion of "the solidarity between men and women and between noble and commoner" (*Borderlands / La Frontera* 54, 56). Indeed, part of Anzaldúa's project in *Borderlands / La Frontera* is to remake and complicate pre-Aztecan interpretations of myths as well as grapple with the legacy of the centuries of the patriarchal, predatory, militaristic Aztecs. Perez makes this point herself a decade prior to her critique of new tribalism in an essay on Anzaldúa's poem "My Black Angelos": "Anzaldúa's privileging of la llorona's Aztecan antecedents presents a more complete and ultimately empowering view of the weeping woman and Chicanas outside the context of the traditional folklore" ("Words" 59). Anzaldúa, therefore, enacts a remaking rather than a romantic retrieval of pre-Columbian myth. As Leisa Kauffman asserts, "it is difficult—if not impossible—to accuse Anzaldúa of exoticizing or of recreating an image of the primitive," when the point in making reference to interpretations of precolonial images and myths is to say "that our binary, hegemonic conceptions . . . are not universal reality, that they do not represent how those categories were always imagined and defined" (66–67). The above said, I do think we need to take seriously Perez's and others' concerns, especially because Anzaldúa's work can be used to exoticize and essentialize the Indigenous past, despite Anzaldúa's intentions. Anzaldúa knew this and talked and wrote about the risks but was willing to take them.

Anzaldúa's artistic preference for, as Bost referred to it, a "precolonial imaginary over postcolonial reality" had a complex political purpose that revisited and recognized cultural identities while deconstructing them. Bost refers to Indigenismo (Indigenism), then, as "a political and cultural creation rather than a simple matter of descent" (*Encarnación* 41). As Anzaldúa tells Inés Hernández-Ávila in an interview, she thought it was important to recognize the Indian aspect that was often denied in Chicana identity as a result of internalized racism while also addressing appropriation concerns by Native Americans: "Some Indian Americans think all Chicanas/os plunder native culture as mercilessly as whites. Who does the appropriating and for what purpose is a point to consider" ("Speaking Across the Divide" 289). Her deep thinking about cultural appropriation is explored in her essay "Border Arte: Nepantla, el Lugar de la Frontera," which reflects on her viewing of an Aztec exhibit at the Denver Museum of Natural History in 1993. There are three published versions of the essay; the first is in a 1993 San Diego Museum of Contemporary Art publication, and two were published posthumously, one in *The Gloria Anzaldúa Reader* and the other in *Light in the Dark / Luz en lo Oscuro*. The *Light*, and later, version of the essay is more substantial and the version used in this chapter.

Border Arte as Decolonial Project

"Border Arte" ventures back and forth between Anzaldúa's recognition of primitivism in and a moving identification with the artifacts before her in the Denver museum. Ultimately, she sees the potential for opportunity in an exhibit "where cultures co-exist in the same site" (49). However, she begins the essay with her clear awareness of the racist and colonialist implications of such a space:

> I ask myself, "What does it mean for me—esta jotita, this queer Chicana, this mexica tejana to enter a museum and look at indigenous objects that were once used by my ancestors?" . . . I am disconcerted with the knowledge that I, too, am passively consuming and appropriating an indigenous cultural. I walked in with a group of Chicano kids from Servicio Chicano Center and now we are being taught secondhand our cultural roots twice removed by whites. The essence of colonization: rip off a culture, then regurgitate its white version to the "natives." (48)

Appropriation by white museum-event organizers is not the only problem on Anzaldúa's mind. As she listens on her museum-assigned Walkman to Edward James Olmos's narration of her tour, one that is occasionally interjected by Nahuatl musical recitations, she also wonders if she herself and other Chicano/a writers and artists are misusing the Nahuatl language and imagery. She is, however, moved by both and says she and other Chicano/a artists "delve into, sift through, and re-work Native imagery" that works on their artistic output, even in unconscious ways (54). Cultures renew themselves from generation to generation, but they are never the same as they were in the past. The delving, sifting, and remaking in "the bewildering transitional space" of nepantla is where border artists create not just culture but also identity (56). Anzaldúa describes the process in detail in the following way:

> Throughout the centuries, one culture touches and influences another, passing on its metaphors and its gods before it dies. Metaphors *are* gods. According to archetypal psychology, we have internalized the old deities, animals, and forces of nature that our ancestors considered gods. We could say that metaphors are allies, spirits (transformative aspects of the unconscious seeking to enter consciousness). (In my case, snake is one of my allies or guardian animals.) The new culture adopts, modi-

fies, and enriches these images, and it, in turn, passes them on changed. In the case of Native American spiritual practices such as the vision quest, the practices, rituals, and ceremonies have been disrespectfully appropriated and misappropriated by whites, Chicanos, and Latinos. . . . The process of "borrowing" is repeated until the images' original meanings are pushed into the unconscious, and images more significant to the prevailing culture and era surface. However, the artist on some level still connects to that unconscious reservoir of meaning, connects to that nepantla state of transition between time periods, connects to the border between cultures. Chicana/o artists currently are engaged in "reading" that nepantla, that border, and that cenote—from which direction and renewal spring forth nepantla, and that border. (55)

Anzaldúa recognizes here that the artist does not preserve a culture but creates one anew for the moment in which the artist lives; "on some level," however, a "border artist" is in touch enough with their cultural origins, as varied as they may be, that a part of past meaning remains. "The border artist constantly reinvents her/himself," she says. "Through art s/he is able to re-read, reinterpret, re-envision, and reconstruct her/his culture's present as well as its past" ("Border Arte" 60). She does not deny the problematics of appropriation; she seems to be acknowledging here that it is impossible for past metaphors and narratives not to be a part of a person's worldview. But appropriation varies by degree and the amount of damage it inflicts.

Removed from the blocked quote above are instances of appropriation that Anzaldúa highlights by "white shamans" and even Mexican writers like Don Miguel Ruiz, who conducts workshops and reaps substantial financial gain from teaching a broad audience about shamanism ("Border Arte" 55). Some who are borrowing from the past are purporting to be practicing it in the present and doing so without regard for the coloniality and global capitalism in which the present resides. Border artists acknowledge their "precarious position" with "feet in different worlds" at once ("Border Arte" 53). This characteristic of the border artist's practice is even evident in the blocked passage above, as Anzaldúa pulls from archetypal psychology, a movement initiated in the 1970s by Jungian-influenced James Hillman, while she is also drawing from Nahua concepts like nepantla and el cenote. Her theorizing is conscientiously a blend of influences, but it's also certainly guided in a considerable way by her desire "to practice the oldest 'calling' in the world—shamanism" but "in a new way" ("Metaphors" 121).

Notable in the blocked quote is Anzaldúa's privileging of images and their meanings: "Metaphors *are* gods," she says, reminding her readers that meaning for her begins with an image. Although she does not directly identify this process as such here, her description of border arte is much like the shamanic journeying she later puts forth in "Flights of the Imagination." A shaman is "a 'walker between worlds,'" she says, "intentionally entering realms that others encounter only in dreams and myth and bringing back information (treasure for healing others, the community, the Earth)" ("Flights of the Imagination" 32–33). Anzaldúa locates the Chicana/o border artist/shaman in contemporary American culture in "Border Arte," identifying the challenges as well as the responsibilities; the "ethnic artist" is positioned as "cultural icon" and "highly visible" and must navigate selling themselves while not selling out to seductive white, capitalist culture (59, 60).

Ultimately, Anzaldúa saw possibilities for an emergence of artwork informed by a blending of cultures, even within colonized spaces. Indeed, she reveals that in these in-between spaces is where border artists emerge and do their work: "The border is the locus of resistance, of rupture, implosion and explosion, and of putting together the fragments and creating a new assemblage" ("Border Arte" 49). To use Mignolo's language, such art can reveal "border thinking" and the experience of border dwelling from the position of and in resistance to the colonial difference. To remain within rigid categories created and articulated by coloniality, one perpetuates them. The task of the border artist, then, is to bring into expression new and dynamic cultures and ways of being that extend from and beyond borders. Inspired by Anzaldúa's "Border Arte," Nancy Tuana and Charles Scott in their recent scholarship explore "the force that 'beyond' can have" for liberatory philosophy ("Border *Arte* Philosophy" 71). I review their efforts next, as theirs is the only substantial published engagement with Anzaldúa's border arte at the time of this writing.

Reading "Border Arte" with Alejandro Vallega's concept of radical exteriority, a way of thinking that comes from and participates with those who are in the periphery of Western life, Tuana and Scott propose groundwork for a "border arte philosophy" that continuously and communally enacts an attunement with experiential, corporeal *sensibilities* that operate beyond systems of oppressions. Distinguished from intellect, sensibility, according to Tuana and Scott, is a prereflective agency and includes "ways of knowing, affective responses, habitual dispositions, bodily comportments, and forms of desire" that are "inherent in specific institutions, rituals, and symbols" and part of "cultural atmosphere" (73–74). "We, you and I, write, live, experience with and through complex lineages and sensibilities," say Tuana and Scott, "but not all of us inhabit/are inhabited by the same weave. Some of us, like Anzaldúa, carry complex lineages that weave worlds of sense from non-Western and Indigenous sensibilities. The differences in our lineages can be a source of tension, but they can also be the path beyond" (77).[14] Attending to these differences and historically overlooked and silenced lineages, sensibilities, and aesthetics is key to this path.

Tuana and Scott's attention to sensibilities can inform how we read the excerpt from "Border Arte" above that describes the transgenerational evolution of images and their meanings as well as Anzaldúa's hints at a shamanic journeying involved in the process. Such ways of knowing and expression operate outside rational sensitivities and articulate a specific blending of lineages and cultures, past and present, from which those expressions come. Tuana and Scott describe the practice of border arte as "representing other worlds of sense" (78). I caution against referring to such work as representation, as this term is often used to mean acting on behalf of something or someone. Each border-arte expression is new and different from what came before it. But I agree with Tuana and Scott that border arte as "continuous reinvention" offers a mechanism to go beyond for those interested in a liberation—beyond the sensibilities and logics of what are traditionally considered to be appropriate articulations of identity and expression but also what are not (78).

Despite what Anzaldúa calls the "obstacles and dangers" of the border artist's journey, she sought to work within the "state of transition between time periods . . . [and] the border between cultures," in a persistent, artistic border-nepantla state ("Border Arte" 55). As she says in the closing of "Border Arte":

> Yes, cultural roots are important, *but I was not born at Tenochtitlán in the ancient past nor in an Aztec village in modern times.* I was born and live in that in-between space, nepantla, the borderlands. Hay muchas razas [there are many races] running in my veins, mescladas dentro de mi, otras culturas [mixed within me, other cultures] that my body lives in and out of. Mi cuerpo vive dentro y fuera de otras culturas [my body lives inside and outside other cultures], *and a white man* who constantly whispers, "Assimilate, you're not good enough," and measures me according to white standards. *For me, being Chicana or any other single identity marker is not enough—is not my total self.* It is only one of my multiple identities. Along with other border gente [people], it is at this site and time, en este tiempo y lugar [in this time

and place] where and when, I help co-create my identity con mi arte [along with my art]. Other forces influence, impact, and construct our desires—including the unconscious and collective unconscious forces and residues of those that came before us, our ancient ancestors. (64)[15]

This position between cultures is why Anzaldúa borrows from what some see as conflicting and even problematic sources to inform her writing. Anzaldúa relied on academic and nonacademic sources, some revered and others critiqued, but certainly when compared to each other, they are very diverse in approach and views. Philosophers, anthropologists, psychoanalysts, poets, and popular public figures, from James Hillman and Henry Corbin to Jean Houston and Carlos Castaneda, show up in Anzaldúa's work, sometimes in the same essays. To her, their influences all live in the conscious and unconscious wells from which our desires and metaphors are formed.

Anzaldúa's sources are Sheila Contreras's major concern in her critique of *Borderlands / La Frontera*; Contreras claims that Anzaldúa's tropes, which she sees as "inversions of accepted conventions," ultimately "do not radically challenge the semiotic order of patriarchy" because Anzaldúa turns to primitivist sources in formulating her thinking ("Literary Primitivism" 58). My reading, especially beyond Contreras's focus on *Borderlands / La Frontera*, is that part of Anzaldúa's point is to emphasize that border dwellers work within a particular, multiply-informed cultural and historical moment that doesn't escape colonialist legacy. Anzaldúa says, "By disrupting the neat separations between cultures [border artists] create a culture mix, una mezcla in their artworks"; however, such work is not an assimilation but the making of something new ("Border Arte" 177).

Contreras argues that in *Borderlands / La Frontera*, "the mythic overpowers the historical in [Anzaldúa's] particular formulation of indigenous identity," but Anzaldúa reminds us that the line between myth and, to use Contreras's term, "material history" is thin, certainly with respect to our individual sense of cultural heritage ("Literary Primitivism" 54). The particular passage to which Contreras refers is when Anzaldúa says, "La India en mí es la sombra [The Indian in me is the shadow]: La Chingada [the fucked one], Tlazolteótl [earth goddess associated with filth and lust], Coatlicue [earth goddess, associated with creating and devouring]" (*Borderlands / La Frontera* 44). Contreras takes issue with Anzaldúa's conflating of Nahua woman Doña Marina, Cortés's interpreter (also known as Malintzín, Malinche, and La Chingada), with Tlazolteótl and Coatlicue, as Doña Marina was an actual person. However, Anzaldúa's choice of naming here is important; the language of the derogatory La Chingada to refer to Marina points to the mythology around La Chingada and that mythology's effects, which Anzaldúa might argue has more influence on contemporary Mexican and Chicana identity than the person Marina and her "material history."

Anzaldúa first refers to La Chingada by her Nahua name, Malinali Tenepat, or Malintzín, and explains that her legacy is disparaged as she "become(s) known as la Chingada—the fucked one. [Malintzin] has become the bad word that passes a dozen times a day from the lips of Chicanos. Whore, prostitute, the woman who sold out her people to the Spaniards are epithets Chicanos spit out with contempt" (*Borderlands / La Frontera* 44). Her aim in this section, "The Wounding of the *India-Mestiza*," the last few paragraphs of chapter 2 of *Borderlands / La Frontera*, is to point out the oppression of women within Chicano culture. The mythology of La Chingada, although based on a person, and the mythology of earth goddesses Tlazolteótl and Coatlicue are all part of one larger defamatory mythology of the Indian woman. The quote that Contreras highlights is given below in its full paragraph for context:

> The worst kind of betrayal lies in making us believe that the Indian woman in us is the betrayer. We, *indias y mestizas* [Indian women and mestizas], police the Indian in us, brutalize and condemn her. Male culture has done a good job on us. *Son las costumbres que traicionan* [It is the customs that betray]. *La india en mí es la sombra* [The Indian woman in me is the Shadow]: La Chingada, Tlazolteótl, Coatlicue. *Son ellas que oyemos lamentando a sus hijas perdidas* [It is they that we hear mourning their lost daughters]. (*Borderlands / La Frontera* 44)[16]

Although Contreras sees juxtaposing "the idea of gendered and racialized subjectivity named *la india* and the numerous goddesses in the Aztec pantheon" as a "slippage" because they don't, to her, "operate on the same discursive level," to Anzaldúa they do (54). We can best understand this by fully appreciating the nagualismo from which she operates.

Anzaldúa's use of Nahua concepts, stories, and traditions were neither attempts to represent Indigenous women nor to tell their stories. She articulated and continues to articulate in her ongoing relationship with readers an art form, border arte, that is (like in the Nahua tradition) always in motion, an art form that operates beyond a particular geographic, cultural, individual, or collective location or even a particular moment in time. "I don't write in a vacuum," she says. "I have helpers, guides from both the outer realm like my writing comadres and invisible ones from the inner world. I write in-community, even when I sit alone in my room. . . . I rely on the part of myself that has this ability to connect with these forces, to the imaginal world. I call this daimon 'la naguala'" ("Speaking Across the Divide" 293).

La naguala, therefore, was a practice of consciousness and art form that connected Anzaldúa to her surroundings but also to el cenote, a well of images, informed by her familial and cultural heritage. This heritage is one that although it can be traced by blood and historical documents is fully dependent on a social location and positioning, one that presented Anzaldúa with food cooked and stories told to her by her curandera grandmother, the same grandmother who said Anzaldúa was "pura indita" (all Indian) when she was born because of the dark blotches on her bottom ("Speaking Across the Divide" 282). This positioning presented Anzaldúa with a family that referred to her throughout her childhood as "la Prieta," the dark one, and with time interacting with los braceros (laborers), indios (Indians) from central Mexico who worked with her and her family in the fields of south Texas. Indian ancestry, by blood, by upbringing, by border dwelling, instilled in Anzaldúa that "to have Indian ancestry means to bear a relentless grief" but also "the promise of psychic integration" ("Speaking Across the Divide" 283). Although Anzaldúa does not claim to be Indian, she does claim Indian heritage through mestizaje, and as she describes in "Metaphors in the Tradition of the Shaman," she saw her writing as a type of shamanic practice of which la naguala, shapeshifting, is an integral part.

Because Anzaldúa summons nagualismo ontology and metaphysics as a personal and political move, with the intention of resisting colonial constructions of selfhood and collective struggle, I suggest that we read her nagualismo as a decolonial practice. Anzaldúa's nagualan consciousness recognizes the self's pervious boundaries and constructedness within relations of power but also enacts the potential to articulate and to hear deeply testimonies and, importantly, to contribute, as an individual and as part of a collective, to the success of social movements to end oppression across difference. Far from a naïve, nostalgic, nativist, or primitivist approach, in her Indigenismo, Anzaldúa was seeking ways to articulate forms of belonging and resistance that weren't bound to colonialist logic.

Anzaldúa's writing projects were her answer to a calling to articulate as an artist a pathway to personal and collective transformation. As she states in "Speaking Across the Divide," "All of my work, including fiction and poetry, are healing trabajos [works]. If you look at my central themes, metaphors, and symbols, such as nepantla, the Coyolxauhqui imperative, the Coatlicue state, the serpent, El Mundo Zurdo [the left-handed world], nos/otras, the path of conocimiento, you'll see that they all deal with the process of healing" (292–293). Debra Castillo claims that Anzaldúa was "a poet as well as, more importantly than, a theorist. It is as poet that she continues to inspire some members of the next generation, even as she angers others. She is not and should not be all things to all people" (265). I propose, in light of Anzaldúa's effort to blend and bend genres, that we not distinguish too rigidly between Anzaldúa as poet and Anzaldúa as theorist. Her poetics were an integral part of her theories, worldview, and activism. In "Let Us Be the Healing of the Wound," she says, "My job as an artist is to bear witness to what haunts us, to step back and attempt to see the pattern in these events (personal and societal), and how we can repair el daño (the damage) by using the imagination and its visions" (304). Anzaldúa's Indigenismo, informed by a particular Indigenous ancestry, deeply shaped her creative process and became even more important to her writing as her life progressed.

Some critics who engage with Anzaldúa's later work, such as those discussed earlier, recognize the decolonial potential of Anzaldúa's writing and concepts. Ohmer, for example, sees Anzaldúa's "now let us shift" as a decolonizing ritual. Ohmer's attention to the nagualismo that informs this work broadens its potential and points to a way to read the essay as an example of border arte and la naguala as a decolonial practice. Ohmer identifies that one of the contributions of "now let us shift" is that it is in part "el ejercicio shamánico" (a shamanic exercise), a term she borrows from Hernán Vidal, who says that shamans find in their journeys into darkness the wisdom of balance and healing to bring back to their communities ("Gloria" 144). Ohmer recognizes that Anzaldúa as a shamanic author/poet/narrator in her "personalized testimonial style" links personal crisis with planet crisis and, in her switch to second person, with reader crisis as well (147–148). As Anzaldúa brings the reader along in the essay, lines are blurred between personal and interpersonal journey, memoir and essay, spirit and body, and the use of rational and intuitive thinking. As she does this, she "transcend[s] the system of values that dominates and colonizes" (150). Ohmer also recognizes that Anzaldúa blends languages and sources:

> "Now let us shift . . . the path of conocimiento . . . inner work, public acts" seams together a number of concepts stemming from the Nahuatl, Spanish and English languages, and epistemologies from Occidental and Oriental ways of thinking. For instance, the symbols originate from the Tarot, the dowsing, astrology, numerology, and Jungian psychol-

ogy. Instead of referring to a specific primary source, Anzaldúa plays with the guiding energies of numerous religions, cultures, superstitions, juggling to allow them to cohabit with her text and within her/your life. (150)

The above passage supports how Anzaldua's essay works as a specific example of border arte, of a writer participating in multiple traditions and cultures to create art and identity that are in constant transformation. As Anzaldúa says, "[t]he multi-subjectivity and split-subjectivity of border artists creating various counter arts will continue, but *with a parallel movement where a polarized us/them, insiders/outsiders culture clash is not the main struggle, where a refusal to be split will be a given*" ("Border Arte" 184, emphasis mine). Invoking Mignolo, Ohmer says that in creating such works, the artist remembers the colonial difference but "moves between such labels" to keep those who belong to a particular culture from becoming part of the larger imperialist project ("Gloria" 142).[17]

As discussed in chapter 1, the concept of la naguala plays a significant role in conocimiento, which we can now read, given Ohmer's analysis, as a decolonizing ritual. The imaginary consciousness and connective potential of naguala, which Anzaldúa derives from her Indigenous heritage and hones from a place of border dwelling, therefore, serve as decolonizing mechanisms. This last chapter section identifies in *Borderlands / La Frontera* the seeds of Anzaldúa's early thinking about la naguala and its decolonial effects. In *Borderlands / La Frontera* Anzaldúa provides justification for appropriating the image of the shapeshifter from Indigenous thought: she is seeking a means to erase the binary between the rational and intuitive and the boundaries and limitation of the colonial, modern, gendered self, and the naguala serves this purpose; it deconstructs what is seen as appropriate paths to knowledge, embodiment, and being. Lastly, this chapter explains how the presence of conocimiento and shapeshifting are evident in the structure of *Borderlands / La Frontera* itself and parallel to *Light in the Dark / Luz en lo Oscuro*.

Seeds of the Shapeshifting Subject

From *Borderlands / La Frontera* to *Light in the Dark / Luz en lo Oscuro*, Anzaldúa consistently claims that complex, relational subjectivity is initiated by the "world of the imagination," which she describes in *Borderlands / La Frontera* as "just as real as physical reality" (59). She sees the split introduced by patriarchy and coloniality between objective, rational modes of consciousness and imaginal, intuitive ones as "the root of all violence": "In trying to become 'objective,' Western culture made 'objects' of things and people when it distanced itself from them, thereby losing 'touch' with them. . . . Not only was the brain split into two functions but so was reality. Thus people who inhabit both realities [rational and imaginal] are forced to live in the interface between the two, forced to become adept at switching modes. Such is the case with the india and the mestiza" (59). To Anzaldúa, myth, metaphor, stories, and images are tools for survival, the survival of an expansive, decolonized way of knowing and subjectivity. The images that Anzaldúa uses to explain the split—rational and imaginal—in *Borderlands / La Frontera* are the eagle and the serpent, and the serpent becomes the first most significant nagual in Anzaldúa's work.

By way of Mesoamerican mythology, particularly the stories of creator goddess Coatlicue/Serpent Skirt, and her brother Huitzilopochtli, whose importance escalated in the time of the Aztecs, Anzaldúa explains the dominance of the eagle—symbolism for the father, sun, spirit, and male—over the serpent—the symbol for mother, earth, underworld, and feminine. She works with this imagery throughout the text. Not only does Anzaldúa seek to honor the serpent but she also simultaneously deconstructs, removes the tensions between it and the eagle, blends them, and queers the serpent; she says, for example, when discussing heterosexual expectations thrust onto female sexuality, "[H]ow does one put feathers on this particular serpent?"[18] How does one face with "tenderness" that which has been forced into the shadow, the underworld, the forbidden? (*Borderlands / La Frontera* 42). She provocatively reveals that a split between the male/female, rational/intuitive is a lie, and she reclaims the shadow, queer side, as she disrupts the binary. The symbol of the serpent is carried throughout *Borderlands / La Frontera* and is most developed in chapter 3, "Entering into the Serpent," where she describes her literal encounter with a snake in "Ella tiene su tono," which Anzaldúa translates as, "She has superpowers from her animal soul" (48). In this prose poem, which is shaped like a serpent, Anzaldúa explains how she was bitten by a rattlesnake that her mother subsequently chops into pieces. The young Gloria reassembles and buries it, and that night she dreams that she becomes the snake: "The serpent, mi tono, my animal counterpart. I was immune to its venom. Forever immune" (48). In her commentary that follows she states:

> Snakes, víboras: since that day I've sought and shunned them, Always when they cross my path, fear and elation flood my body. I know

things older than Freud, older than gender. She—that's how I think of la Víbora, Snake Woman. Like the ancient Olmecs, I know Earth is a coiled Serpent. Forty years it's taken me to enter into the Serpent, to acknowledge that I have a body, that I am a body and to assimilate the animal body, the animal soul. (48)

The snake—the shadow side, the feminine, the animal, the body, unconscious, the imagination, that which she fears but also embraces with fervor—is more than a metaphor or nod to or appropriation of her Indigenous roots. Here and throughout Anzaldúa's work, imagining the snake is a way of knowing, one that takes her literally into the body, the imagination, and Coatlicue states. She says in chapter 4, "Come little green snake. Let the wound caused by the serpent be cured by the serpent," or in other words, delve into the darkness, the shadow side of self (unknown, instinctive, irrational, that is usually projected onto someone or something else) in order to come into one's sexuality, queerness, fullness (68). By *Light in the Dark / Luz en lo Oscuro*, Anzaldúa has developed her theory of conocimiento, cyclical stages of consciousness involving "inner work [and] public acts," a process prompted by the presence of la naguala. She discusses in "Flights of the Imagination" a shamanic journeying into "el cenote," or the "inner, underground river of information" where "shamanic images" reside, a journey aided by the snake naguala (28, 24). At the end of her life, Anzaldúa's image of the snake is her call to "imaginal musings," metaphors full of energetic and materializing force that give her direction and purpose ("Flights of the Imagination" 35). Importantly, personal and social transformation and healing, to Anzaldúa, are brought on by this creative process. La naguala, as a practice of consciousness, selfhood, and subjectivity, initiates that journey. The snake, la víbora, as naguala is discussed in more detail in chapter 4.

In addition to the obvious appearance of the shapeshifting in chapter 3 of *Borderlands / La Frontera*, a structuralist reading reveals a shapeshifting nature of and pattern in Anzaldúa's texts themselves. *Borderlands / La Frontera* and *Light in the Dark / Luz en lo Oscuro*, written about a decade apart, follow a similar form, a textual conocimiento. Each begins with a historical event that created a monumental breakage and devastating, shocking moments that ripple throughout decades, centuries, and generations. *Borderlands / La Frontera* describes, of course, the history of the US-Mexican border, and *Light in the Dark / Luz en lo Oscuro*, the collective trauma of September 11, 2001. These events mark the arrebato, the rupture and fragmentation involved in the initiation of stage 1 conocimiento, an ending of "un susto" (trauma) gives way to the beginning of the texts ("now let us shift" 547). Chapters 2, 3, and 4 of each text describe the inner journeys of nepantla space and Coatlicue states—woundings—inner struggles with identity, selfhood, and nos/otras. Chapters 5 and 6 of *Borderlands / La Frontera*, "How to Tame a Wild Tongue" and "Tlilli Tlapalli: The Path of Red and Black Ink," respectively, describe the role of language and the writing process in the reconstruction of self, introducing theories that are fleshed out in *Light in the Dark / Luz en lo Oscuro*'s chapter 5, "Putting Coyolxauhqui Together: A Creative Process." The final chapters of the texts, *Borderlands / La Frontera*'s "La Conciencia de la Mestiza: Towards a New Consciousness" and *Light in the Dark / Luz en lo Oscuro*'s "now let us shift" are chapters that pave a path to possibility, reassembly, and hope and reinforce the shapeshifting nature of reality and survival.

Although Anzaldúa had not yet fleshed out her theory of conocimiento nor of la naguala when she wrote *Borderlands / La Frontera*, the stages and cyclical nature of conocimiento are present in the text, as is the importance of shapeshifting. She closes "La Conciencia de la Mestiza: Towards a New Consciousness" with a memory of her and her family's farmwork and a metaphor for the remaking of a people: "Growth, death, decay, birth. The soil prepared again and again, impregnated, worked on. A constant changing of forms, renacimientos de la tierra madre" [rebirths of the mother earth] (113). For Anzaldúa, la naguala, this constant changing of forms, is present in the natural world in the quest for self-in-relationship and in the survival of cultures and people. La naguala is present in the making of and response to texts and art—border arte. Introduced and developed in *Borderlands / La Frontera*, more than a metaphor, the coiled serpent, shedding its skin, becoming something new, despite being dismembered, buried, and cast as evil and abject, offers Anzaldúa, as border artist, a powerful means for resistance to Western modes of knowing and, more important, a means to creativity and survival.

CHAPTER THREE

Connections with Arab American Feminism

I am a cultural worker. I write stories and essays.
Each one comes with a different taste and
texture, and I want you to feel each one and
taste each one, to let the words slide into our
bodies, to know with certainty that my words
are written not out of a sense of duty, but with
love and tenderness, anger and passion.

—Joanna Kadi [Joe Kadi]

For me, writing begins with the impulse to push
boundaries, to shape ideas, images, and words
that travel through the body and echo in the
mind into something that has never existed.
The writing process is the same mysterious
process that we use to make the world.

—Gloria Anzaldúa

From her earliest writings and activism until her death, Gloria Anzaldúa was invested in "break[ing] the impasse" between and bringing together differently racialized groups of feminists to work in coalition against oppression ("[Un]natural bridges" 245). Her investment in finding strategic common ground among variously situated groups, however, was balanced with a commitment to create opportunities that gave voice to how individuals and groups of people experienced oppression in divergent ways. "Our goal is not to use differences to separate us from others, but neither is it to gloss over them," she says (245).[1] To Anzaldúa alliance work among feminists shifted during her years in liberation movements. Two years into the twenty-first century, she looked back to the 1981 groundbreaking volume *This Bridge Called My Back: Writing by Radical Women of Color*, which she and Cherríe Moraga edited and that is reflected in her preface to the 2002 *this bridge we call home: radical visions for transformation*: "Twenty-one years ago we struggled with the recognition of difference within the context of commonality. Today we grapple with the recognition of commonality within the context of difference" ("Preface: (Un) natural bridges" 2). Another twenty years later, using categories to name our personal and collective experiences is even more complicated, as is working across those categories when we do. How do we, as feminist activists, affirm real differences in the conditions of our lives and experiences of oppression while reaching toward and moving with each other in solidarity?

Many of us still turn to Anzaldúa's work for advice on this question. I turn to her now, to the preface mentioned above, and find a paragraph where she is pondering how "we are interconnected with all life" (5). She writes of prodding at a sea anemone and watching it tremble and contract into a ball: "We all respond to pain and pleasure in similar ways. Imagination . . . has the capacity to extend us beyond the confines of our skin, situation, and condition so we can choose our responses. It enables us to reimagine our lives, rewrite the self, and create guiding myths for our times" (5). Using imagination, we tell particular stories, of being prodded and of our own prodding, of despairs and desires, and we can use them to build bridges. When we hear stories from others, we might not relate to the circumstances, but we do relate to the feelings a journey invokes—fear and joy, isolation and connection, rejection and belonging, and being in-between. We also hear in these stories, however, what life feels like to be in a specific location at a certain moment in time. A location that is not our own. We know that when we do not honor that experience, even and especially that which is opaque to us, we render someone invisible. So we listen with care and feel with all our senses each and every word. We know that feminist movements survive and are effective when there is a balance in speaking and hearing, contracting and expanding, when the narrative is both one and many, and when each narrative is something we learn from. We call upon and enact the imagination in telling and hearing stories, and in the process emotions are awakened, emotions that we recognize in others, too. In turn, we see and make connections.

The quotations highlighted at the beginning of this chapter reveal a desire by the authors to summon feelings and share worlds with their words. Joanna Kadi (Joe Kadi) and Anzaldúa demonstrate surprising similarities in approach to storytelling despite their vastly different cultural locations, one Arab Canadian and one Chicana. Within their works is a similar process of a radically relational self-in-the-making, but these writers speak from experiences and conditions separated by many miles and different histories and traditions. In uncovering the distinctions in situations and insights that arise in the work of diasporic Arab women writers, this chapter attempts to add nuance and richness to the expansiveness of subjectivity discussed so far with relationship to Anzaldúan nagualan consciousness.

Bringing Anzaldúa into conversation with Arab American and Arab Canadian women writers and activists,[2] specifically, serves several purposes. First, feminist discussions of relational selfhood and feminist theorizing, in general, have overlooked writings by Arab women, even in attempts to include voices by women of various cultural backgrounds; therefore, this chapter aims to help redress this oversight. Arab American women writers and activists have exposed the precise barriers to their visibility in US feminist discourse, many related to the Eurocentrist and Orientalist tendencies and anti-Muslim racism of the West and to tensions between Zionist and Palestinian feminists.[3] Importantly, like Rabab Abdulhadi, Evelyn Alsultany, and Nadine Naber, the editors of *Arab and Arab American Feminisms: Gender, Violence, and Belonging*, who assert that they go beyond an "add-and-stir" approach or resist the problematic "*adding* [of] Arab and Arab American feminist perspectives to the landscape of existing models of U.S. feminisms" (xxxi), the focus here is on how late twentieth- and twenty-first-century Arab American women writers offer a particular, transformative take on subjectivity, relationality, and coalition politics. Due to their unique positionality, as Carol Fadda-Conrey explains, Arab American writers of today reenvision selfhood, belonging, and citizenship in ways that resist assimilationist and nationalistic approaches to subjectivity, for example, "[b]y problematizing the binary constructs (such as 'us vs. them' and 'over there vs. over here')" and producing, instead, what she proposes are identities that are "transnational and transcultural" as well as "revisionary and radical in nature" (*Contemporary* 3, 27). Fadda-Conrey demonstrates a change in perspective in writings by second- and third-generation, US-born (1950s and onward) Arab Americans who transform the nostalgia for and visions of the Arab world articulated by their parents and grandparents; these newer generations of Arab Americans write of a transnational identity, one that is not torn between Arab and US locations but informed by both.

The subjectivity expressed in the writings of Arab American women is similar to Anzaldúa's, for example, in its attention to the negotiating of multiple, shifting cultural influences. Indeed, Arab and Arab American women writers, such as Smadar Lavie, Fadda-Conrey, and Hanadi Al-

Samman, find in Anzaldúa's concepts of borderlands, mestiza consciousness, and borders, respectively, useful means for explaining the experience and consciousness gained from being in between two or more cultures. This chapter, however, focuses on links to the radical relationality present in Anzaldúa's account of nagualan consciousness, specifically, to reveal subjects-in-the-making that bridge time and locations and blur boundaries between persons and objects. Also similarly to Anzaldúa's nagualan process, the authors foreground writing itself and journeying into the imagination for wisdom and connection, retrieving images, stories, and metaphors as practices of a subjectivity that are always in motion.

Arab American women writers are positioned at not only multiple intersections of identity but also in identity locations that shift and are difficult to define, even in a temporal way. Christina Najla LaRose, for example, shows how Evelyn Shakir, an originator of Arab American literary studies, complicates Nancy Hartsock's standpoint theory, the notion that "group knowledge is locatable in time, space and particular cultures" by pointing out that Shakir's autobiographical narrative voice is an "intergenerational interlocutor," one in which she shifts between the voices of many subjects, even those long gone, and shifts between "various actual and imagined locations," pasts, presents, and futures (237). LaRose refers to this as Shakir's "imaginary topographies." I agree with LaRose but add to her analysis that narratives by Arab American women, particularly, echo an intergenerational influence not just of people but also of other aspects of culture, for example, basic material aspects, such as food, recipes, and postcards. Perhaps, this is an aspect of all diasporic experience, but its presence in Arab American women's work is highly prevalent and palpable and what led Kadi to the title for the groundbreaking anthology *Food for Our Grandmothers: Writings by Arab-American and Arab-Canadian Feminists*.[4] Fadda-Conrey, too, has commented on food as a "connective bridge" in Arab American women's writing and also sees food as an "important distinguishing tool between one national and ethnic affiliation and another" as well as a metaphor for hybrid experience ("Arab American Literature" 201).[5]

This chapter uncovers and emphasizes the intergenerational influences in Arab American (and in the case of Kadi's book, also Arab Canadian) women writers' work, revealing subjects that interact with people as well as objects, in moments of the present as well as in the past, expanding on and not just providing an example of the concept of nagualan consciousness and practice, practices accessed by nonrational means, including by way of the body. Therefore, a second purpose for reading Arab American women writers with Anzaldúa in mind is the opportunity to explore metaphysical aspects of a nagualan-like, decolonial selfhood, in general, while also recognizing the specific, concrete reality of a culturally based group in the United States, one that offers a unique take on subjectivity that resists Western humanist, colonial constructions of subjects. Negotiating bicultural and/or multicultural upbringings and lives and the marginalization and oppression that have intensified since the beginning of the twenty-first century, Arab American women contribute in original ways to an articulation of an expansive selfhood and also of post-oppositional identity politics.

Thirdly, therefore, the voices of Arab American women also help to flesh out and complicate the newly introduced idea of post-oppositional politics. In proposing the concept, AnaLouise Keating offers a long-overdue analysis and recognition of the theoretical contributions of the writers of *This Bridge Called My Back: Writings by Radical Women of Color* in "developing and enacting nuanced politics of interconnectivity" (*Transformation Now!* 38). This chapter raises other examples and their implications in addition to *This Bridge Called My Back*—in which Arab feminists did not have a presence—by bringing into the conversation insights that emerge from memoirs, essays, and critical works of Arab American women writers who were writing during the time period of that book and afterward.[6]

In addition to exploring how these writers narrate relational subjectivities that expand Anzaldúa's descriptions of nagualan consciousness, this chapter explains how Arab American women writers articulate what I link to Keating's three lessons for the development of post-oppositional consciousness: making connections through differences, positing radical interrelatedness, and listening with raw openness. These articulations provide clear, practical examples of how a consciousness with nagualan features works toward post-oppositionality and the potential for coalition. While it might seem complicated, even contradictory, to appeal to identity while also reaching in the direction of post-oppositional consciousness, I argue that it is not only conceivable to do so but it is also necessary. Recognition of differences in the experiences and circumstances of oppression renders these differences real and visible, exposes particular systemic problems, and can reveal similarities in practices of resistance and survival among the differently oppressed. Naming and honoring differences also provides a foundation for building trust and articulating multivoiced rather than assimilative responses and goals and for implementing wholly new tactics.

The connections between the work of Anzaldúa and Arab American writers advanced in this chapter begins with discussion of Arab American feminisms, in general, followed by emphasis on Anzaldúa's contemporaries Shakir and Kadi. My analysis is humbly cautious in comparing these writers inspired by two distinct cultures in America. Avoiding assumptions of sameness and seeking to honor the specificities of their unique contexts, I identify connections in the complexities with which these writers practice self-identification and formation. I bring them together for the reasons specified at the beginning of the chapter but also in part to recognize the contributions of both Arab *and* Latina/x writers to feminist scholarship and activism and in part the relationship between them in articulating voices, stories, and experiences of what Laila Halaby calls, in her poem by this name, "browner shades of white" (204). A specific link between Arab and Latina/x persons is articulated in one of the poem's stanzas:

> My friend who is black
> Calls me a woman of color
> My mother who is white says I am Caucasian
> My friend who is Hispanic/Mexican-American understands
>   my dilemma.
> My country that is a democratic melting pot
> Does not. (205)

Again, in pointing out the links between these two identities, each informed by two or more cultures, I simultaneously recognize their very different histories, languages, cultural and religious influences, and group-based experiences in the United States. Of course, Anzaldúa's term and concept of "la naguala" relate to her particular ancestry, but what I suggest here is that we can find links and potential for decoloniality in *how* those affiliated with group-based experience write about their *practices and processes* of identity formation informed yet also limited by ethnic, racialized, and gender categories.

Highlighting these practices brings into relief how the authors discussed here can claim an Arab American woman's experience that contributes to a fluid selfhood and nagualan-like consciousness without claiming a fixed Arab American woman's identity. In other words, these writers experience intersectionality but also recognize that experience as constructed by coloniality and in the case of Arab American experience, Orientalism, as introduced by Edward Said.[7] María Lugones suggests that although the concept of intersectionality plays a necessary role in explaining power relations, including the power relation between white women and women of colors, another logic that does not depend on categories created by coloniality is necessary in imagining and living possibilities that will effectively resist oppression. Lugones calls this logic one of "fusion," which is "lived and understood relationally" and disrupts the logic of categories upon which, she argues, even intersectionality relies ("Radical Multiculturalism" 77).[8] In other words, oppressions are always already fused and not "combined fragments" (76). However, even Lugones, who claims that intersectionality is still within the "logic of oppression," points out that intersectionality demonstrates how "women of color are not seen precisely because the categories [i.e., Black and women] are not seen to intersect" (75). This tool is critical to understanding the invisibility of Arab women's experience discussed later in the chapter. I embrace Lugones's call, however, to find new logics and mechanisms with which to resist oppressions and seek to contribute nagualan consciousness to this effort.

What can follow, therefore, are coalitional opportunities among those who recognize that although marginalized experiences are particular and varied, communication and resistant practices among different groups can be shared and broader collectives formed. As Lugones says, "[s]ince the fusion is a resistance to multiple oppressions, one can also appreciate the ways in which others have conceived, given cultural form to, theorized, expressed, embodied, their resistance to multiple oppressions" ("Radical Multiculturalism" 77). It is in the spirit of Lugones's understanding of categories of identity as experientially real but socially constructed tools of oppression and of her call for "non-dominant resistant circles,"[9] that I honor and work with Arab American women's writing. Although it is tricky to discuss a particular intersection of experience—Arab, American, woman—and claim that writing from this intersection or fusion suggests a fluid, decolonial identity, it is possible and productive to do so.

Lastly, the effort to bring Arab and Latina/x feminists together is also done in part to align with Anzaldúa's persistent efforts throughout her life to work across differences, as mentioned at the beginning of the chapter, even in the face of opposition to such attempts. As Keating notes, "[a]t a time [1960s and 1970s] when separatism was a familiar political strategy among oppositional groups . . . Anzaldúa maintains her allegiance to all of the groups while rejecting their mono-thinking perspectives, politics, and rules" (*Transformation Now!* 14–15). Also, Anzaldúa's influence on Arab American feminists is well noted, for example, in the case of Kadi, who in an interview with Nadine Naber credits Anzaldúa and Moraga's *This Bridge Called My Back* for inspiring the vision for *Food for Our Grandmothers*, which showcases narratives of Arab women that *This Bridge Called My Back* left out, helping to fill the void in feminist scholarship by and about Arab women identified by Carol Haddad in 1983 at the National Women's

Studies Association Conference.[10] Just three years after the publication of *Food for Our Grandmothers* came *Bint Arab: Arab and Arab American Women in the United States* by Shakir, who later published, among other things, the memoir *Teaching Arabs, Writing Self: Memoirs of an Arab-American Woman*.

In addition to Kadi's and Shakir's texts, this chapter explores Diana Abu-Jaber's 2016 memoir, *Life Without a Recipe: A Memoir*, and works by other more contemporary writers in order to cover a chronological breadth of writing. Amal Talaat Abdelrazek, who identifies a lack of critical discussion on Arab American literature even in the twenty-first century, points out the emphasis on "hybridity and diaspora" and "border crossings" in the writings of Leila Ahmed, Mohja Kahf, Halaby, and Abu-Jaber and claims that their work moves toward a "rearticulated politics of difference," the result of "living in two worlds but belonging to neither" (12, 17). Abdelrazek says, "These women, all of whom search for an integrated hyphenated identity, straddle cultures, fight double battles, and recognize that any location comes closely intertwined with gender, racial, and political context" (17). This context Abdelrazek describes resonates with post-oppositionality, demonstrating the impossibility of naming and belonging to fixed, single, and, therefore, opposing locations or identities. Abdelrazek and other critics point to the work of Said and Homi K. Bhabha and feminist writers of color, such as Patricia Hill Collins, Chandra Mohanty, and Gayatri Spivak. Abdelrazek mentions Anzaldúa's early work in *Making Face, Making Soul / Haciendo Caras: Creative and Critical Perspectives by Feminists of Color*, but I turn to Anzaldúa's later theorizing for thicker descriptions of "inclusivity" mentioned in Abdelrazek's critical work as a means for thinking through the immense nuances and value of the shifting subjective processes present in Arab American women writers' texts.

Arab American Literary Scholarship

Although a thorough review of Arab American literary output and criticism is beyond the scope of this chapter,[11] this section draws attention to some distinguishing characteristics of that history that influence the writings and theorizing discussed later in relationship to Anzaldúa. Also in an attempt to stay with the narrow purposes of the chapter, I will not pursue a comparison of the heightened experiences of cultural, political, and policy barriers faced by both Mexican and Arab Americans in recent decades. However, the discrimination and dehumanization both groups face are intensified at this historical moment and have implication for times to come, and although the histories and backgrounds of each group (and within each group) are vastly diverse, the need for more nuanced understanding and visibility of these experiences is of crucial importance today to the academy and beyond.

While Chicano literary criticism began to burgeon in the 1960s and early 1970s with the establishment of such journals as *El Grito* (1967) and *Aztlán* (1970), it wasn't until the 1990s that such a movement took hold for Arab American writers, propelled by the first publication of *Al Jadid* (1995), a quarterly magazine of Arab culture and arts in the United States and abroad, and *Mizna* (1998), a journal of Arab American literature and art. Numerous works of poetry, novels, anthologies, and drama and academic articles also proliferated in the 1990s, although an Arab American literary tradition can be traced back to the beginning of the twentieth century in the foundational works of Ameen Rihani and Gibran Kahlil Gibran.

Since the beginning of the twenty-first century, Arab American literature has greatly thrived, despite and certainly in part in resistance to an increase in anti-Arab racism and Islamophobia in the United States. Most Arab American authors, even those who are bilingual, write in English, which, among other factors, differentiates them from Arab writers; however, the cultural, national, ethnic, and religious backgrounds that make up Arab American experience are numerous and varied. Lynn Darwich and Sirene Harb observe that the late nineteenth and early twentieth centuries exposed "a collective sense of urgency in the identification and representation of a multitude of Arab American experiences within the fabric of the United States" (300). This attempt to highlight the diversity in Arab experience was "essential as a starting point" but was also a "defensive standpoint" in "reclaiming space within the United States" and "recovering a sense of legitimacy" in articulating an Arab *and* American experience (301).

Noting the importance of attempts to confront stereotypes and myths, Darwich and Harb also point out that such efforts risk perpetuating essentialist interpretations of Arab American life. Amira Jarmakani, whose work is discussed later in the chapter, explains that Arab American feminists' energies are often derailed and their theorizing unheard because they have to spend so much time responding to and correcting stereotypes and misinformation about Arab American women, which creates an additional problem of reinforcing a false binary. But particularly after 9/11, confronting essentialist interpretations of Arab American writing and experience was and still is sometimes necessary.

Today, critics like Darwich and Harb propose moving away from "essentialist, celebratory, or reclamatory" readings of Arab identity and positionality. More specifically, in their reading of Randa Jarrar's coming-of-age novel *A Map of Home*, they reveal a form of analysis that "examines the characters' experiences, not as typical struggles of identity and belonging but as tense *processes* of gendered and classed racialization, self-representation, and political determination" (302–303, emphasis mine). Darwich and Harb, therefore, look at how race, class, national origin, gender, and religion intersect in particular locations and influence particular moments in characters' lives, offering a highly nuanced take on agency and power in Arab American experience. As a result, Darwich and Harb contribute an original take on such issues as gender and body regulation, racialized and gender violence, and the relationship of both to global neoliberal demands and to scholarship on the novel and Arab American studies, more generally. Their work, like Fadda-Conrey's discussed earlier, is invested in anti-essentialist approaches to literary production that takes into consideration the vast variation in the experience of Arab Americanness.

Like Chicana writers, such as Anzaldúa, who invoke the histories and mythologies of female figures like Malinche, la Virgen de Guadalupe/Coatlalopeuh, and Coatlicue, Arab American writers call on Scheherazade,[12] the heroine of the series of folktales *One Thousand and One Nights*, whose skillful storytelling won over the sultan Shahrayar, saving her own life and the soul of the ruler, and call on historical women like Muhammad's wife Aisha and the Egyptian queen Cleopatra to explore tropes and stereotypes, recast them in feminist perspective, or mobilize as feminist theory. Susan Muaddi Darraj raises all three figures in her essay on Third Wave and Arab American feminisms to assert that such figures are read in the West as exotic sex objects or as weak, veiled, and voiceless women, using these cultural mythologies as a starting point for introducing the failures of American feminism to fully understand and appreciate the complexities of Arab and Arab American women's situations. Jarmakani explores Orientalist representations of Arab womanhood within the context of the expansionist, militaristic, and imperialist aims of the United States with relationship to the changing power dynamics between the United States and the Middle East since the early twentieth century. Working with Said's central thesis in *Orientalism* and other poststructuralist, postcolonial, and feminist theories, Jarmakani makes a strong case for how US narratives about the veil, harems, and belly dancers function as myths and obscure the realities of Arab women's lives.

Some scholars assert that Arab writers use cultural icons as theoretical tools or to remake myths, similarly to Anzaldúa. In her work on trauma and authorship, Al-Samman argues that when Scheherazade is raised in contemporary diasporic Arab women's life writing, the trope works to revisit and transform the literary erasure of generations past, revealing a transgenerational subject that resists centuries of traumatic threats to Arab women.[13] These references to and critical work with historical figures and literary tropes serve as means for the exposure of misrepresentation and elision of Arab women's lives and as a tool for reimagining and rewriting Arab women's experience.

In Arab American women's writing, scholars note a variety of philosophical ethics and apply a range of theoretical approaches in their readings of texts. Broadly speaking, contemporary critics articulate interest in anti-essentialist, anti-Orientalist understandings of Arab American experience and identities; writers' complex relationships to the Arab world and diasporic perspective; trauma and other experiences of war and military involvement, including US military involvement, in the Middle East; food and cultural memory and identity; treatment of Islam and Muslims in US culture; Arab American's complex relationship to non-European "whiteness" and racial status; and gender identity and politics as they intersect with Arab culture and Arab American experience. Although contemporary Arab American literary scholars tend to offer readings that are rich in cultural, feminist, postcolonial, and more recently, queer critique, links to the revival of materialist ontologies are yet to be pursued at this writing.[14] My own reading of Arab American women's writing seeks to simultaneously answer the call for more-nuanced, anti-essentialist readings of Arab American experience while bringing that experience under the lens of posthumanist interests and, relatedly, an Anzaldúan approach to a radically relational, nagualan consciousness.

Arab American Women Writers and Nagualan Consciousness

The voice and subjectivity in writings by and about Arab American women's diasporic experience resonate in specific ways with Anzaldúa's descriptions of nagualan consciousness. Anzaldúa's account, like the accounts of the Arab American women writers to be discussed here, resists Western, humanist, and colonialist constructions of subjectivity as enclosed and unitary. Although each Arab geographic region differs with relationship to a colonial past, the influence of and relationship to a Western gaze, though varying in extent and particulars, is present across Latina/x and Arab American experience. I argue that Anzaldúa uses the language of her heritage, that of the earliest Mesoamerican society, not to appropriate or romanticize it but to enact a decolonial ontology and epistemology. Arab American women invoke the Arabic language and myth as well in their works in English and resist privileging Western forms of being, knowing, and achievement. One author after another turns, for example, to her grandmother's cooking, storytelling, and other daily activities as sources of knowledge, metaphors for describing her experience, and major influences on her self-development, in general. Consider the reference to Kadi's grandmother, referred to as "Gram" or "Sittee" (Arabic for grandmother), in a reflection on weaving a multicultural heritage, Arab and Canadian, into a cohesive selfhood:

> I know it is possible and I believe it is necessary to create maps that are alive, many-layered, multi-dimensional, open-ended, and braided. Gram combing that long hair, dividing it into three equal parts, twisting and turning and curving the pieces. Braiding tightly enough so that each hair stays in place, but not so tightly that it hurts. It is difficult finding that balance.
>
> It is difficult finding that balance. Take three strands—one that is Gram, one that is me, one that is the force of history—twist, turn, and curve; do not pull so tightly that it hurts; do not weave so loosely that strands escape. It is difficult finding that balance. (introduction, xiv)

Kadi is honoring Gram's "beauty, endurance, and usefulness," represented by the use of her hands, while also finding in the image of Gram's braiding a way of describing the many cultural forces at work on Kadi's subjectivity, and the tension present when negotiating them all, represented by the repetition of, "It is difficult finding that balance." Strands of a braid demonstrate the complexity of how single parts become one, not an amalgam but a multipleness. Two themes of nagualan consciousness can be found here: reference to the body, as nagualan consciousness is informed by corporeal experience; and the use of an image or imaginal consciousness in demonstrating a process of becoming a subject. Like Anzaldúa, who becomes the crashing wave and lighthouse described in chapter 1, Kadi becomes the braid. For Kadi, the process of the braid's formation is like Kadi's own attempts, in complex relationship to the grandmother and a specific history, to claim a selfhood that is intimately, invariably linked with others and context. References to the body and multipleness of self can tie to phenomenological readings of subjectivity, like Mariana Ortega's; however, as discussed in chapter 1, nagualan consciousness includes not only a sense of oneness with other persons but also with nonhuman objects and processes, such as dreaming, and creative, imaginative practices, such as writing and art. Kadi's work, like the others discussed further on, is full of—is guided by—the latter.

To Kadi, maps are "alive" with "both physical and political features," and "*Food for Our Grandmothers* can also be understood as a map" (xiii). Kadi is blurring the distinction between sentient and insentient beings and things and bringing attention to their power and agency. Requesting readers to understand the text as an actant in the Latourian sense, Kadi says the book is a physical thing that is alive. Kadi calls forth Sittee, or Gram, and, in the opening sentence of the introduction, a daydream—a memory—of childhood of sitting "in a wooden desk, its top scarred by the pens and knives of students who had gone before" Kadi. Readers witness Kadi in the act of presenting them with the text and its authors as subjects that transgress time and location, conjuring up, even in a physical sense, the presence people and locations from an earlier time. "Dig out a map of my old high school. Try to re-trace those corridors, try to re-cast those sound waves echoing off walls lined with yellow lockers," Kadi recollects, before remembering the experience of growing up Lebanese in Canada. "Lebanese, Not Black. Not white. Never quite fitting in. Always on the edge" (xvi). Being "on the edge" allows Kadi to develop a sense of facultad in the Anzaldúan sense, an intense awareness of surroundings, a "survival tactic" as Ortega calls it (*In-Between* 37) but also something else—a shifting, intuitive consciousness that merges with the palpable presence of the past, a subject that senses by way of memory and imagination people and places of the past and present.

Anzaldúa's poem "Immaculate, Inviolate: *Como Ella*" similarly brings to life, with vivid corporeal imagery and a blend of past and present tenses, a speaker's memories of their grandmother. Smoke, fire, and heat are carried through this bilingual poem, as the speaker recounts how her grandmother was burned, physically and psychologically. Mamagrande survived a kerosene accident and the pain of serving a husband who did not meet her needs and fathered children with other women. In the closing two stanzas, the speaker describes when she gets too close to fires, she almost glimpses her grandmother's face. As the speaker feels the heat, she empathizes with her abuela's situation, saddened by her lifetime of silence, powerlessness, and hardship hidden behind her "parchment skin" and "clouds of smoke" (132). Felicity Amaya Schaeffer reads these passages as leaving a "sense that future generations will inhale the rage that must be suppressed in the moment, some unsure of where it came from and why to them" (1022). Proposing that the poem "both imagines and enacts intergenerational solidarity" as readers engage with its meaning, Schaeffer sees Anzaldúa, informed by "kinship with family but more so through a kin relation with the elements all around her," as having an "acute ability to queer, in startling and sensual ways, being, as inherited and lived within a dazzling array of multispecies and multiforms" (1022). The speaker did not attend her grandmother's funeral and ponders that her grandmother must have suffered, and readers grasp the ongoing, inextricable link between the grandmother and granddaughter, one that defies time, space, and even death. Theirs is a shapeshifting relationship that works with ephemeral and enduring earthly and psychic elements, bodies, memories, and feelings that are both multiple and one. As the title suggests, the relationship is also a sacred one, as the speaker carries on with her life as her grandmother did, with "dignity" and "pride" despite generations of oppression.

Arab American women writers add to and transform the Anzaldúan sense of naguala/shapeshifting as subjects that invoke generations of experiences and imagine futures that do not depend on binary categories of identification. One of the unique ways in which Shakir demonstrates the fluidity and multiplicity of subjects in her work is in her final chapter of *Bint Arab*, "Collage." "Collage" consists of sections of commentary from her interviewees, not ordered by individual voices but by topic. In this way a single person's voice shows up several times throughout the chapter, but her story comes in fragments, interspersed between the voices of others. Each individual voice is given its own paragraph, with a pseudonym underneath. This collaging technique leaves the reader with the notion that they are hearing many specific yet interrelated voices and stories, the sense of many but also one, each voice as important as the others. Shakir shows that within Arab American communities, women share some traditions, but expectations and responses to them are varied, especially between the generations. LaRose describes this chapter as Shakir's strategy for creating "counter fictions," by including contradictory (normative and counter) discourses juxtaposing each other. She also points out Shakir's "intergenerational interlocutor" at work here, compiling "fragments of memory" and "new take[s] on the old" (257).

Shakir, her interviewees, and the writers in *Food for Our Grandmothers* invoke the words of their relatives, mostly mothers/mamas and grandmothers, "sittees," as co-creators of the texts. The shapeshifting subject described by Anzaldúa as transformed by the imagination and empathetic communication with others takes on deeper meaning considered within the context of Shakir's chapter. In this last section, by leaving out an overarching narrator or her own commentary, Shakir gives way to a many-voiced subject that is still identifiably Arab American and female despite the differences and contradictions among the generations of experiences represented by the stories. She describes this complexity succinctly in the epilogue, which takes the form of a letter to her deceased mother; she calls the book a "houseful" of bint Arabs (Arab women), a gift of sorts to her mother, "full of voices tumbling over one another. Point and counterpoint, yes and no. . . . Hearts divided between two urges. The need to make a getaway . . . the need to belong" (196). The image summoned here allows the reader to imagine a collective of multiple parts, sometimes conflicting and sometimes in sync and always in motion, depicted by the action of tumbling. Not only do the multiple voices connect but past, present, and future also do, expanding the subject's temporal boundaries.

Lebanese American writer Therese Saliba breaches boundaries of time by invoking memories of her deceased grandmother's voice but also delves into the imaginal and spiritual realms of subjectivity by bringing her grandmother back to life in a description of her "phantom appearances" in "Sittee (or Phantom Appearances of a Lebanese Grandmother)," Saliba's nonfiction essay in *Food for Our Grandmothers* (7). Notably, Saliba closes her essay with this reflection:

> Sittee appears to me now at night standing beneath a lamppost, her shadow spreading up the stairs of my apartment building. I walk down the steps toward her, calling her name. She motions to me to follow and together we glide along the sidewalk, my fingers reaching for the fringes of her crocheted shawl fluttering in the night wind. She is taking me somewhere, I don't know where. As we wind our way through the deserted alleyways of the bazaar, past tables of jewelry, perfume, and ceramics, past shops without vendors, I reach for her hand and we stand together beneath the domed archway of the night, speaking Arabic, her language I have come to know. (17)

As described in chapter 1, nagualan consciousness lends itself to mystical wisdom, including that which comes through dreams, bodily sensations, and imaginal experiences, even wisdom that on a rational level seems absurd or impossible. Saliba does not belabor how she came to this encounter with her grandmother, therefore underplaying the question of the "reality" of the experience. In nagualan consciousness, the body responds to images, concrete *and* imagined, and Saliba demonstrates here how this image of interacting with her grandmother after her grandmother's death plays a profound role in her selfhood and development; the relationship with her grandmother continues into Saliba's adulthood, and that relationship is a material, active one. Although in the short passage above, Sittee's image is ethereal and not quite tangible, represented by the "shadow" and just out-of-reach "shawl fluttering," Saliba's surroundings are concrete, her walk lined with "jewelry, perfume, and ceramics," suggesting that her grandmother's presence is palpable in the objects Saliba associates with her, even though her Sittee's physical body has long left (17). The relationship to the grandmother here, like the one in Anzaldúa's poem "Immaculate, Inviolate," is a blend of material, immaterial, and sacred experiences. Saliba's example demonstrates the "connectionist view" of naguala, one that expands beyond Enlightenment humanist conceptions and participates with not only people but also images and objects (Anzaldúa, "now let us shift" 569).

Saliba, author and narrator of "Sittee," exhibits an intensely embodied subject in this story; her negotiations between her American surroundings and her Lebanese history are told mostly in descriptions of the scents, sights, tastes, and touch of a land she never visited but to which she was privy by way of her Sittee. Her memories of Sittee are of lemon jasmine, dyed red hair, the taste of honeyed pastries, pistachio and pine nuts, and kibbee (a meat dish), as well as the squeeze of Sittee's hand. Fadda-Conrey recognizes the patriarchal, gendered dimensions and implications of such memories—Saliba's and others—that celebrate the immigrant domestic and domestic sphere; however, Fadda-Conrey also points to how second- and third-generation Arab Americans interrogate and remake such roles as they reflect on and are critical of them.[15] Saliba's expansive take on subjectivity, one that moves beyond rational, enclosed constructions of selfhood, relationships, and subjects, resists patriarchal, Western worldviews and offers an embedded, embodied account of identity and development that negotiates among people, time periods, and cultures.

Saliba and other writers like Jordanian American Abu-Jaber, who conjure family and food in their narratives, are described by critics as departing from conventional text that do so in order to restore one to an authentic identity, which, in turn, perpetuates essentialist notions of ethnicity and nationality. More specifically, Carol Bardenstein argues that Abu-Jaber's memoir *The Language of Baklava* "maintains a critical distance from simplistic nostalgia" and "never collapses the fluidity and complexity of these relationships [between characters and locations] into fixed, essentialized poles or binaries that are so common in the cookbook-memoir genre, such as homeland and hostland, before and after, loss and recuperation" (161). Bardenstein adds that Abu-Jaber and other post-1990 Arab American writers depict "complex articulations of transnational identities and affiliations in unsettled flux" in their works, breaking ground in written expression of multiethnic subjectivity (162). I extend Bardenstein's and Fadda-Conrey's analyses by emphasizing not only the transnational subjects present in Abu-Jaber's work but the posthumanist and decolonial dimensions of those subjects as well by exploring Abu-Jaber's 2016 memoir *Life Without a Recipe.*

Like Abu-Jaber's other works, the relationships with family members and food are particularly pervasive in her latest memoir. In chapter 1, she is demonstrating to her daughter how to crack an egg as they embark on a baking project. The egg certainly serves as a metaphor for Abu-Jaber's deep connection to her origins and musings on her legacy, as she ends the scene with a memory of her own grandmother teaching her to do the same thing, but the intense descriptions of the relationship between the child and the egg—the cracking—lends itself to a posthumanist reading that reveals an expansive subjectivity at work, one that is intra-active or emerging from within the process in which the egg, daughter Gracie, grandmother Grace, and Abu-Jaber herself are sharing a materialization.[16]

Abu-Jaber opens the scene: "Her small hand curves like eggshell: satin skin, round fingers, dimples in place of knuckles. The brown egg echoes her holding hand. My breath is there too, inside the curve of her holding, waiting for the crack[. . . .] I watch the small hand hover with treasure. The treasure isn't so much the egg, it's the cracking. It's using the sharp knife, prizing cookies off the hot tray, flipping the pancake. If it's difficult and risky, it's delicious" (15). In the process of the cracking, which Gracie does with too much vigor and does again gently with her mother's help, Gracie and her mother experience together a shared moment that enlarges their sense of becoming in the world, one that Gracie is just beginning to experience and that Abu-Jaber learned from her grandmother. Even the way that Abu-Jaber describes Gracie's hand, with the article "the" instead of "her," is as if the hand is a part of a moment and not attached to an individual person. "The small hand hover(s)," and later, "(t)he hand lifts, hesitates, then smashes the egg," a hand seemingly driven by something other than Gracie alone, guided not only by a young girl's will but a mother's temperate supervision and the multifaceted egg (15). The peculiar statement that Abu-Jaber makes about her own presence in the egg-cracking process, "My breath is there too, inside the curve of her holding, waiting for the crack," invites worthwhile consideration. Abu-Jaber places not just herself but the air in the room (as breath, so part of her being, as well) between her daughter and the egg. The crack, therefore, creates a transformation for all involved.

The image and language of "the crack" can serve not only to express a co-constitutive subjectivity in action involving close family members but also can be understood with relationship to Anzaldúa's mentions of "cracks" in "Geographies of Selves" (79). Anzaldúa uses the language of cracks, rajaduras, to describe the space between Western, binary constructions of subjects, those with personal and political implications, and the opportunity for change and community building. According to Anzaldúa, "[a]n identity born of negotiating the cracks between worlds, nos/otras accommodates contradictory identities and social positions, creating a hybrid consciousness that transcends the us versus them mentality of irreconcilable positions, blurring the boundary between us and others. We are both subject and object, self and other, haves and have-nots, conqueror and conquered, oppressor and oppressed. Proximity and intimacy can close the gap between us and them" (79). Here Anzaldúa is discussing the tension between assimilation into dominant culture and protecting one's "ethnic cultural integrity," while in Abu-Jaber's scene the self/other divide is specifically between daughter and mother (and the memory of a grandmother); however, Abu-Jaber's scene provides a specific example of a nagualan consciousness at work, the type of "hybrid" awareness or practice that Anzaldúa is calling for above, that can be created in particular moments involving particular persons and their contexts (79). The "crack" is an in-between place, an awareness of the intimate connections between the persons and objects in moments and spaces. For example, returning again to Abu-Jaber's opening scene, even a bowl becomes an actant, as Gracie gazes into it after asking her mother about what an egg becomes: "Tilting the big ceramic bowl, she [Gracie] might be considering the beginning of life, the ends of the cosmos. The whorl at the center of the batter. A bowl is a place to find meaning, I think" (16). The bowl itself is lending meaning and possibilities to Gracie, reminding the reader that objects themselves can participate in consciousness.

Lastly, Abu-Jaber's opening chapter offers a take on selfhood that is porous yet also experiences a sense of separateness or in-the-flesh "me-ness," another complex characteristic of la nagualan consciousness. For example, Gracie and her mother do have some variations in their approaches to baking and to life—Gracie, after all, stabs the yolk repeatedly with a fork while Abu-Jaber, "wary of that hard white thing" as a child, tried to hand her first egg back to her grandmother, indicating that within the midst of dynamic, co-constitutive relations, a person experiences a lived sense of a complex single selfhood, too (17). In this scene Gracie and her mother are teaching each other about concepts that are at the heart of Abu-Jaber's written self-expression: desire, love, and perseverance, states of experience that can only be fully fulfilled in relationship. Although Abu-Jaber's writing about food, cooking, and family functions in ways that other multicultural "food memoirs" do, as expressions of ethnic community, identity, rituals and traditions, Abu-Jaber's *Life Without a Recipe* is also a narrative of expansive, shapeshifting subjectivity, where the scents, sights, touches, tastes, and sounds of food play as much of a role in the scenes as the characters' thoughts and conversations with others. For Abu-Jaber, food, including the egg in this scene, functions like the braid in Kadi's example, by offering a potent image to express the nagualan subjectivity process.

Anzaldúa also works with food imagery to share experiences of family, gender, and culture growing up at the US-Mexico border. In the bilingual poem "Nopalitos," meaning little cactus leaves, the speaker appeals to readers' senses not only to pull them into her location but also to express her intuitive ways of knowing and a vast sense of selfhood that intimately engages with her surroundings. Scents of "dust," "orange blossoms," and "mesquite burning" open the poem while the speaker spends hours "defang[ing] cactus" as tiny needles lodge and remain embedded in her thumb (134). In an extensive reading of the poem, Carolina Núñez-Puente says that Anzaldúa invites readers into a dialogic, in the Bakhtinian sense, in her use of chronotopes,[17] which are amplified by lyrical play with scents, sounds, sights, and personification of natural elements, such as the "bleeding nopal" and "sighing leaves" (134). Anzaldúa's use of allusion, alliteration, synesthesia, zeugma, and themes, as Núñez-Puente observes, are impressive, as Anzaldúa brings readers in to "bridge time-spaces in the best of all possible dialogical scenarios" (149). Núñez-Puente and others have also noted the blending of Christian and Nahua imagery and other ways in which Anzaldúa blurs boundaries between binaries. What I see as particularly significant about this poem is the relationship between the speaker and her surroundings, as she is "pierced" by that with which she interacts, even in physical ways (134).

For most of the autobiographical "Nopalitos," the protagonist, who has returned to her rural southwest Texas home after a "long time" away, is laboriously preparing nopalitos for chile colorado, all while taking in the scene around her. The speaker is washed by the laughter of the women gathered on their porches ("Their laughter swells over the garden, *laves me*") and is also scolded by them, and the speaker is more interested in listening to the "grillos" (cicadas) than the women. Despite the tension between the now well-traveled and educated speaker and the people of her village, she is part of them and is especially part of the land, as the "thorns embedded" in her skin indicate. "Though I'm part of their camaradería am one of them," she says (135). Separate but implanted, as the "I" goes missing in the second phrase. Like the mother-daughter duo in Abu-Jaber's story, cooking rituals and cultural traditions ground the speaker to her community. Attending to dogs, flies, wind, a stick, chickens, flowers, sunlight, and more in this seven-stanza poem, the speaker is hyperaware of her location and exhibits an expansive sense of place, a shifting body-self.

Kadi's braids, Shakir's collages, and Saliba's and Abu-Jaber's, like Anzaldúa's, use of food and attention to bodily sensations are metaphors rich with meaning with respect to relational subjectivity, providing powerful, concrete images of how something or someone can be singular yet simultaneously and intricately connected to something or someone else. Neither a braid nor a collage exists without its individual parts; each link stands out yet blends in. The food in Saliba's, Abu-Jaber's, and Anzaldúa's examples heightens readers' awareness of the senses, the undeniably material way in which the body-self physically engages with its context. A person's practice of nagualan consciousness, which, as Anzaldúa says, requires "alternat[ing] between hyperempathy and excessive detachment, a seamless change from one form to another" can be witnessed in these texts ("Putting Coyolxauhqui Together" 250). Indeed, the examples provided here are just a few of what emerge as consistent themes in these authors' writings.

The next section links Arab American women writers with postoppositionality and the potential for coalition work by way of nagualan consciousness. Substantial attention is given to Keating's writing on post-oppositionality and three "bridge" lessons in *Transformation Now!* since addressing post-oppositionality, a phrase that she coined, is one of the proposed purposes of the book, but more important, these three lessons or skills provide a theoretical and practical foundation from which social-justice efforts can grow. Within this framework I investigate the development of nagualan consciousness in coalition.

Arab American Women Writers and Post-oppositionality

An exploration of Arab American women's writing, with attention to expressions of post-oppositionality, reveals the practical, politically progressive implications of identifying and promoting nagualan consciousness. This section takes up Keating's three *"Bridge"* lessons as groundwork for establishing coalition and strengthens those lessons by linking them with

Arab American women's writing as examples. Keating honors the authors of *This Bridge Called My Back* by theorizing three ways in which "radical visions for transformation," can be built (*Transformation Now!* 38). Those lessons are (1) "making connections through differences," (2) "positing radical interrelatedness," and (3) "listening with raw openness" (38).

Commenting on lesson 1, Keating describes Latina/x and Black writers like Mirtha Quintanales, Andrea Canaan, Audre Lorde, Rosario Morales, and Anzaldúa as those whose work not only attends to difference but also "refines difference in potentially transformative ways" (*Transformation Now!* 38). These writers "expose (often to themselves as well as to their readers) their own previously hidden fears [of those who are different from themselves] and desires—fears and desires that have seemed so different, so shameful, that they must be entirely hidden" and go on to reveal "a type of intellectual humility by acknowledging the limitations in her knowledge"; they then take a risky step of "reaching *across* this gap to make connection," finding commonalities but not sameness in the experiences of women of colors from varying backgrounds (39).

Acknowledging and transforming difference into common ground are frequent themes in Arab American women's writings, as well. For example, Abdelrazek demonstrates that Mohja Kahf's poetry "[o]ffers a notion of Arab Muslim women's difference not as static or definitive but, rather, as an opportunity for dialogue and conversation" (92). Abdelrazek points out that the Muslim American speaker in Kahf's poem "My Grandmother Washes Her Feet in the Sink of the Bathroom at Sears" uses the opportunity of a conflict between her grandmother and "white Sears matrons" to "see beyond the rigid barriers put up by human ignorance," realizing that "despite their differences, all people share a common humanity" (92). The speaker's grandmother is preparing her feet for prayer by washing them in the sink of the store's bathroom, which the "Middle West[ern]" others find appalling and unclean (Kahf 27). As the only person in the scenario who speaks the languages (Arabic and English) of each of the two conflicting parties, the speaker is called on to translate the angry words that the women are leveling at each other (Abdelrazek 92). The speaker reflects on the situation:

> My grandmother knows one culture—the right one,
> As do these matrons of the Middle West. (Kahf 27)

The speaker recognizes, as she is situated "between the door and the mirror" and can see "multiple angles," that her grandmother and the others are "decent and goodhearted women" (27), so instead of translating the angry words she does the following: "I smile at the Midwestern women as if my grandmother has just said something lovely about them and shrug at my grandmother as if they had just apologized through me" (28).

Abdelrazek aptly says, of this decision to misrepresent the conversation, that the speaker "knows above all how to speak the language of love," and "[i]nstead of merely asserting the value of one's pure identity, the speaker suggests a hybrid one that opposes dualistic Western thinking" (92). At the end of the poem, the speaker opens the door of the bathroom, and all exit into "the great common ground" of the sales floor or, as Abdelrazek reads it, "humanity" (93). The speaker in Kahf's poem exhibits what Keating would describe as a post-oppositional consciousness, realizing that a binary-oppositional approach to the situation does not offer an adequate solution. This speaker attempts to understand each party's difference, even their ignorance, and offers a bridge (the open door) onto common ground.

The challenges and complexities of "making connections through differences" is, perhaps, the most difficult of the lessons that Keating identifies in *This Bridge Called My Back*. In the process of developing nagualan consciousness, Anzaldúa says that empathizing and seeing someone's circumstances from their, not your own, point of view are the keys to compassion and, in turn, transformation. Making connections requires "honoring people's otherness" and movement to a "roundtable" ("now let us shift" 570). The position of in-between, for example, as "Not Black. Not white," to use Kadi's language (*Food* xvi) and "Mexican from an Anglo point of view" and "lesbian and raised Catholic, indoctrinated as straight" in Anzaldúa's *Borderlands / La Frontera* (101), allows one to embrace ambiguity, identify how rigid categories of identity are too stifling, reframe conflicts, and move to coalitional strategy. In an earlier project I bring together la naguala, particularly the aspect of recognizing deep interconnectivity, with Lugones's "On Complex Communication" in order to explore the liminal conditions within which a subject is motivated to make the shift to an alliance with others ("Focus on the 'I'"). I argue that a self-in-coalition recognizes difference, recognizes a shifting self-across-selves, and recognizes the resistant strategies of others. Although the scene in Kahf's poem is not one involving feminists of color working for change, it does offer insight into a first step of recognizing difference without defensiveness from the consciousness of someone between two extremes. Kahf, as artist and the poem's speaker, engages in multiple shifts—across languages, cultures' expectations, and generations—and finds middle ground that doesn't obscure the myriad of experiences that inform an all-too-common type of conflict that occurs in everyday America.

Of all of Keating's "*Bridge*" lessons, the second, "positing radical inter-relatedness," is the easiest to identify in all of the works of the Arab American women writers described to this point. The deep sense of connection to people, places, food, and objects expressed by narrators is one of the most noticeable themes in their writing. Important to note, however, is that the practice of post-oppositional politics and radical interrelatedness is difficult, tricky work and requires big risks. Most at risk is the chance that a person or marginalized group might sacrifice their particular voice, identity, analysis, and strategic activity to further misrepresentation and oppression in an attempt to work across difference.

In the past and currently, oppositional politics play a major role in il-luminating the voice and position of oppressed groups. As even Keating observes, there are times when "oppositional consciousness, politics, and thinking have been necessary to our survival, enabling us to resist and sometimes partially reform oppressive social practices and structures" (*Transformation Now!* 5). For Arab American women, distortions of their realities and risks of erasure are palpable. For example, Amira Jarmakani points out that Arab American feminists experience "being simultane ously invisible and hypervisible," given the highly publicized, misinformed perceptions of Islam as "hyperpatriarchal" and affiliated with terrorism and "an incomplete and monolithic understanding of Arab womanhood," all perpetuated by the cultural mythologies of the veil, the belly dancer, and the harem ("Arab American Feminisms" 227, 232, 231). Jarmakani states, "We are not merely silenced; we are wholly displaced and, there-fore, ontologically elided, by sensationalized news stories and images of oppressed and exoticized Arab women" (237). How, then, do women-of-colors scholars and activists make visible the realities of particular oppressed groups while working together to confront and dismantle the social constructedness of these groups and mechanisms of broader sys-temic oppression?

Jarmakani suggests a mobilization of "the politics of invisibility," grounded in Chela Sandoval's differential or nonbinary form of opposi-tional consciousness.[18] The politics of invisibility is conscious of ways in which speech and visibility as "counterdiscourse" might "run the risk of legitimating the problematic assumptions of the very discourses they re-sist" (Jarmakani, "Arab American Feminisms" 240). Jarmakani states that, therefore, silence and invisibility can be mobilized as strategies. To be more specific, she says, "Simply advocating for a rejection of current stereotypi-cal categories and narratives would inevitably lead to the establishment of equally limiting categories of representation, and spending energy to create a counterdiscourse will perhaps unwittingly reify the false binary that already frames much of public understanding" (240). At the center of Jarmakani's and Sandoval's theories is the recognition of the multiple-ness and flexibility of subjective experience and of identity categories. In *Transformation Now!* Keating recognizes Sandoval's differential conscious-ness as "beautifully illustrat[ing] the non- and post-oppositional forms of theorizing" that she sets out to explore in her text. Jarmakani's politics of invisibility provides an example of a differential consciousness that is informed by a specific group–based experience but recognizes that the elision that is part of the experience is imposed by coloniality and occurs for other nondominant groups as well.

For example, Jarmakani makes reference to the politics of invisibility in the work of Japanese American feminist Mitsuye Yamada, who wrote in *This Bridge Called My Back*, "No matter what we say or do, the stereotype still hangs on. I am weary of starting from scratch each time I speak or write, as if there were no history behind us, of hearing that among the women of color, Asian women are the least political, or the least oppressed, or the most polite" (68). Both Yamada and Jarmakani claim to feel like they were "starting from scratch," having to identify and dispel the myth of the stereotype before moving forward. In the stereotypes, women are "not seen as thinking, theorizing individuals" (Jarmakani, "Arab American Feminisms" 236). That moment of starting from scratch requires a cre-ative response that depends on the particular situation, in that particular moment, and it begins with a seeing of the self and identity as shifting and recognizes that an oppositional, corrective reply might reinforce a binary, incomplete, and inaccurate representation of experience. It is in this recognition of nondominant differences and in acting from it that persons in coalition participate in what Keating identifies as *"Bridge"* lesson 2, "radical interrelatedness."

Keating argues that the twenty-first century requires a new form of politics and resistance, that of a "radical interrelatedness," which is not a call for assimilation or accommodation; it is a call for rethinking ourselves as subjects. It is a call for truly listening for and understanding difference *and* a call to connect in recognizing and pursuing shared ground and goals. She reminds her readers that "we are interrelated and interdepen-dent—on multiple levels and in multiple modalities: economically, so-cially, ecologically, emotionally, linguistically, physically, and spiritually" (*Transformation Now!* 47). Of *This Bridge Called My Back*, Keating says that "interconnectivity" is "the inspirational force behind the book" and that it has "concrete ethical implications" (*Transformation Now!* 47, 49).

Building on Rosario Morales's analogy in *This Bridge Called My Back* of women of colors being in "the same boat" despite their differences, Keating states, "We are all in the same boat, floating on the same water, tossed about by the same waves, battered by the same storms: We all rise or sink together" (*Transformation Now!* 49). Although finding common ground is the ultimate goal in this lesson, it is not always easy or even possible, especially when facing hostility and hatred. The act of recognizing and getting on the boat together is complicated. Sometimes it seems safer to remain on the shore, even when the shore is on an island; some survive journeys, and others do not, even in the same boat. How does one know when taking up some form of oppositional strategies is necessary, and when it is not? Keating challenges us to think very carefully about this.

In this section of the "*Bridge*" lessons, Keating describes a painful event that served as a reminder to her of how her oppositional approach, honed in the academy, was harmful in many ways. She recounts a tension that materialized on a listserv among the authors of *this bridge we call home*, the follow-up text to the first *This Bridge Called My Back* that she and Anzaldúa edited. The conflict began when some contributors voiced serious concerns about the authorship being open to people who were not women and not women of colors and escalated into an explosive argument between pro-Palestinian and pro-Israeli contributors. Anzaldúa and Keating eventually shut the listserv down, with Keating noting in retrospect, "it's not always possible to build bridges and create communities" (*Transformation Now!* 51).

Keating describes seeing flaws in both sides of the argument and explains her first response: "I noted my strong desire to react oppositionally, to fight back, to counter the contributors' angry words with my own anger, to meet aggression with aggression, to give what I was receiving" (*Transformation Now!* 50). She was hurt, wrote reactionary e-mails she did not send, and then became physically ill. Anzaldúa addressed the conflict in the preface of the book (at the request of the Arab American authors), stating that the event "churned a liquid fire in our guts" and "masked feelings of fear," but she also recognized "generous, conciliatory responses" from some contributors ("Preface: (Un)natural bridges" 2). However, one of the Palestinian contributors, Nada Elia, was "seriously disappointed" in Anzaldúa's response, saying Anzaldúa underplayed "the hatred" that emerged during the conflict (154). Elia, writing about the struggle in her essay "The Burden of Representation: When Palestinians Speak Out," felt silenced by the shutting down of the listserv and marginalized by the editors' suggestion that another listserv be created for political discussion. Although the situation ended with the closing of the listserv, the tension was not resolved.

I spend time on this especially uncomfortable conflict for two reasons. First, because this chapter seeks to bring attention to often-overlooked Arab American writers engaging in feminist discourse, accounts of this particular conflict are crucial to note, as Arab American feminists had no presence in the first work, *This Bridge Called My Back*, and a small presence in the second, a presence that unfortunately was threatened by the misunderstanding and hostility they faced on the listserv; some contributors considered withdrawing their pieces. Both Keating's and Elia's accounts suggest that the pro-Israeli contributors, too, felt misunderstood and attacked. However, no one withdrew their pieces, and the project went on, but so did the uneasiness. This incident is a reflection of some of the specific difficulties that arise for Arab American women working to move from margin to center in feminist, women-of-colors discourse.

The second reason this conflict is mentioned here is to help to demonstrate the immensity of the task of "positing radical interrelatedness." Keating writes candidly of the listserv events in order to expose her own struggle with reacting oppositionally, a learned us-versus-them reflex and barrier to hearing and understanding others, and seeking resolutions and alliances, as well. By writing about her struggle, she demonstrates the "intellectual humility" she says post-oppositional politics requires and argues that "because binary oppositions have their source in the dominating culture and support its values and worldviews, our oppositional politics cannot be as transformative as we might assume. Indeed, oppositional politics can become poisonous and self-defeating" (*Transformation Now!* 51). This event speaks to the complications and complexities that can emerge in working across differences toward radical interrelatedness; deciding to put aside oppositional tactics or being silent when you are being misread and harshly criticized might not always be a viable approach. However, as Keating reminds us, "oppositional thinking erodes our alliances and communities," and coalitions require a move from "binary-oppositional to relational approaches" in order to succeed (*Transformation Now!* 8, 52). Certainly, for women of colors to come together and create strategies for change on broad, massive scales, post-oppositional thinking and tactics are necessary.

"*Bridge*" lesson 3, "listening with raw openness," involves the "intention to listen deeply and open-mindedly" (*Transformation Now!* 52). Keating says, "It sounds so obvious," but she reminds us that this task is particularly challenging for groups who work hard to discover their authentic voices and break out of silence (52). Keating recalls the well-known example of Audre Lorde's "Open Letter to Mary Daly," which questions whether Daly had really read deeply the works of Black women. Keating calls lesson 3 "listening with raw openness" to underscore the work and sometimes pain involved when we put aside our defensiveness. This act of listening is a crucial part of the nagualan process, in which "compassion triggers transformation" (Anzaldúa, "now let us shift" 569). Anzaldúa says, "This shift [nagualan transformation] occurs when you give up investment in your point of view and recognize the real situation free of projections—not filtered through your habitual defensive preoccupations" (569). Given Anzaldúa's description, "listening with raw openness" is, perhaps, the linchpin of shapeshifting/nagualan practice. According to Keating, the us-versus-them binary breaks when we admit to the limits of our own thinking and allow ourselves to learn from others. On a more specific level, the divisions we place between identity categories begin to erode as well.

In *Teaching Arabs, Writing Self,* Shakir grapples with binary categories of ethnic identities but also of teacher/student. Listening with raw openness profoundly transformed her thinking about these classifications. As an American-born woman of Lebanese descent, Shakir traveled to the Middle East to teach and thought she would "understand—even share" the students' "cultural instincts" (68). However, her assumptions were immediately debunked. They did not see her as one of them, and in poem after poem, story after story she taught, her students came up with interpretations she had to fight hard not to dismiss as "misreading" and "nonsense" (72). But Shakir took her students comments seriously. In the text she explores how the role of teacher and student, in her words, "turn[ed] inside out and back again, like the cupped hands of an Arab woman dancing" (72).[19] Here she is referring to teaching as a "two-way street," her teaching others, and they teaching her as she described her years as an Arab American teaching in Lebanon, Syria, and Bahrain (72).

Two of the stories about learning from students that Shakir shares in the book include themes of not only listening with raw openness but of the other two "*Bridge*" lessons, too. In the first story, a student asks Shakir if she is proud of being Lebanese. Shakir responds with an "Oh, yes," following the comment with praises for the landscape, the hospitality, and focus on family. Shakir then realizes that she was just trying to prove herself and fit in. The student, seeming unsatisfied with the answer, says, "Don't you know about the war? . . . Muslims and Christian and Druze all killing each other. How can you be proud?" (*Teaching Arabs* 57). Shakir follows this quote immediately with her second story:

On another day, a young woman, who I knew to be Christian, was eager to tell us a story. "Doctor, two years ago I was struck by the Evil Eye. I had the mark of an eye on my arm"—she indicated the spot—"and no medicine could heal it."

"It's all in your mind," sneered a young man. The class looked from him to her; they'd never been so attentive.

"No, no," she insisted, twisting around in her chair. "It was really the Evil Eye, not even the priest could help me."

"What happened?" asked several voices.

"My family bought medicine from an old Druze lady and I drank it." She paused, milking the moment, and then announced, "The mark disappeared the next day!" The class was spellbound, not wanting to believe, and yet. . . . And then another young man spoke up.

"I am Druze," he said, and we gave him our full attention. "Some of our people," he said, "have the same beliefs. But they get their medicine from an old Christian woman."

The class erupted in laughter. More moments like that, I thought, and there would be no fighting to shame us. (57–58; ellipses in original)

In both stories Shakir is recounting the wisdom she learned from her ethnically diverse young students about understanding difference but reaching through it to find common ground, seeing radical connections between each group's needs and traditions, and, lastly, their deep listening to one another, emphasized here with the comment, "we gave him our full attention." Shakir's memoir is full of stories of learning from others that demonstrate her willingness to be vulnerable and open to new ideas and to complicate her own understanding, even as a seasoned professor and mature adult, that she had much to learn, including from young people.

Shakir also applies post-oppositional thinking to the category of self and writer—self is the writer and the written about. Throughout the text she describes her struggle in search of herself as an Arab or an American and comes to the conclusion that she is both, saying of her time in the Middle East, "I'd been expecting a mirror and found a window. It just took a while for me to know the difference. . . . In looking at my students, I wasn't merely staring at my own face. Though, yes, I could still detect a family resemblance" (*Teaching Arabs* 87). In the above passages, Shakir demonstrates "raw openness" to listening to her students and interrogating her sense of self and her assumptions, including assumptions of sameness among her students and between her students and herself. With respect to nagualan consciousness, Keating's listening with raw openness can be read as a function of shifting awareness from "the ego" or "customary point of view" to a connectionist view," or the self-other merger, that then prompts a move to nepantla where the "knower" incorporates the experience into a changed self (Anzaldúa, "now let us shift" 569). In this way, nagualan consciousness is a practice, an act of choice, a shifted self, one expressed, in the case of Shakir above, in the act of writing ("now let us shift" 569).

Keating's lessons provide a framework for thinking about how subjects can move into coalition by describing practical skills required to do so. The radically shifting nature of and art forms generated by nagualan consciousness put forth by Anzaldúa offer ways of thinking, epistemologically and ontologically, about the type of selfhood needed to enact such capacities. The instances of negotiations of subjectivities provided here bring Arab American women's writing into conversations of complex yet day-to-day concrete processes of self and coalition. By focusing on examples, I attempt to move what might sound abstract and even anodyne into achievable goals. Reaching across and connecting through differences, positing radical interrelatedness, and listening with raw openness are, indeed, difficult to imagine in practice and present many challenges and risks, particularly in Western cultures that reinforce oppositional thinking about identity and belonging. However, seizing what work across difference looks like in art and in action is critical in the move to coalition.

Political movements in the United States, feminist and beyond, have much to learn from the often-marginalized, even among women of colors, Arab American women writers, whose understanding and practice of subjectivity, of writing, of relationship making, and of community building offer blueprints for moving beyond binaries and oppositional thinking about identity. I offer here just a few examples of creative works that demonstrate this point. Now is a critical time to call on Arab American feminists' strengths and skills, in women-of-colors coalitions and beyond, for the benefit of a greater, more inclusive American community. Arab American women writers demonstrate how subjects communicate across not just persons but across periods of time, locations, and ways of thinking and being. The subject is embodied and also acutely embedded in its surroundings in ways that help to prompt a movement toward radical interconnection and coalition necessary for positive, large-scale change.

Arab American authors, such as Shakir, Kadi, Abu-Jaber, Kahf, Jarmakani, and others discussed in this chapter, join Anzaldúa in demonstrating new ways of moving past what Lugones calls "the logic of narrow identity," the idea that individuals belong, primarily, to one fixed identity, the logic upon which US social-justice work is historically based ("On Complex Communication" 75). Although they experience the realities of living in such logic, they exercise the imaginal consciousness, what Anzaldúa calls "the dreaming naguala," to access images or symbols and metaphors that initiate new ways of being and relating that enlarge sense of self and community ("Putting Coyolxauhqui Together" 253). Despite difficult barriers, even among themselves as women of colors, they persevere and work together. Anzaldúa states, "Before holistic alliances can happen, many people must yearn for a solution to our shared problems" ("now let us shift" 573). Moving beyond oppositional thinking and strategies is critical to finding that common ground.

CHAPTER FOUR

"Reaching Through the Wound to Connect"

Trauma and Healing as Shapeshifting

> Betrayed for generations, traumatized by racial denigration and exclusion, we are almost buried by grief's heavy pall. We never forget our wounds. La Llorona, our dark mother with her perpetual mournful song, has haunted us for five hundred years—our symbol of unresolved grief, an ever present specter in the psyches of Chicanos and Mexicanos. . . . If you name, acknowledge, mourn, and grieve your losses and violations instead of trying to retain what you've lost through a nostalgic attempt at preservation, you learn not just to survive but to imbue that survival with new meaning. Through activist and creative work you help heal yourself and others.
>
> —Gloria Anzaldúa

> I am a two-thousand-year-old Arab woman. They tried to bury me in the desert, but they failed. They killed me several times, but I always resurrected myself from the ashes to fly, and to write.
>
> —Ghada Samman

> Resilience is unveiled when we are triggered, injured, heartbroken, attacked, challenged. . . . Resilience is perhaps our most beautiful, miraculous trait.
>
> —adrienne maree brown

Although experiences of loss, adversity, pain, and trauma might seem for some to be unlikely places from which to build theories for self-transformation and social justice, resilience is, indeed, born from such circumstances, as adrienne maree brown suggests in her epigraph. This chapter develops the idea of a transgenerational, relational, shifting subject introduced in chapter 3 by investigating the role of acute and insidious trauma, including what Marianne Hirsch calls "postmemory,"[1] or "generation after" trauma, in the lived experience and artistic expressions of subjects. In Nahua terms this concept is understood as "susto" ("soul wounding") or, more specifically, "susto pasado" ("past trauma"), meaning "the extended impact of trauma" (Gonzales 202).[2] Furthermore, I strengthen how writing and other art forms serve to heal and transform subjectivity as personal and collective experience with potential for decolonial coalition work.[3] In the narration, performance, and witnessing of traumatic memories and postmemories, those memories are remade, and the narrator and witness take power over them; the traumas become transformed. Of course, this link between art and trauma recovery is not new; scholars and practitioners have documented the role of creative expression in healing from trauma in numerous disciplines and mental health practices, from neurobiology to art therapy. Many of these discussions, however, focus on individual, psychological healing in the tradition of Enlightenment humanism.[4] Trauma, however, is a relational and collective experience and process; its existence is ever-present, and effects are transtemporal and transspatial. This chapter's broad aims are twofold in that it explores how the relational subject is motivated in fundamental ways by loss and trauma, even traumas not experienced directly but by way of cultural, transgenerational postmemory/susto; and how artistic response and, more precisely, shamanic shapeshifting response, to trauma initiate a subjective and decolonial agency, transformation, and healing that is place and time specific.

When focusing on artistic expression, particularly writing, as a form of resistance and activism, I do not wish to diminish other necessary, activist means for resisting and dismantling coloniality and oppression. My interest is in offering a theoretical foundation for exploring selfhood, subjectivity, agency, and collectives in posthumanist and decolonial forms and from which to build ethical actions and movements. What I propose more specifically is that a decolonial praxis informed by Indigenous thought can be found in articulations of nagualan selfhood and subjectivity in the writings of Gloria Anzaldúa and that praxis is motivated by a "wound" or rupture. I place this praxis within Walter Mignolo and Rolando Vazquez's understanding of "decolonial aestheSis," or a response to the modern "aestheTics" and its implications, which include a regulation of sensation and perception by way of European Enlightenment.[5] Decolonial aestheSis is "a heterogeneous, historico-embodied move" that "departs from an embodied consciousness of the colonial wound and moves toward healing."

For Anzaldúa, the site of trauma, directly and indirectly connected to the colonial wound, is the place from which most of her writing and theorizing begins, from her earliest works to her last, and the language, theme, and practice of creative expression and naguala/shapeshifting show up to play a major role in enunciating (to use Mignolo's term)[6] how recovery and transformation move selfhood into new, relational, always-in-motion forms of subjectivity. In other words, the text itself is engaged in, not a representation of, naguala/shapeshifting at the time of its writing and in being read or witnessed. This artistic expression is a decolonial one, an aestheSis, that is aware of the trauma of coloniality and enacts a practice of transformation that operates outside and holds the potential to transform modern ways of knowing, aesthetics, and being.

Writing from Wounds and Refashioning the Cosmos

To set up consideration of Anzaldúa's process of articulating or writing wounds as naguala/shapeshifting, I turn to how her poetic expression is in line with the process metaphysics of Nahualism, which, as chapter 1 explains, holds that artistic creation and change-of-form, or shapeshifting, is at the heart of any transformation, including teotl's regenerating of the cosmos. A recurring theme in Anzaldúa's work is that wounds are a place at which we can connect, create, and, therefore, heal, and this process of healing is a shapeshifting, shamanic journey, a journey of resistance to oppression and destruction, of hope for change, and of transformation. Also notable here are the expansiveness and agency of subjects. She says in the chapter "Let Us Be the Healing of the Wound" in *Light in the Dark / Luz en lo Oscuro*:

> Our actions have ripple effects on all people and the planet's environment. We are accountable for all the wars, all human disasters—none of us are blameless. We ourselves have brought this great turmoil upon ourselves. We are all wounded, but *we can connect through the wound that's alienated us from others.* When the wound forms a cicatrix, the scar can become a bridge linking people split apart. What happened may not have been in our individual control, but how we react to it and what we do about it is. Let's use art and imagination to discover how we feel and think and to help us respond to the world. (21, my emphasis)

Anzaldúa says next that it is in nepantla that we create: "We write and make art, bearing witness to the attempt to achieve resolution and balance where there may be none in real life. In nepantla we try to gain a foothold on los remolinos [the whirlwinds] and quagmires, we try to put a psycho-spiritual/political frame on our lives' journey" (21). In nepantla, one of the three types of motion-change or dynamics of reality according to Nahua metaphysics is where the cosmos get woven; nepantla processes "join, interlace, interlock . . . mix, fuse, shake, or weave things together" with "mutuality and reciprocity" and in ways that are "creatively destructive and destructively creative" (Maffie 364).[7] Those participating in the nepantla process are always in transition, always already moving from one prior status to something new while retaining the old; so in this way, participants in nepantla are not only creating some*thing* but they are also *part of the creation*, always part of the energy-in-motion that is teotl. Human persons are in and of nepantla. Maffie describes nepantla in this way:

> Nepantla-processes destroy their participants' prior status as fish or foul while simultaneously creating something that is neither fish nor fowl . . . the confluence of two rivers transforms rivers A and B into a new river, C. By mixing together A and B, the confluence destroys A and B while also creating something both ontologically and conceptually novel: C. Since C incorporates and preserves A and B, it follows that C is neither A nor B yet at the same time both A and B. Thus C is irreducibly ambiguous. (364)

Weaving fabrics is a nepantla process as it simultaneously constructs and destroys; threads are no longer independent in the resulting cloth but are something new. Artistic endeavors are processes that contribute to the constant transformation of teotl, as the maker takes existing materials and creates from them; in the act of creating, the artist is intimately *part of* the creation as well, changing and being changed by the project. Writing, painting, and performance all fall under this refashioning—the nepantla process. Reinforcing this idea, Anzaldúa says in "Preface: Gestures of the Body," "The writing process is the same mysterious process that we use to make the world" (5). Returning to the "Let Us Be the Healing of the Wound" quote above, we see how something new is made from not only the physical materials used by the artist/s but also the imaginal, affective, psychological, and physical materials that make up the artist/s themselves. For the writer on a shamanic journey, the writer, text, and, as discussed later, the reader participate in the refashioning activity of teotl.

Numerous scholars document that transformation for the shaman is born from crisis, illness, pain, and trauma but that such conditions are not usually considered pathological, as illness is seen as an invitation into a higher consciousness where wisdom is gleaned.[8] The process of entering into an awakened state of consciousness (emotional intensity or "trance") brought on by unexpected crisis or illness or induced deliberately is a defining characteristic of the shamanic journey. Anzaldúa describes these trance-like instances from which she gains knowledge in a number of her essays and stories. She also enacts them in the process of writing.[9] Anzaldúa offers descriptions of these moments in her use of the Coatlicue state as a plunging into darkness and depression and the fragmented Coyolxauhqui imperative that provokes the need to remember, repair, and heal. She also describes these states as hauntings by Llorona (as mentioned in this chapter's first epigraph) and visits by her nagualas during drug-induced and hypoglycemic states, dreams, and near-death experiences.

In her later work on conocimiento, a wounding is stage 1, what she calls "el arrebato," a "rupture, fragmentation," or susto, that introduces struggle but also opportunity ("now let us shift" 546). An instance of el arrebato can be "a frightening event, close call, shock, violation, or loss" that serves as an awakening and a chance to discover wisdom ("Let Us Be" 20). Her associating of conocimiento with the shaman's journey is straightforward as she closes her description of stage 1: "You must, like the shaman, find a way to call your spirit home" ("now let us shift" 125). The practices and rituals of "calling back the spirit" after susto or what Patrisia Gonzales discusses as the "ceremony of return" are well documented by scholars in studies of the ancient Nahuas, Zapotecs, Mixtecs, and Latinos (201, 211). For Anzaldúa, calling the spirit to the body is a process of transforming images in the mind into the written word. The drive is instinctual, and the process is equally bodily and textual. In an early (1981–1982) unfinished, unpublished autobiography, "Esperando la Serpiente con Plumas / Waiting for the Feathered Serpent,"[10] Anzaldúa describes writing this way in a section called "Struggling to Emerge":

> Struggling to recreate the image of spirit and body being one within the other, to lay bare their overlaying and interweaving threads. Like wind we cannot see but know is there when the curtains of an open window billow, the ^the^ [sic] spirit of the words move in the body. They are as material as one's flesh and as palpable. The hunger to create, the intent is as substantial as muscle and bone. (35)

Here Anzaldúa invokes the two ways the cosmos is transformed: by artistic creation (writing) and by shapeshifting, a transforming of the artist into the artist's invention. Narrative and writer move and change together, manifesting the self-generating force of teotl and refashioning the cosmos. This next passage, in the same section as the quote above, clarifies the intensity of the physical relationship between not only the body and the writing but also the cosmos, body, and writing, as well. The reference to blood emphasizes the pain of the inner work and disorder—the sacrifice—that is also part of the process: "The chaotic profusion which the writing brings up, the writing must clear up":

> I write in red. Ink. Blood. Intimately knowing the smooth touch of paper, its muteness before I spill my blood on it. I write on the insides of trees. Trees, the lungs of the earth. Trees, that white slice of flesh so much like mine. I daily battle the muteness and the red. Daily *will* the words to emerge. Daily take myneck [sic] in my hands and shake it until my voice wakens and the cries pour out, daily coax out the "presence" or spirit of the poem, my larynx and soul are sore from the constant struggle. (35)

Readers of *Borderlands / La Frontera* will recognize both passages above as versions of paragraphs that became part of "Tlilli, Tlapalli / The Path of Red and Black Ink" (*Borderlands / La Frontera* 93–94). These less-refined drafts emphasize even more so than the final, published passages the relationship among earth, body, and text and the physicality of the process of "the ceremony of return," the soul wound's healing ritual. The term "spirit," for example, is removed from the passage in the later text, and the term "tree" used only once. The unpublished writings demonstrate that Anzaldúa had a sense of herself as a shaman from her earliest efforts. By the final version of "Tlilli, Tlapalli," her understanding is clear: "The writer, as shape-changer, is a nahual, a shaman" (88). What follows is a review of how Anzaldúa's writing serves as a textual shaman's shapeshifting journey and refashioning of the cosmos, the cyclical process of crisis/wound/susto to healing, and how the naguala is critical to this practice, particularly, in the form of la víbora, the snake.

From her earliest works, including the 1981 mixed-genre collection *This Bridge Called My Back: Writings by Radical Women of Color*, which Anzaldúa edited with Cherríe Moraga, the relationship among writing, wounds, and trauma is ever present and emphasized. Moraga writes in the preface, "The materialism in this book lives in the flesh of these women's lives: the exhaustion we feel in our bones at the end of the day, the fire we feel in our hearts when we are insulted, the knife we feel in our backs when we are betrayed, the nausea we feel in our bellies when we are afraid, even the hunger we feel between our hips when we long to be touched" ("La Journada" xl). The "physical and psychic struggle" or "theory in the flesh," as Moraga referred to it, written in the pages of *This Bridge Called My Back*, still serves as a feminist blueprint for resisting patriarchal, racist, and colonialist restraints on expression (xli). In *This Bridge Called My Back*, Anzaldúa introduces readers to "La Prieta," an autohistoria (self-history) organized around significant moments of being wounded and subsequent healing.

In "La Prieta," Anzaldúa recounts several traumatic events that shaped her, calling them images that "haunt" her, "the old ghosts and old wounds," and these events frame the structure of the essay (198). The essay's form accentuates these traumas, small and large, as she begins many of her paragraphs with them and often with ellipses preceding the first sentence, indicating a disruption or interruption in the flow of the experience and of the writing. Her father's accident and sudden death, being bullied, being robbed, her early menarche and subsequent problems, her mother's victimization *and* tendency to take it out on her—these occurrences give way to the fear, shame, pain, and powerlessness that shape her coming of age. The traumatic images that visit her share in common their associations with blood, with a wound: "The bloodshed on the highway had robbed my adolescence from me like the blood on my diaper had robbed childhood from me." However, her healing is of her own accord, even unwittingly: "And into my hands unknowingly I took the transformation of my own being" (200). Significantly, Anzaldúa processes her experiences of trauma and survival in relationship to how she is read racially and as a queer woman, feeling like she is misunderstood and doesn't belong anywhere. Her "white and non-Chicano friends" ascribe "mythic qualities" to her strength and power and fail to see the realities and difficulties in her circumstances, which create distance between them (204). Yet, she insists that excluding people as potential friends and allies based on "color, class, and gender" is a misstep, remarking that two people whom she loves—Randy and David, who are white and male—experience traumas of oppression, including internalized homophobia, alienation, and powerlessness, with which she can identify (206). They, too, can be a part of the bridge she is seeking to build.

The traumas highlighted in "La Prieta," informed by a rich cultural legacy and immediate context, enlighten her vision of subjectivity and of her coalitional activism. The "mixture of blood and affinities" calls on her to identify with others who experience shifting but not the same identities (209). She says, "Not all of us have the same oppressions, but we empathize and identify with each other's oppressions" and form a "network of kindred spirits" (209). To her this outsider experience, what she refers to in this essay as "El Mundo Zurdo" or "the Left-Handed World," is necessary and ultimately positive and brought on by a rupture in consciousness. In this last section of "La Prieta," Anzaldúa says that by traveling the "two-way movement" of "going deep into the self and an expanding out into the world" that "a simultaneous recreation of the self and a reconstruction of society" occurs (208). She follows with, "And yet, I am confused as to how to accomplish this" (208). However, a little more than twenty years later, with the publication of "now let us shift," she clarifies the process and offers what she calls the seven stages of conocimiento, "inner work, public acts." Anzaldúa's autohistoria "La Prieta" and "now let us shift," in content and structure, express a cyclical process that moves from wounds to recovery, from flights of the soul and imagination to reintegration and re-creation. Rupture/susto initiates a self/collective journey toward healing, a shaman's journey, a participating with the regenerative motions of teotl. In between "La Prieta" and "now let us shift" is *Borderlands / La Frontera*.

In the opening of *Borderlands / La Frontera*, Anzaldúa introduces readers to the reference to a wound for which she is most known, "la herida abierta" (the open wound), the US-Mexican border, "where the Third World grates against the first and bleeds" (25). Scholars have written about Anzaldúa's theme of wounds, particularly this reference and others in *Borderlands / La Frontera*. Some explore Anzaldúa's use of Coatlicue and Tlazoteotl in discussion with the internalization of the mark or wound inflicted by colonization, the susto pasado that lingers from generation to generation. A few connect these images to shamanism.

George Hartley draws from the work of Andrea Smith on colonial control over and exploitation of the bodies of women of colors in analyzing Anzaldúa's poem "Matriz sin tumba o 'el baño de la basura ajena'" ("Womb Without Tomb" or "The Bath of Other People's Trash") as "homage" to Tlazolteotl (goddess of trash or filth), noting the speaker's "trauma of the inability to speak" and that like trash she is "tossed by the wind" (41, 45). Hartley says that Anzaldúa uses this "trashed condition" or wound as an opportunity for growth, an encounter with the Coatlicue state, turning "the woman of color's rejected womb into a source of decolonizing regeneration" (47). In the violent last half of the poem, then, the scene of excision of the womb is refashioned as a "Nahua ritual" or "limpia" (cleansing ceremony), a "purification" or washing away of the negativity, evil, and hate of coloniality that causes susto (47).[11] Hartley identifies this process again in *Borderland / La Frontera*'s chapter 6 where Anzaldúa describes another encounter with Tlazolteotl, a "surrender[ing] to what lies in the darkness inside her," where the poet is ultimately transformed into a shapeshifter (53). Here Hartley acknowledges the potential of Anzaldúa the writer as shaman and nagual: "This transformation of the poet into a nahual is the precursor to developing the capacity to transform her culture as it undergoes the painful shocks of cultural shifts and to recognize these shocks and shifts as creative change" (53). Hartley does not focus on the philosophical status of the selfhood and subject created in Anzaldúa's position as nahual and practice as a "curandera [healer] of conquest"; I propose that her writing practice and work as shaman, or curandera, shifts what we understand as the Anzaldúan subject even ontologically (58). Exploring the significance of wounds in the creative movement of nagualan consciousness adds depth to this discussion by expanding our understanding of the process and its connection to nagualismo, or shamanism.

The details of this movement from wounds to creative output and healing also reveal a subject's sense of control over and agency in individual and collective transformation. The wounds or ruptures that Anzaldúa discusses are often not self-imposed (earthquakes, physical violations, racism, illness, and death); however, the journey to creative response that follows *is* a choice and one she elects each time she writes, despite the barriers. As she says in the earlier blocked quote, "What happened may not have been in our individual control, but how we react to it and what we do about it is" ("Let Us Be" 21). She also says in "now let us shift," as mentioned in chapter 1, "When a change occurs your consciousness (awareness of your sense of self and your response to self, others, and surroundings) becomes cognizant that it has a point of view and the ability to act from choice" (568–569). Although wounds are brought on by external circumstances, our responses to them, like those that are a part the shaman's journey, are at least partly within our control, according to Anzaldúa. Perhaps, part of why some readers are drawn to Anzaldúa's writing is the optimism and hope in this aspect of her worldview: the power in change and the power to make change together, despite the pain and repressiveness of wounds. She sees pain in the same vein as love with respect to giving way to affiliation: "Although all your cultures reject the idea that you can know the other, you believe that besides love, pain might open this closed passage by reaching through the wound to connect. Wounds cause you to shift consciousness—they either open you to the greater reality normally blocked by your habitual point of view or else shut you down. . . . Like love, pain might trigger compassion—if you are tender with yourself, you can be tender to others" ("now let us shift" 571–572).

This unexpected and peculiar connection between love and wounds shows up in Anzaldúa's unpublished short story "Sleepwalkers," a manuscript she was working on before and after the publication of *Borderlands / La Frontera*. The story opens as Prieta, who, we learn later, is dying from internal bleeding after being beaten by "the Opposition/menshadows," is riding in a getaway car. Next to her is a stranger, a woman healer, with whom she locks eyes in the rearview mirror. The attraction is instant, and what follows is their exit from the car, a journey through the dark Texas night to the woman's apartment, and a scene that for Prieta is an experience that is simultaneously intensely painful and erotic. The sensual connection is a nonnormative one, two women—the healer in "two inch heels" and "blue suede skirt" and Prieta in "jeans and briefs." They are avoiding the 1980s oppression and violence of the US Southwest, moving together at night when it is easier to hide, like other "sleepwalkers" "for whom night was day and day night" (1, 3).

Once the two women reach the safety of the apartment, Prieta has to completely give over to her companion, as her lungs are succumbing to the injury, and she realizes that she is on the brink of death. Her healer tells her, "The only thing is that my healing you depends on you believing that I can heal you," but Prieta realizes that the healer, too, must trust that Prieta will be honest with her: "Aren't you afraid I may not believe you?" The two must believe in each other in order for Prieta to heal and in order for the curer to help. They connect through the wound, one inflicted by outside Oppressors but internalized. Bleeding at the mouth, like the nagual jaguar that vomits fire, Prieta exposes the "gateway" to transformation, "reaching through the wound to connect" to her healer, offering a chance for transformation, an opportunity to transport themselves to a safer place and connection, where they can escape the violence of their current world, including that which they have internalized, and live out their imaginaries and desires together and uninhibited ("Werejaguar" 7; "now let us shift" 571). Although "Sleepwalkers" is a fictional story, this one, like Anzaldúa's other stories, includes autobiographical elements, indicated by protagonist Prieta's presence, Anzaldúa's nickname since childhood and speaker in her memoirs, as well. In sharing this story with her readers, Anzaldúa is revealing a deep wound through which they, too, can connect with her, empathizing with her situation, feeling the fear, pain, and passion felt by Prieta in a vulnerable moment.

Moving through wounds, therefore, offers not only opportunities for healing but also for connection and relationship; the movement is neither easy nor linear, however. Anzaldúa warns of the potential for "desconocimiento" or "excessive dwelling on wounds," which she says takes the form of "leaving the body" and "re-enacting past hurts" in the mind ("now let us shift" 572). Mariana Ortega, too, suggests, "Trauma does not necessarily lead to transformation or more knowledge; it could just leave us fragmented and dead" ("Wounds of Self" 243). However, like Anzaldúa, Ortega sees the potential to connect in the expression of wounds through writing: "[S]ometimes the wound can be transformative for me as well as for others as I narrate and share my experience with you" (243). La Prieta's experience in "Sleepwalkers," trusting a companion in the midst of her being most vulnerable serves as an example of connecting at the wound and healing from the wound in relationship to others. I return to Ortega's ideas shortly, as she undertakes *Borderlands / La Frontera* in her exploration of words, wounds, and healing.

A few other scholars in addition to Hartley have connected wounds with shamanic process in *Borderlands / La Frontera*. Sarah Ohmer explores communities of African and Indigenous descent and how texts serve to remake or what she calls "re-member" a "collective culture memory" to manage "repressed sexuality and other traumas" and to heal ("Re-membering Trauma" 8). Like Hartley, Ohmer works with Anzaldúa's poetry in *Borderlands / La Frontera*, focusing on the nineteenth-century lynchings and rapes of Tejanos and Tejanas in "They Called Them Greasers" and chapter 3 of *Borderlands / La Frontera*, "Entering into the Serpent." Ohmer reads the Olmec serpent mythology as the way in which Anzaldúa moves from fear to acceptance of her body and sexuality. (Later this chapter explores the serpent as a critical process of entering into el cenote, as well.) Ohmer says that Anzaldúa likens writing, as a shamanic act, to shapeshifting (7). Approaching illness from a shamanic point of view, Ohmer sees illness and trauma as offering "a transformative initiation" to "enhanced psychic sensitivity" and, subsequently, "the hidden and highest potentials for human existence" ("Re-membering Trauma" 341). I add to this perspective as the last section of the chapter develops the decolonial potential of trauma and writing.

In her analysis of Anzaldúa's "wounded and wounding words" in *Borderlands / La Frontera*, Ortega takes up Roland Barthes's idea of "punctum," or "the sting, the speck, the cut that wakes us and alerts us to look further, to investigate, to understand, to care" ("Wounds of Self" 236).

Although Barthes was interested in the photographic punctum and said that images communicated more than words, Ortega thinks that words can reveal a punctum, too. She asks to what extent can punctums be not only deeply personal but shared and says that Anzaldúa's written expression of "life in the borderlands" and "liminal existence" captures lived experience in ways that are translatable and transformative, reaching others with her words, offering "an invitation to an intimate encounter" (240, 242). They are "word[s] that pierce, that wound," and such words are ways to connect and transform the self and collectives (246). Although Ortega does not discuss Anzaldúa's writing as a shamanic process, in the final paragraph of the article she notes Anzaldua's reference to becoming a "nahual" or "herself transformed" and her writing an offering of "communication and transformation" (246).

To Ortega the punctum is a way of thinking about selfhood and relationship whereby the self is personal *and* shared, what she later calls "the multiplicitous self" in *In-Between*. The self, therefore, is understood as "an existential dilemma that always involves the personal, the political, [and] the theoretical" instead of "the criterion that explains same-selfness over time" ("Wounds of Self" 238). Traumatic and other powerful punctums found in words offer options for appreciating and connecting with one's own and someone else's experience. Ortega's phenomenological account of the communicative and transformative power of words that come from wounds helps us to see the patterns and value in Anzaldúa's writing as a lived personal and shared experience. But also, understood within the motion-change dynamics in Nahua metaphysics, Anzaldúa's reference to becoming nahual, "able to modify and shape primordial energy," as she says in the passage that Ortega cites, enacts a shaman's journey from susto to growth, an artistic creation (writing) within which she is part of and participating with teotl (96). Her use of "primordial energy" is a telling phrase and suggests that Anzaldúa was purposely using her writing, art, and self as artist to contribute to an always, already life force.

This shamanic creative pattern of movement from wounds to healing is evident in much of Anzaldúa's published and unpublished writing, far more than can be covered in this chapter. Before returning to one of her unpublished pieces that displays this form, I recognize a recent growing number of works by those who explore spiritual and/or shamanic healing in Anzaldúa's writing in not only *Borderlands / La Frontera* but beyond. Among the first of these publications is Betsy Dahms's *Letras Femeninas* article, in which she identifies a "shamanic praxis," one that recognizes the shaman as a "wounded healer,"[12] in not only *Borderlands / La Fron-*

tera but in some of Anzaldúa's other published and unpublished works ("Shamanic Urgency" 10). Dahms's 2012 article predates the publication of *Light in the Dark / Luz en lo Oscuro*, although Dahms does address one essay, "Putting Coyolxauhqui Together: A Creative Process," that appears not only in *Light in the Dark / Luz en lo Oscuro* but in the 1999 *How We Work*, edited by Marla Morris, Mary Aswell Doll, and William F. Pinar. In her close reading of *Borderlands / La Frontera* and some of Anzaldúa's stories, interviews, and essays, Dahms concludes that as a writer Anzaldúa was a practitioner of shamanism.

Relying on Mircea Eliade's 1962 publication *Shamanism: Archaic Techniques of Ecstasy* as "the most comprehensive study of global shamanism" at the time, Dahms highlights the "two-way movement within her person and outward into her community" as Anzaldúa's shamanic process ("Shamanic Urgency" 10, 11). Publications on shamanism and Mesoamerican metaphysics since Dahms's article provide support for her argument about shamanic process. A notable aspect of Dahms's claim is her emphasis on Anzaldúa's use of the Nahuatl term "patalache" or "woman-loving woman" to describe herself; Dahms traces the idea of patalache/queer as border crosser and also as shaman in Anzaldúa's writing and says, "Anzaldúa viewed her particular mixture of male and female qualities as a gift that afforded her new knowledge," allowing her the metamorphic, shapeshifting qualities of shamans (14).

This "gift," to which Dahms attends, can be seen in Prieta in "Sleepwalkers" when she participates in her own healing, as well as in "Puddles" when Prieta, who has a sense for reading queerness, shapeshifts into a lizard. The character of Andrea, too, in "El paisano is a bird of good omen" exhibits shapeshifting qualities. Dahms also identifies in Anzaldúa's poetics the shamanic transformation of the writer by way of the writing itself, particularly in "Speaking in Tongues: A Letter to Third World Women Writers." Dahms mentions the concept of shapeshifter, using it as a synonym for shaman,[13] and also notes the role of the snake and snakebite in *Borderlands / La Frontera* as Anzaldúa's initiation into shamanism.

Other more recent works take up Anzaldúa's later writings in relationship to wounds, spirituality, and recovery. I discovered two right before this manuscript went into production, an indicator of scholars' increasing efforts to bring the spiritual aspects across Anzaldúa's oeuvre into academic conversations. Engaging Anzaldúa's theories of conocimiento and El Mundo Zurdo as "queer of color worldmaking," Robert Gutierrez-Perez makes sense of and enacts healing within the simultaneous process of grieving and writing scholarship about the June 12, 2016, Pulse nightclub massacre in Orlando, Florida (384). A scholar of rhetoric and communications, Gutierrez-Perez discusses the "emotional and spiritual labor" of living through the time of the event and finds in conocimiento a mechanism for describing his and other queer-of-color experience, from susto to recovery, in theorizing, writing, and publishing about the massacre (384). Gutierrez exposes a "violence of intersectional heteronormativity" in the academy in his "archiving [of] the processes that queer people undertake to make worlds that exist alongside the master narrative" (385). Although Gutierrez-Perez does not focus on healing as shamanic activity in this piece, I note it here as a clear and specific example of how Anzaldúa's writing, understood as a healing ritual, can serve as means for creative and effective activism, decolonizing of the academy, and even physical and spiritual survival.

Also recently, Christina Garcia Lopez identifies in Chicanx literature, including Anzaldúa's late writings published in *The Gloria Anzaldúa Reader* and *Light in the Dark / Luz en lo Oscuro*, a healing spirituality and decolonial potential that are reflections of curanderismo, a blending of Indigenous Mexican spiritual traditions and Catholicism that developed in colonial Mexico. Lopez invokes the ritual of "calling the soul back" (mentioned earlier in this chapter in reference to Gonzales's and Hartley's work) but rearticulates it as a conscious practice by Chicanx writers in their storytelling to heal traumas or splits (self/environment, body/soul, etc.) imposed by colonialism (5).[14] She refers to "calling back the soul" as a "willful move toward a reintegration and transformation of consciousness that carries the potential to radically restructure how we experience and move through our lives," a move that she says can be initiated by scholars and creative writers (14). In this regard she sees stories as "medicine" and possibilities for "spiritual decolonization" of the academy (14).

Garcia Lopez identifies Anzaldúa's reference to desconocimiento as an example of the concept of soul loss. Her work with Anzaldúa is carried throughout the book, but she gives the most substantial treatment to "Let Us Be the Healing of the Wound" as "a culturally specific framework of susto" (26). Garcia Lopez explains that Anzaldúa narrates "a personal and collective fragmentation" and, subsequently, a cultural healing or limpia practice, using writing as a spiritual tool (37). I agree with Garcia Lopez's claim here and see it as part of Anzaldúa's larger textual conocimiento pattern, that of the shaman's journey, found in her essays but also her stories and poems and in the structure of her books. I see the naguala, as story and writer, as an integral part of this practice.

I now return to Anzaldúa's unpublished autobiography "Esperando la Serpiente con Plumas" as I close this section on Anzaldúa's writing from the wound as a shamanic act, as some of the most telling connections between her ontology and Nahua metaphysics are revealed in this manuscript. Incomplete and nonlinear, meant to be "read like a poem or a novel," this selection offers an intimate look into Anzaldúa's thinking and writing process in the early to mid-1980s, after the publication of "La Prieta" and before *Borderlands / La Frontera* ("First draft, Esperando la Serpiente" 1). "Explanation, analyses, and theory are included but they are not the main roads traveled here—the path of process is," she notes (1). More like raw musings than an orderly draft, "Esperando" displays Anzaldúa's worldview and writing process and the links between them. She says this of the relationship among humans, creativity, and the cosmos: "I believe there is order and structure in the universe and that we see this in the cycles of nature. As we change and evolve so does the planet. And so does the Creative Live [*sic*] Force. . . . I see evolution in a planet, person, or grop [*sic*] as the unraveling, unfolding of _____ [*sic*] creative process. The stiffling [*sic*], limiting, and crippling of creative powers and potentials for growth is de-evolution the only evil in the world" (3). The definitive claim that stifling creative power is the only evil seems less like hyperbole when understood within a Nahua framework, where form-change and regeneration are driven by creative endeavor. Creativity feeds life, movement, and change, but the path—the shaman's path—like any birth, requires rupture, pain, and sacrifice, a journey inward toward wounds in order to regenerate and heal them. In the outset of "Esperando," Anzaldúa says, "The aim of this book is to put back together parts of our ^the^ [*sic*] flesh severed from us. To heal our deep, deep wounds. To return to the things we allow ourselves to be split from" (2). She implicates the body, the breath, in the process—"inhalation" as a "going inward, exploring the inner path" and "exhalation, a moving outward, sending away"—and says this process is enacted "as a group, not just as individuals," a bodily, singular and collective, two-way shamanic movement (2).

Although Anzaldúa's allegiance to the spiritual and ontological traditions of her Mesoamerican roots is what is emphasized here, true to her border-arte practice that combines the influences of past and present, situating her in her particular cultural moment, there are many references to other diverse inspirations, such as the I Ching, the ancient Hawaiian belief in Aumakua, the Tarot, numerology, and Plato. However, most of the references in and the process of the writing adhere to her path as shaman and to what she identifies as her "ancestral spiritual traditions" of the "Coahuilteca, Aztec, Maya, [and] Navajo" (1). As her work develops, this allegiance seems to become stronger, as her final writings that make up *Light in the Dark / Luz en lo Oscuro* indicate. Her references to the naguala shift as well, emphasizing its role in the creative process.

Referring to the impulse to write as the "Coyolxauhqui imperative," Anzaldúa says in the preface to *Light in the Dark / Luz en lo Oscuro* that she is driven to write in order to "reconstruct oneself and heal the sustos resulting from woundings, traumas, racism, and other acts of violation que hechan pedazos nuestras almas [that tear our souls to pieces], split us, scatter our energies, and haunt us" ("Preface: Gestures of the Body" 1). She also says of the process that writing is "an act of calling back the pieces of the self/soul that have been dispersed or lost, the act of mourning the losses that haunt us," in line with the Nahual curing/spirit ceremony of limpia that Garcia Lopez identifies in "Let Us Be the Healing of the Wound," but the reference here is an even more obvious one (Anzaldúa, "Preface: Gestures of the Body" 2). Still practiced today by Indigenous peoples in Mexico and their descendants in the United States, the limpia, or "sweeping" ceremony, also called "levantando la sombra," or "raising the shadow / calling the spirit back," involves retrieving the spirit "from the place of traumatic recurrence" (Gonzales 206). This Mesoamerican ceremony is seen in many variations across time, groups, and languages. For Anzaldúa, writing from the wound, revisiting "traumatic recurrences," is guided by the naguala, what she calls in "Preface: Gestures of the Body" the part of consciousness involved in "active imagining," or ensueños (dreaming while awake), and also "the making of images" (5). An "inner sensibility" that directs her life, the naguala—together with the imagination—compels the creativity process (4). However, the naguala can also take her in unproductive directions: "Often my naguala draws to me things that are contrary to my will and purpose (compulsions, addictions, negativities), resulting in an anguished impasse. Overcoming these impasses becomes part of the process" (4). The naguala, the "animal in you and your animal companion, yourself and other," therefore, appears to have unbridled potential to take consciousness to great expanse and depths, to places that are difficult to delve into and discover, the shaman's journey or soul flight ("Putting Coyolxauhqui Together" 249).

In her late essays Anzaldúa explains how she calls on the Nahua concept of nahua/shapeshifting to tell stories. "My text [*Light in the Dark / Luz en lo Oscuro*] is about the imagination (the psyche's image-creating faculty, the power to make fiction or stories, inner movies like *Star Trek*'s holodeck)," she says in "Preface: Gestures of the Body" (5). The naguala that seems to be especially connected to this process is la víbora, the snake. A discussion of la naguala as a decolonial writing practice follows the next section, which is a closer look at la víbora in *Light in the Dark / Luz en lo Oscuro*.

"El Nagual in My House": La Víbora and Journeys of Imagination

Although Anzaldúa's discussion of the serpent in her writing is vast,[15] it is in her essays that were unpublished until they appeared in *Light in the Dark / Luz en lo Oscuro* that she describes the serpent in most detail as a naguala that is key to the creative process. Prevalent in the chapter "Flights of the Imagination,"[16] as the title suggests, is Anzaldúa's focus on the role of images, the imagination in the development and broadening of consciousness, especially in its linking of personal and collective unconscious to consciousness. The unconsciousness about which Anzaldúa speaks is connected to the archetypal psychology of Carl Jung and James Hillman but is also informed (and I argue primarily so) by nagualismo/ chamanería, which she describes in "Flights" as a Mesoamerican "alternative epistemology" that involves journeying to "worlds" outside of "ordinary reality" by "interrupting the flow of thoughts and interpretations of the everyday world" in search of wisdom, direction, connection, and even healing ("Flights of the Imagination" 32).[17] Integral to this journey is a passage into el cenote, or the "unconscious reservoir of meaning" where shamanic images reside, the source of creativity, and the well from which transformation stems (55). Underscored in this section is how the naguala, particularly the image of the snake, serves as Anzaldúa's vehicle to el cenote. Ultimately, I bring into relief la naguala's role in the imaginal work that is critical to the Anzaldúan subject, a major project that Anzaldúa is working through in her last essays.

The peculiarities of and differences between each shapeshifting animal form in Anzaldúa's essays and stories indicate that particular images play certain roles in and induce specific states of experience. For example, the jaguar is one that Anzaldúa reported showed up in her dreams when she was experiencing a hypoglycemic episode in her sleep, the one who greeted her on the brink of death, serving as guide and protector ("now let us shift" 556). La lechuza, the owl, awakened her from "hyper-rationality" ("now let us shift" 556). Anzaldúa connected some "visionary experience[s]" with becoming an eagle that would "gather information from looking down at the ground" ("Last Words?" 284). In "Flights of the Imagination," la víbora, the snake, as nagual, is explained as the vehicle to the unconscious, the underworld, and el cenote and adds more depth to the practice of nagualan consciousness described in "Putting Coyolxauhqui Together" and "now let us shift." In "Flights of the Imagination," Anzaldúa discusses several meetings with the snake. When she encounters la víbora as her "guardian spirit," her consciousness "flows out" into it (27). As the snake symbolizes the life of the unconscious, it becomes the path from consciousness to el cenote, where, as Anzaldúa describes in "Border Arte," "the source of creativity, dreams, fantasies, intuitions, and symbolic events" exists (55). Along the journey, nepantla, "the bridge between compartments" where transformation occurs, emerges. What becomes clear in this chapter is that for change to occur, resources must be collected from the deep pool of el cenote. In other words, shamanic journeying, braving the path of conocimiento, is not achieved without a dive into "the Mayan well,"[18] the "ocean of uncanny signs" of personal and collective, ancient and contemporary wisdom ("Border Arte" 57, "Putting Coyolxauhqui Together" 244).

The image of la víbora, therefore, enacts the journey to and presence in the well of imagination; to gain wisdom requires a deep sensing, an openness to "[t]he creative rush of ideas, the sudden flash of an 'other' reality rising out of the sea" ("Putting Coyolxauhqui Together" 244). As an experience of expansiveness or totality, being in el cenote with others (nepantleras) and with an awareness of one's surroundings prompts a deep listening to others, a sensing of oneness within the context and content of the well. In this sense, in the cyclical journey of conocimiento from ego state to merger (naguala) to a woven-ness or new outcome (nepantla), el cenote is part of the merger. This cyclical journey is important as we look at the self as a subject of experience.

Anzaldúa's relationship to the snake was not always a positive one, and the meaning of the snake/serpent shifted throughout her work. In "Flights of the Imagination," Anzaldúa reveals that as a girl her mother told her: "Don't go out late at night; a snake will enter your vagina," which meant, "'Don't go out late at night; a man will rape you" (26). Anzaldúa traces the origins of the connection between rape and a snake to the sixteenth century and cites Rosan Jordan, who explained that women were warned not to go into lakes or rivers or else larva and even sperm would get inside of them. In a 1983 interview with Christine Weiland, Anzaldúa describes a conversion she had in her thinking about snakes that coincided with her thinking about the female body: "The female body and serpents are two of the most feared things in the world, so I used the serpent to symbolize female sexuality, carnality, and the body. Snakes used to represent to me the body and everything that was loathsome, vile, rotting, decaying, getting hair, uri-nating, shitting, all the conditioning I've had—that all people have—about the body, especially the female body" ("Within the Crossroads" 102). After her "conversion" she sees the female body and, subsequently, snakes, dif-ferently and in a positive light. In her later work, including *Borderlands / La Frontera* and in "Flights of the Imagination," she associates snakes with Serpent Woman, La Llorona, a nagual with facultad.

"Flights of the Imagination" is an important addition to Anzaldúa's theorizing on the naguala in its particular emphasis on the work of images and the imagination in self-knowledge, knowing, and transformation. Her image of the snake serves as the call to the unconscious, to el cenote, the deep well of personal and collective metaphors and their meanings. To Anzaldúa, creative response begins with an image, and the "serpent spirit" is her vehicle to the "imaginal musings," metaphors full of energetic and materializing force that give her direction and purpose (35). Importantly, the creative process brings on personal and social transformation and healing. La naguala, as a practice of selfhood, subjectivity, and conduit in the artistic process, facilitates the movement in the journey.

Writing from Wounds and Decoloniality

This chapter now turns to a focus on the role of writing wounds and trauma in decolonial theory and action, keeping these overarching assump-tions in mind: Anzaldúa's writing is a shamanic journey that she initiates, in conversation with her writing comadres and other inspirations and that readers continue; the act of writing from the wound, from the place at which we feel most vulnerable, injured, confused, different, and afraid, is a significant aspect of the Anzaldúan writer-shaman-subject; and this writing process is a journey of imagination, selfhood, and collective subjectivity with time- and place-specific decolonial potential. I see Anzaldúa's writing, as border arte and shamanic process, not as an attempt to revive or repre-sent a precolonial process but to enunciate, in Mignolo's sense, to create something new that resists humanism and modernism, that is enacting decoloniality. To clarify, Mignolo explains enunciation in this way:

> When you start from the enunciation and think decolonially, you shall run away from representation, for representation presupposes that there is a world out there that someone is representing. This is a basic as-sumption of modern epistemology. There is not a world that is repre-sented, but a world that is constantly invented in the enunciation. The

enunciation is constituted by certain actors, languages, and categories of thought, beliefs, and sensing. The enunciation, furthermore, is never or only enacted to "represent" the world, but to confront or support previous existing enunciations. That is, enunciation is enacted and framed in other options (e.g., could be disciplines, could be systems of ideas like liberalism or Marxism, could be artistic conventions, etc.). (Gaztambide-Fernández 198–199)

With Mignolo's clarification in mind, we can understand Anzaldúa's writing as supporting shamanic practice, not as a representation or appropriation of it, particularly since she goes to great lengths to articulate that her art form is a blending of influences of her particular cultural moment. She is, however, enacting and framing her work, in my reading, in the traditions of Mesoamerican metaphysics, and part of why she is doing so is to resist coloniality.

With imagination at the heart of her process, as "real" as matter, she embraces and makes possible the type of decolonial imaginary articulated by Emma Pérez, who says, "Without the imaginary, the decolonial occludes so much and expunges, for example, brown imaginaries of desires and pleasures" (245). Stories like "Sleepwalkers" are expressions of such desires and pleasures and take seriously the imaginary, that which has been silenced and not yet voiced and that which simultaneously resists the established colonial imaginary. Additionally, even when the concept is understood in a Western, measurable sense, as Pérez argues, "the imaginary is real precisely because it creates the materialist conditions" (245). Recently, Pérez extended her understanding of the decolonial imaginary by proposing that we tend to what she calls "the will to feel": "What if the will to feel is the will to be different, as 'feelings' compel us to express differently in a world that anticipates 'logic,' the 'rational mind,' and unfeeling to explain our lives, even when there is no logic, no rationale, no real explanation that can fulfill expectations grounded in that which is not part of one's experience, or phenomenological way of being" (247). She suggests that "the will to feel has its own truth" that "encapsulates so much more than the sensory" and asks, what if we use the pain and "woundedness" associated with "psychic, physical, emotional, and historical trauma, which feels as real as present-day emotional abuse" to "drive critique and analysis consciously, with an astute awareness?" (248). Complicating her theory, Pérez reminds us of the difficulties in decolonizing the imaginary when desire lives inside it, a desire that is conditioned by decoloniality. "Is decolonial desire even possible?" she asks. "Can desire ever be truly authentic?" (248, 249). To get to that decolonial, "sacred" desire made heinous and shameful by coloniality,

Pérez says to delve into and feel the pain of the colonial wound (251). She says that, perhaps, in moments of "impasse," in the Lauren Berlant sense in which impasse is "a stretch of time in which one moves around with a sense that the world is at once intensely present and enigmatic," decolonial desire can be freed and give pleasure (qtd in Pérez 251). Pérez likens impasse to "in-between space," "nepantla," and "interstices," invoked by other writers to refer to a "stretched out present" (251). Embracing wounds and memories, blood memories, at the impasse, in nepantla activity and engaging with historical trauma offer much potential for freeing a repressed imaginary and for transformation, according to Pérez.

As I pore over Anzaldúa's drafts and published writings, I'm convinced that her writing was an attempt to take herself and her readers to this impasse, writing through the wound, on the shaman's path, to uncover not only her own desires and new knowledges but to shapeshift, to transform herself, to influence others, and the world around her. "The creative process is an agency of transformation," she says in "Flights of the Imagination" (35). In other words, writing itself has agency and the potential to transform; it is nepantla motion-change activity, and the writer operates as a nagual-shaman, a conduit, to bring the new results into being. "It's not on paper that you create but in your innards, in your gut and out of living tissue—*organic writing* I call it. . . . It [a poem] works when it surprises me, when it says something I have repressed or pretended not to know," she discloses in "Speaking in Tongues" (33). Therefore, writing works when the writer is most vulnerable, when they allow the wounds that live in the body to reveal themselves. Writing and other forms of art that come from the colonial wound express "the will to feel," or that which cannot be articulated by rational means or in conventional ways or from colonial imaginations. "Words that do not forget the wounds that the self carries have much to say," says Ortega in "Wounds of Self" (242). Those words can change the writer and also the reader.

Anzaldúa communicates an awareness of and engagement with her readers in a number of ways, an obvious one being her use of second-person singular and plural. Her use of second person as a reference to herself, as in "now let us shift," pulls the reader into her experience as speaker. In other instances, such as "Speaking in Tongues: A Letter to Third World Women Writers," the usage of the second-person plural is directed at the reader, in this case women of colors, but the effect of the writing is that any reader is put in the position of hearing Anzaldúa's claims and pleas as directives and is called on to take responsibility for making change. "Find the muse within you. The voice that lies buried under you, dig it up. Do not fake it, try to sell it for a handclap or your name in print," she says as she closes "Speaking in Tongues" (35). Her advice to be authentic has a broad reach; however, and importantly, by using second-person plural, Anzaldúa communicates that the named "we" in "Speaking in Tongues"—mujeres de color (women of color)—are a visible and effectual alliance. She reveals, "I have never seen so much power in the ability to move and transform others as from that of the writing of women of color" (33). Therefore, another way Anzaldúa conveys a careful regard for her readers is in her stance that the type of change that writing can generate has enormous transformative potential. Without the reader, change is limited to its influence on the writers themselves.

Tiffany Ana López's term "critical witnessing" is useful here to clarify the potential influence that readers have in writing's dynamic impact. She says that some Latinx writers, including Anzaldúa, craft their works about trauma in ways that point not to "resolution" but to "making meaning" and "instigating change" in relationship with their readers (205). Critical witnessing means to be so "moved" by an experience with a text that one takes up action intended for personal and social transformation. Looking specifically at children's books, López notes how writers place themselves as critical witnesses and invite their readers to witness critically, as well. "Critical witnessing is more than a focused act of looking or bearing witness. . . . Critical is an operative word here, for it is what characterizes this form of witnessing as engaged in a pedagogy of social justice whereby the story instructs in order to reconstruct" (206). López makes a powerful case for how Latinx children's literature, like Anzaldúa's, voices and records the weight of cultural trauma and violence on children and offers guidance for survivors.

López says that in *Borderlands / La Frontera* and in her children's book *Friends from the Other Side / Amigos del Otro Lado*, Anzaldúa puts herself in the position of passing on survival skills by "imbuing her protagonist Prietita with the characteristics of the new mestiza as a critical witness" to the character of Joaquín and the violence and impoverishment he faced (216–217). The reference to "the other side" in the book is related not just to the "other side of the border" but to "a new location of thought, a narrative space driven by empathy and understanding, rather than presumptions born from stereotypes, fear, or ignorance," according to López (218). Writing, then, offers witness and instills witnessing skills, as well as producing the potential for activism.

With López's critical witnessing in mind, I turn now to the idea that readers of Anzaldúa's work participate in its role as creative motion-change, in being moved—emotionally—but also moved to act. "Reading puts you into a trance. The skills required in reading are to empathize with characters, to imagine or play in your mind the scenery, get involved," Anzaldúa instructs (appendix 3, 177). Critical witnesses bear witness to the writer-shaman-subject's journey, and by way of naguala shapeshifting—in the merger—the reader feels empathy and maybe even feels what the speaker feels; this sense is temporary, however. Readers also feel their individual deep reactions based on their memories and experiences. Anzaldúa says, "The aim of good writing is to decrease the distance between reader, writer, and text without 'disappearing' any of these players" ("Flights of the Imagination" 41). A reader enters into a complex relationship with the writer and the text in a way that creates movement, an energetic force particular to a specific moment in time.

Recall from chapter 1 the Rosiek, Snyder, and Pratt commentary on radically relational agency and power in Indigenous thought: that it emerges in connection with not only persons but also "animals, rivers, places, and stories" (12). In the process of nepantla motion-change, in the weaving, at the "impasse," decolonial desires, subjects, and radically expansive realities are uncovered, discovered, and unfolded. Writing and reading as a decolonial project include as subjects writers, readers, texts, places, and cultural and political context. According to Jarrett Martineau and Eric Ritskes, "the task of decolonial artists, scholars and activists is not simply to offer amendments or edits to the current world, but to display the mutual sacrifice and relationality needed to sabotage colonial systems of thought and power for the purpose of liberatory alternatives" (ii). Such a project requires a fundamental examination and rethinking of what is meant by desire and agency, in the personal and collective sense. This chapter argues that experiencing deeply, by way of writing and/or reading, the wounds that are directly and indirectly associated with coloniality is a vehicle toward untethering those desires and agencies. Anzaldúa, whose writing practice is rooted in Indigenous practices and metaphysics, understands this about wounds and their potential to heal. "Perhaps the wounds are the opening to sacred desire," Pérez poses. "Perhaps these residual colonial wounds entice a brown desiring imaginary, willful and willing, pushing us to new realms of psychic/sexual pleasures previously negated and judged as shameful because they are not the 'norm'" (251). The complexities of decolonizing desire and the imaginary are profound and include considering how the senses and aesthetics themselves are colonized.

This last section of the chapter considers that Anzaldúa's writing is a decolonial act because it resists and disengages from modern, Western humanist, and colonial conceptions of artistic practice and aesthetics. I support that claim with the argument that her work falls into the realm of what Mignolo and Vazquez refer to as decolonial aestheSis, which "seeks to recognize and open options for liberating the senses" (qtd. in Ferrera-Balanquet, Moarquech, and Rojas-Sotelo). They emphasize the distinction between aesthetics and aesthesis to highlight that not only is our sense of what is beautiful and tasteful informed by coloniality but our senses and perceptions are as well: "Decolonial aestheSis refers in general to any and every thinking and doing that is geared toward undoing a particular kind of aesthesis, of senses, that is the sensibility of the colonized subject. What decolonial artists want is not to create beautiful objects, installations, music, multimedia or whatever the possibilities are, but they create in order to decolonize sensibilities, to transform colonial aestheTics into decolonial aestheSis" (qtd. in Gaztambide-Fernández 201). Mignolo explains that there is a foundational relationship between decolonial aestheSis and healing, as patriarchy and racism, what he calls "two pillars of Eurocentric knowing, sensing, and believing," are "embedded and embodied" in our world, creating a denigration that becomes internalized, creating a wound (qtd. in Gaztambide-Fernández 206). Healing means undoing that sense of inferiority; decolonial artistic creativity and aesthesis and building collaboratives are the path to healing. In other words, exposing the source of the wound is part of the process of decoloniality: one has to understand how they have been colonized in every sense (including the senses!) in order not to be regenerating and reinforcing the colonial matrix of power.

How, then, does Anzaldúa, more specifically, la naguala as a practice and a consciousness, decolonize the senses? "We must empower the imagination to blur and transcend customary frameworks and conceptual categories reinforced by language and consensual reality," Anzaldúa says in "Flights of the Imagination" (45). New selves, lives, and projects will cost us the old ones, she also explains; this is the price, the sacrifice, to get to the sacred, to the wound. "Writing is a given. All else yields before it, except your health, and there will probably be times when you'll sacrifice even that," also says Anzaldúa, a prescient message given her untimely death ("Putting Coyolxauhqui Together" 243). For Anzaldúa, delving into el cenote, into wounds and the imagination, although unrelenting and often painful work, can decolonize the senses and generate artist creations that are offerings of hope and healing and contributions to decolonizing the world.

Writing for Anzaldúa was not an attempt to entertain or instruct; it wasn't simply a career or means for a living or advancement. Writing was her activism, her contribution to changing the world. The cosmos.

Anzaldúa's influence on the project of decoloniality ranges from decolonizing the senses to decolonizing reality. Her processes and subjects are rooted in the shaman's cyclical journey of inner work and public acts, involving the imagination and the wound. She engaged with writing as a creative and spiritual process and as a shamanic ritual, to go straight to the wound and to heal it. "Nuestra tarea [our homework] is to envision Coyolxauhqui, not dead and decapitated, but with eyes wide open. Our task is to light up the darkness" ("Preface: Gestures of the Body" 8). And those of us who take up her work as readers and scholars, by journeying with her, light up the darkness, too.

Toward New Potentials
of Imagination

Suffused with the poetic, the arts can be
revolutionary language or vital energy,
midwifing mental and shared social spaces
beyond colonizations of unjust power.
—Laura E. Pérez

Imagination opens the road to both personal
and societal change—transformation of self,
consciousness, community, culture, society.
—Gloria Anzaldúa

Of the many themes in this book, one is most pervasive: that accessing
and liberating the decolonial imagination offer much untapped potential
for refashioning selfhoods, identities, bodies, relationships, social-justice
coalitions, and even realities. For writers like Anzaldúa, artistic endeavors
and inventions are primary means for such refashionings: "If reality is only
a description of a particular world, when a shift of awareness happens
we must create a new description of what's perceived—in other words,
create a new reality" ("Flights of the Imagination" 45). Those descriptions require new languages, identities, stories, and truths. They involve
new ways of understanding and relating to ourselves and each other. As
subjects formed by coloniality, by way of direct and transgenerational
experiences, uncovering and expressing authentic ways of being, knowing,
relating, and living are complex challenges. How do we reimagine and
reenact selfhoods and collective subjects—agencies that reach beyond
coloniality's limitations and destruction? How do we imagine and remake
a more livable and liberating future? How can writing and other works of
art break ground and lead the way in creating new and wildly habitable
and thriving worlds? Answers to these difficult questions still remain, of

course, but like others working to discover them, I offer this glimpse into Anzaldúa's writing as a shapeshifting, shamanic pathway to radical new ways of enacting agency and change.

I have found in Anzaldúa's use of la naguala, the shapeshifter, a new form of consciousness and practice that simultaneously honors the influence of her specific heritage, the cultural moment in which she lived, and the legacy of her life's work. La naguala for Anzaldúa was a means for expanding the experience of and possibilities for the self, an "inner sensibility" and "hyperempathetic" consciousness ("Preface: Gestures of the Body" 4; "Putting Coyolxauhqui Together" 250). She referred to her naguala as "an image, an action, or an internal experience" ("Preface: Gestures of the Body" 4). In other words, the shapeshifter is a guide that can appear in the form of an *image* (the jaguar, werejaguar, lechuza, lizard, snake, etc.) that subsequently initiates a shift or movement/*action* (writing, social-justice work), and transforms the experience of selfhood or *internal experience* (induces intense sense of merger, expansiveness, and empathetic feeling but also pathways to experience of wounding, isolation, and even death). These images, actions, and experiences are part of and produce energy as real as matter in a continuous motion-change dynamic within which everything participates. Because it is part of and beyond personal experience, the concept of la naguala, of shapeshifting, offers a means for understanding the vulnerability, permeability, and transformability of selves and human bodies, the expansiveness of subjectivity, and the power in and potential of imagination and creative activity overall. Felicity Amaya Schaeffer referred to la naguala as "the supreme border crosser, or walker between worlds" and a "skill latent in all of us" (1020). My hope for this extensive study is to help to expand and spark that potential.

In this book I have sought to unpack some of the ontological, philosophical, and metaphysical dimensions of la naguala and suggest that Anzaldúa's work, in line with Nahua metaphysics, offers a way out of dualisms, even those of matter/nonmatter, matter/spirit, matter/social, and matter/language, by considering the possibility of a tertium quid, a substance/energy as real as but different from what we consider to be matter. I also offer an example of how shapeshifting might show up in the writings of others influenced by life in a different ethnic American borderland that reveal transgenerational, temporal, and spatial subjectivity. In Anzaldúa's thinking about the work of the border artist, unapologetically informed by a blending of cultures and past and present moments, I see an example of how to address issues and problems of appropriation and primitivism. Border arte is crafted from and must be considered within the peculiarities of its making, and border artists work to communicate new sensibilities and expressive forms, not to revive a stagnant, romanticized past. And lastly, la naguala plays a role in shamanic response to trauma/susto and initiates decolonial agency and healing, an undoing of internalized oppression and a generating of new desires and imaginary. Importantly, writing becomes the healing process and living product of the writer-shaman's journey through the wound/rupture, the upheaval. "Through the act of writing, you call, like the ancient chamana, the scattered pieces of your soul back to your body," Anzaldúa says ("now let us shift" 573). Readers, as critical witnesses, continue the writer's journey when they engage with the writer's words and are inspired by them to create their own art and other acts. Informed by their own lineages, wounds, and present moment, readers take up their own particular work, their personal and collective path to transformation. Anzaldúa calls readers into this shapeshifting journey; within the closing passages of "now let us shift" (575–576), a "ritual . . . prayer . . . blessing . . . for transformation," written in first- and second-person plural (first is demonstrated here), is an example of this invitation:

> May the roaring force of our collective creativity
> > heal the wounds of hate, ignorance, indifference
> > dissolve the divisions creating chasms between us
> > open our throats so we who fear speaking out raise our
> > > voices
> > > > by our witnessing, find connections through our
> > > > > passions . . .
> May the words and the spirit of the book, our "giveaway" to the
> > world,
> > > take root in our bodies, grow, sprout ears that listen
> > > may it harm no one, exclude none
> > > > sabemos que podemos transformer este mundo[1]
> > > > filled with hunger, pain, and war
> > > > into a sanctuary of beauty, redemption, and possibility
> > > > > may the fires of compassion ignite our hands
> > > > > sending energy out into the universe
> > > > > where it might best be of service
> > > > > may the love we share inspire others to act.

Anzaldúa initiates the shapeshifting shamanic journey not only by her words in this poetic blessing but also by the shape of the words on the page: the full poem/ritual unfolds into the form of a snake, calling readers to enter into the coiled serpent of depth, darkness, and the devouring earth, the vagina dentata, "the creative womb from which all things were born and to which all things returned" ("Entering into the Serpent" 56). Into el cenote, "the architecture of the imagination," where knowledge lies, la víbora, Coatlalopeuh/Guadalupe, Cihuacoatl, La Llorona leads the way (appendix 3, 177). At the end of the piece, Anzaldúa and her readers "step through the doorways between worlds leaving huellas [footprints] for others to follow," indicating the cyclical and inclusive nature of the journey ("now let us shift" 576). Stories and other writing forms were for Anzaldúa her art and her gift, her effort to help cure an ailing world, but they were also a means for expanding the self: "Storytelling and reading and listening to stories is not only how we make sense of ourselves, our lives, and our place in the world, and how we make the Self. Storytelling is healing when it expands the autohistorias (self-narratives) of the teller and the listeners, when it broadens the person that we are" (appendix 3, 177). The use of the first-person plural in this last sentence is curious and can be read a couple of ways. "When it broadens the person that we are" can be understood as the speaker addressing each person individually, as in "broadening the personhood of each of you," or it can also be read as "broadening the person we become together, as one subject." Reading Anzaldúa's parting blessing—"now let us shift" was one of her last published essays—within a Nahua framework, we can understand the statement as both, as selves as separate senses of being and as collectives. Writing, here, is a vehicle for shifting self, others, and reality.

Unbinding and nurturing oppressed imaginations can bring into being realities that better suit and serve more-diverse lives, allowing for many more possibilities in desires, sexualities, and bodily potentials. Such imaginaries can also resist dominant ones aimed at narrowing and normalizing lives. Imaginative endeavors have a broad reach and are critical to every field, including science, engineering, computers, and medicine. As Eli Clare reminds us, "Many medical technologies shift over time, moving from imaginary to real, ambiguous to reliable" (91). These technologies can be both liberating and dangerous. Clare, a trans man with cerebral palsy, calls into question our definitions of defectiveness and cure, recognizing both as socially constructed and bound to ideology. His critique is informed by the insight that the "medical-industrial complex" is moving toward a future, an "imaginary future," within which "disability has been cured" (25). "Disability shapes who we are," he says, and for many, "curing" their disabilities is a threat to their existence (26). More specifically, Clare explains, "At the center of cure lies eradiation and the many kinds of violence that accompany it. On the surface, this claim appears hyperbolic. Many lives, including my own, depend on or have been made possible by cure and its technologies. As it supports and extends life, the restoration of health seems to be the opposite of eradication. But cure arrives in many different guises, connected to elimination and erasure in a variety of configurations" (26). Addressing the many implications and questions raised by Clare's claims requires more depth and discussion, but I introduce his work here to bring into focus the range, power, and effects of imagination when it comes to determining what is normal, natural, and acceptable, even in a scientific and medical sense. Clare also offers an important reminder of how defectiveness has been used to serve racist, classist, homophobic, and transphobic forms of violence, determining which lives are subject to institutionalization, enslavement, imprisonment, and eradication. I find it provocative and telling that Clare uses the language of "imaginary future" juxtaposed with a scenario that seems very possible, in a couple of different sections of his chapter. He says that in the "imaginary future," "we, or future generations like us, wouldn't exist. I feel neither triumph nor progress but loss" (26). His nonnormative experience allows him to see himself in the dominant imaginary, which is forecasted and voiced as progressive and good, but he tells a different story, one of his own and others' experience with defectiveness, carefully woven, crafted, and shared with readers.

The language of imagination shows up in various places throughout Clare's book, not only to paint a picture of dystopian realities but also to assert a glimpse of a world that allows for more diversity of bodies: "Once fatphobia, ableism, sexism, racism, classism, homophobia, transphobia, and xenophobia, and all the rigid constraints placed on body-mind variation are dismantled,[2] what will we desire? This question overwhelms me. It requires an impossible flight of imagination" (183). Anzaldúa uses these same words—flights of imagination—in *Light in the Dark / Luz en lo Oscuro* in order to "rewrite reality," calling on what might seem to be an impossible mix of teachers, including Bernardino de Sahagún, Carlos Castaneda, Carl Jung, James Hillman, her mamagrande Ramoncita, and even John Keats (23). Perhaps, part of her point in doing so is to demonstrate that we cannot escape backwards to some idealized precolonial existence, and we cannot completely leave behind the influence of coloniality either, projecting ourselves into a future we have not realized. One can, however, engage the imagination in the present, in generating ensueños (fantasies/daydreams) that, in turn, create new worlds of experience. These flights or shaman's journeys were processes Anzaldúa took very seriously and describes in detail, in different ways, in each chapter of *Light in the Dark / Luz en lo Oscuro*. For her, flights of imagination are not flights *from* the barriers of oppression but involve processing and healing from them to overcome their limits and create new perceptions and dimensions of reality.

Although Clare suggests that the answer to "what will we desire" after oppressions are dismantled is an "impossible flight of imagination," he does go on to give the task a try (183). He begins with an unequivocal stance against a list of horrendous historical and present injustices he has spent the better part of the book describing—from bullying, gawking, and growth-attenuation treatments to institutionalization and inconceivable situations of dehumanization and slavery. Then Clare imagines a "world reconfigured" where "cure" is nuanced and "one tool among many" and a place where "our body-mind desires will spread through us, as vibrant and varied as a tallgrass prairie in midsummer" (184). His flight of imagination seems to take the route that Anzaldúa suggests, a journey into the depths of darkness and unspeakable oppression in order to imagine what healing from it and creating a new reality can be. Clare gives voice to the victims of the social construction of defectiveness and imperfection and shares a new framework for understanding the ideology, politics, and violence of cure.

Like Anzaldúa, Clare expresses an appreciation for and intense connection to nature and the environment in his politics and poetics. A visit to a tallgrass prairie in Wisconsin serves as a framing metaphor for thinking through the concepts of natural and unnatural, as the thirty-acre tallgrass prairie, once a huge agribusiness cornfield, is in the process of being restored after years of efforts by activists. The land, originally belonging to the Dakota people, was damaged by almost two hundred years of destruction by plows and pesticides but now burgeons with plants and wildlife. Thinking about the absence of bison today, Clare wrestles with what is natural or normal about a place that holds within it all its manifestations over the centuries, including the cycles of damage and restoration leading to its status today. "Maybe the earth just holds layer upon layer of history," he says. Closing the book with another visit to the prairie, Clare is "thinking not of concepts but of beings," of grasses, butterflies, sparrows, coyotes, and more that he "imagines" (186). He realizes the "illogic of *natural* and *unnatural*, *normal* and *abnormal*" and finishes his musings with this paragraph: "This little pocket of restored prairie is not a return to the past nor a promise to the future, although it may hold glimmers of both. Rather it is simply an ecosystem in transition from cornfield to tallgrass, summer to winter. I feel the old corn furrows underfoot, the big bluestem waving above me, my own heart beating, imperfect and brilliant. I walk—a tremoring, slurring human, slightly off balance, one being among many. Could it all be this complexly woven and yet simple?" (187). Clare opens and closes his text with a juxtaposition of bodies and ecosystems; more specifically, he reflects on how history and present moment affect and resonate in both, that neither can be deemed natural, but in their motion-change, weaving process, the unfolding or becoming-ness offers liberation. For nepantleras, for those who experience shifting and multiple, oppressed positionalities and identities, the intense, "hyperempathetic" journey to authentic selfhood and desire means being in the middle of the contradictions, the past and present, and imagining and making something new of them both (Anzaldúa, "Putting Coyolxauhqui Together" 250). As a writer, Clare is employing the border artist's journey, decolonizing the realities of ableism and cis and class privilege while also communicating a keen consciousness of racial and environmental injustice. Clare's writing, integrating the personal, historical, and political, invites the reader into his and other's stories and a shapeshifting journey of "grappling with cure." Storytelling like Clare's nurtures and expands our imagination and, in turn, our sense of connection, agency, and hope.

The role of images, stories, and writing in transforming lives and realities carries much weight throughout this book. Perhaps, you have asked yourself if the imagination is overemphasized. Anzaldúa wrote that it wasn't until after the publication of *Borderlands / La Frontera* that she came to realize she was unconsciously attempting to practice shamanism in a new way; she wanted to transform deeply imbedded, damaging metaphors by way of writing ("Metaphors"). As a "poet-shaman" she found that misinformation and ailments in individuals and society could always be linked to the persistent metaphors of the culture. Cures, she said, "were about extracting the old dead metaphors" *and* creating and sharing new ones ("Metaphors" 122). "We can share ourselves through metaphor—attempt to put, in words, the flow of some of our internal pictures, sounds, sensations, and feelings and hope that as the reader reads the pages these 'metaphors' will be 'activated' and live in her," Anzaldúa explains ("Metaphors" 122).

Similarly, writer-activist adrienne maree brown believes her writing articulates a narrative that has the power to refashion reality. She asks herself "if art is enough of a contribution" and concludes, "I see that I am charged to write about the revolutions I long for, and that any writing I do, even if it isn't explicitly political, is still a transformative act. I apply this to my songs, my self-portraits, my poems—understanding that when a Black, queer, thick artist woman intentionally takes up space, it creates a new world" (30). Also like Anzaldúa, brown, who fleshes out what she calls "emergent strategies," or "how we intentionally change in ways that grow our capacity to embody the just and liberated worlds we long for," is influenced by a diversity of teachers and sources, like activist and philosopher Grace Lee Boggs and science-fiction author Octavia Butler (24). Highlighting the importance of collaboration, change, recovery, and resilience, brown's ideas are highly imaginative yet straightforwardly practical. Of key importance to her theorizing is "the medicine of possibility" in science fiction, especially visionary fiction, which she "reads as political, sacred, and philosophical text" (37). Brown sees critical lessons in even the most incredible worlds of fiction, and she says her own book is "an offering of experiential learning" (272). A glimpse of nagualan consciousness and practice can be read in brown's process, like here, as she addresses her readers in the last paragraphs of the book: "It [her book] has shaped me, shaped those I am living my life with, and hopefully shaped you, dear reader. It changed the world, even if it is/was only in tiny ways that can't be seen, measured" (272). Brown, working with the idea of fractals—that small-scale patterns "reverberate to the largest scale"—saw her work as an offering, as part of an evolving, palpable conversation, like Anzaldúa, who believed her stories are "'enacted' every time they are spoken aloud or read silently" and that a story "dedicates itself to managing the universe and its energies" (brown 52; Anzaldúa, "Tlilli, Tlapalli" 89).

The radical philosophical and even metaphysical implications of the works of Anzaldúa and later writers like Clare and brown can be easily missed and dismissed given our embeddedness in Western, humanist scholarly frameworks. We read their stories of connection and transformation as symbolism, but if we look more closely at their sources and proposals, we can read narrative and metaphor as foundational to how we construct self, subjects, and lived experience. Anzaldúa's border arte, heavily influenced by nagualismo and her concept of la naguala, has received little attention to date but holds potential for broadening our understanding of the depth and breadth of her contributions. Reaching outside disciplinary constraints and linear, rational writing processes, Anzaldúa and other writers of colors are offering theories and strategies for imagining and creating decolonial lives and worlds, shifting the shape of subjectivity and reality.

You have the power to shape-shift not only yourselves
but the whole of the world. You, each one, are
endowed with gifts you don't even yet know, and you,
each one, are what love and the possibility of a world
in which our lives truly matter looks like.

—Patrisse Khan-Cullors and Asha Bandele

I am writing the last chapters of this book in a middle of the COVID-19 pandemic and a rise in a wave of the Black Lives Matter movement. Our usual lazy Midwest summer heat feels angry and anxious. I was supposed to be traveling this week for work, but, instead, I am quarantined with twin eleven-year-olds in a world turned on its head, writing with them in stereo, the prospect of traveling seemingly another lifetime away. Instead, it looks like the work to do is right where I am, right where we are, within our own families and communities. Avoiding a virus but leaning into another ill, both of which can be difficult to feel and see depending on your vantage point and both of which are bound to implications related to race, class, ableism, and politics. Both reveal how pervious, vulnerable, and connected we are.

I go searching for *This Bridge Called My Back* in my endless piles and finally find it at the bottom of a stack. Holding everything else up. I revisit the voices of women of colors refusing to be buried. There is a sea change, and it is speaking from a wound that is generations old, that lives in flesh and bones, that knows. Listen. Anzaldúa says, "I write because I want to leave a discernible mark on the world" ("When I Write I Hover" 238). She also says, "Forget the room of one's own—write in the kitchen, lock yourself in the bathroom" ("Speaking in Tongues" 31). I have read those lines lots of times in the last few months. You, my reader, might or might not write. You make and do other things that matter and matter a lot, actions that create movement and transformation.

My mother, who died four years ago today—the date I write this—had a T-shirt that said, "Bloom where you are planted." She was a gardener, painter, and cook, when she wasn't tending to my sister, who, like Clare, has cerebral palsy. My mother was grounded to home and made that home a place that brimmed with immortality. The summer Mom unexpectedly left us, her gardens persisted more beautifully than ever. My niece, Mom's granddaughter, tends to them now with her own flare, getting rid of some plots and establishing new ones, creating another "layer of history." My sister and I move the St. Francis statue; someone adds a big, blue, laughing Buddha. Those gardens are different each year, depending on care, rainfall, and sun, bugs and birds, but Mom's presence, the presence of the persistent force of life she nurtured, lingers and yet is constantly transforming.

A virus threatens us, trying to keep us in our homes this year, but we don't always stay inside; a violent, centuries-old trauma drives us to the streets of our communities to resist white supremacy. We realize that we, as individuals and as a collective, can change the course of both ills. We engage in impossible flights of the imagination, from our homes and communities, writing speeches, making signs, making masks, marching, and chanting. It's all art. Art that speaks from a wound that when we come together begins a healing, a tilling of the ground, our spirits, and our love for each other, so that we may all, eventually and freely, bloom.

Notes

Preface

The quote is from Gloria Anzaldúa, "Lechuza," folder 19, box 72, Gloria Evangelina Anzaldúa Papers, 1942–2004, Benson Latin American Collection, University of Texas at Austin.

1. See Zaytoun, "New Pathways Toward Understanding Self-in-Relation," in which I open with this reflection. The passage in *Borderlands / La Frontera* to which I connect the image is in "Entering into the Serpent": "So I grew up in the interface trying not to give countenance to el mal aigre, evil non-human, non-corporeal entities riding the wind, that could come in through the window, through my nose with my breath. I was not supposed to believe in susto, a sudden shock or fall that frightens the soul out of the body. And growing up between such opposing spiritualties how could I reconcile the two, the pagan and the Christian?" (60).

2. "Putting Coyolxauhqui Together" (2015), 105.

3. The idea that "change is the only constant" is often attributed to pre-Socratic Greek philosopher Heraclitus of Ephesus, but this notion is at the heart of Indigenous Mesoamerican metaphysics dating back to the Olmecs, whose origins predate Greek civilization by several hundred years.

4. "Flights of the Imagination," 35.

5. I borrow this idea from Emma Pérez, who says, "The imaginary is real precisely because it creates the materialist conditions" (245). I suggest in this book, however, that the line between the imaginary and the material can be blurred, even metaphysically.

6. Preface, *Borderlands / La Frontera*.

7. In the final editing phase of this book, I discovered philosopher Andrea J. Pitts's *Nos / Otras: Gloria E. Anzaldúa, Multiplicitous Agency, and Resistance*, not

yet released at the time of this writing. Pitts's text, like this one, explores agency and Indigeneity in Anzaldúa's writing, among other topics. I look forward to opportunities for these two texts to be brought into conversation with each other.

Introduction

Readers of *Borderlands / La Frontera* will recognize in the chapter title the nod to the title of chapter 7, "La Conciencia de la Mestiza: Towards a New Consciousness," which I invoke to communicate that the consciousness emphasized in the current book is part of, yet builds on, Anzaldúa's theorizing of mestiza consciousness.

The epigraph is from "Let Us Be the Healing of the Wound" (20).

1. Following AnaLouise Keating, who was inspired by and uses Indigo Violet's concept "women of colors," I also adopted the term for use in this book to highlight the point that many differences exist among marginalized groups of people of color (Keating, *Transformation Now!* 207). María Lugones refers to the term "women of color" as a "coalitional identity," not a "racial descriptor"; I adopt the term women of "colors" to emphasize this distinction, as well. See Lugones, "Radical Multiculturalism and Women of Color Feminisms."

2. Nagualismo is a Mesoamerican shamanism or spiritual practice. Nagualismo's definition and Anzaldúa's use of the term is discussed in more detail in chapter 1.

3. I use the terms "self" and "selfhood" to refer to an individual person's sense of "me-ness," or a first-person experience. My focus on self is in line with that of Anzaldúa, who says in the preface of *Borderlands / La Frontera: The New Mestiza* that the book speaks of her "existence" or her "preoccupations with the inner life of the Self, and with the struggle of that Self amidst adversity and violation; with the confluence of primordial images; with the unique positionings consciousness takes at these confluent streams; and with [her] almost instinctive urge to communicate, to speak, to write about life on the borders, life in the shadows." The exploration of selfhood in this book takes on the experience of oppression and colonial wounds, sources of creative response to hardship, and the need to connect and communicate as it informs selfhood and sense of agency. Subjectivity more broadly refers to consciousness and agency that are not necessarily limited to individual persons. Both concepts are discussed in more detail throughout the text but especially in chapter 1.

4. These concepts and the complexities of their meanings are addressed throughout the book. There are controversies and critiques around the uses of nepantla and mestizaje, particularly, in scholarly discussions. The following brief definitions are simplistic but offer readers a sense of the terms. "Nepantla," a Nahuatl term, refers to being in-between but also to intermingling. Anzaldúa uses the Spanish term "facultad" to express an acute awareness of surroundings and "nos/otras" to discuss the complex links between us and them and self and

other. "Mestizaje" refers to the ethnic, racial, and cultural mixing that occurred as a result of Spanish colonization.

5. The Nahua are the largest Indigenous group in Mexico; the Aztec and Toltec are of Nahua ethnicity.

6. Because the term "Indigenous" is used broadly to refer to peoples who are the original inhabitants of an area and their descendants, and such populations are geographically, ethnically, and culturally very diverse, its usage is complicated. As Linda Tuhiwai Smith states, "The term 'indigenous' is problematic in that it appears to collectivize many distinct populations whose experiences under imperialism have been vastly different" (*Decolonizing Methodologies* 6). However, the term is useful in bringing visibility to the numerous communities worldwide that have struggled against settler colonialism. Despite her warnings about the term, Tuhiwai Smith also recognizes, "[i]n some contexts," including North America, "the word 'indigenous' is a way of including the many diverse communities, language groups and nations, each with their own identification within a single grouping" (*Decolonizing Methodologies* 6). Originally used in the 1970s by the American Indian Movement (AIM) and the Canadian Indian Brotherhood, the term has "enabled the collective voices of colonized people to be expressed strategically in the international arena" (*Decolonizing Methodologies* 7). This recent term also emerged in the naming of Indigenous Studies in the academy. In my work with Indigenous Studies in this text, I mostly engage with nagualismo and Nahua studies and the complexities associated with the concept of shamanism.

7. For their discussion on this topic, see Alexander, *Pedagogies of Crossing*, and Keating, *Transformation Now!*

Chapter 1. La Naguala in Theory and Practice

Earlier versions of parts of this chapter were published in *MELUS*, vol. 40, no. 4, Winter 2015, 69–88, in the article "'Now Let Us Shift' the Subject: Tracing the Path and Posthumanist Implications of la Naguala/the Shapeshifter in the Works of Gloria Anzaldúa."

The epigraphs are from Gloria Anzaldúa, "Flights of the Imagination" (41), and Roberto Sirvent, "Interview with María Lugones" (4), respectively.

1. Although Anzaldúa did not call herself "indian," she did claim "indigenous ancestry, one of mestizaje" ("Speaking Across the Divide" 282). She discusses a history of and relationship between Native and Chicana identities and the concept of Indigeneity in detail in "Speaking Across the Divide" in *The Gloria Anzaldúa Reader*. In this piece, a dialogue with Inés Hernández-Ávila, a version of which was originally published in the Fall–Winter 2003 issue of *Studies in American Indian Literatures*, Anzaldúa explains that she feared that by claiming Indigenous ancestry and connections that she and other Chicanas could "unwittingly contribute to the misappropriation of Native cultures" and "contribute to the cultural erasure, silencing, invisibility, racial stereotyping, and disenfranchisement of people who

live in real Indian bodies" ("Speaking Across the Divide" 286). But she also felt that it was "imperative" to give voice to the issues, no matter how complicated, of mixed-heritage identities.

2. Anzaldúa uses the term "nagualismo" broadly to refer to Indigenous worldviews and, in its specific sense, the aspect of shamanism concerned with the nagual, the shapeshifting human and the animal spirit guide. She references nagualismo in "now let us shift" as "a Mexican spiritual knowledge system where the practitioner searches for spirits signs." She calls "la naguala" the "maker of spirit signs" and "an aspect of self unknown to the conscious self" (577).

My discussion of decoloniality follows Walter D. Mignolo and Catherine E. Walsh's definition that exposes and articulates the refusal of and resistance to the enduring legacy of colonialism. According to Mignolo and Walsh, decoloniality "is a form of struggle and survival, an epistemic and existence-based response and practice—most especially by colonized and racialized subjects—*against* the colonial matrix of power in all of its dimensions and *for* the possibilities of an otherwise." They go on to say, "Decoloniality denotes ways of thinking, knowing, being, and doing that began with, but also precede, the colonial enterprise and invasion" (17).

3. For more on this interpretation, see Daniel Brinton, *Nagualism. A Study in Native American Folk-Lore and History*. Scholars have debated the meaning of nagual (also spelled nahual and nahualli) but overall, in its broadest sense, agree that the term refers to transformation and changing form. See James Maffie's discussion in *Aztec Philosophy: A World in Motion* (39–42). For scholarship on the complexities of Nahuatl interpretation, see Jongsoo Lee, "Nezahualcoyotl and the Notion of Individual Authorship in Nahuatl Poetry" and *The Allure of Nezahualcoyotl: Pre-Hispanic History, Religion, and Nahua Poetics*.

4. Because there are two published versions of both of these pieces, "now let us shift" (2002, 2015) and "Putting Coyolxauhqui Together" (1999, 2015), I clarify that for the purposes of this chapter (and throughout the book), which includes a historical take on Anzaldúa's use of the term "naguala," and to avoid confusion, I am quoting from the versions of these two essays that were published first. Anzaldúa was revising both essays to be included in her dissertation, which she was writing at the time of her death. Those essays became the final two chapters of the posthumously published *Light in the Dark / Luz en lo Oscuro: Rewriting Identity, Spirituality, Reality*; "Putting Coyolxauhqui Together" is chapter 5, and "now let us shift" is chapter 6.

5. In claiming that Anzaldúa resists humanism, I am not suggesting that she is against the human or human rights or, importantly, struggles for women, queer people, and people of colors to be treated as fully human persons. My focus is on how her work debunks and deconstructs "the subject" and overall concept of subjectivity of humanisms based in Enlightenment principles that privilege individualism; a universal human reality; reason as the primary guide for understanding the world; and human life over and above other life forms and at

the expense of the environment. More details are presented in the section on posthumanism in this chapter.

6. I turn to both phenomenology and Indigenous metaphysics to explain Anzaldúa's work with the concept of creativity. First, phenomenologically, Rosa Aurora Chávez-Eakle refers to creativity as "the generation of new things or ideas or the transformation of those previously existing" ("Relevance of Creativity"). According to Chávez-Eakle, the process of creativity involves first the "association-integration" stage, or the linking of "previously unrelated elements of inner and outer experiences, forming new associations among what is perceived through the senses, thought, memories, ideas, and emotions." The "elaboration" phase involves "transform[ing] the associations into tangible works," and, lastly, "communication" involves sharing the result with others, which, in turn, sparks others to be creative, too. In Nahua metaphysics, creative activity of humans takes place in unison with the creative, regenerative activity of the cosmos and is "fundamentally transformative" (Maffie 38–39). Creative and artist processes are, therefore, at the heart of living and of the universe. I say more about this process as the chapter develops.

7. Anzaldúa refers to the imagination as "the ability to spontaneously generate images in the mind" and "the psyche's image-creating faculty, the power to make fiction or stories" ("Flights of the Imagination" 36; "Preface: Gestures of the Body" 5). She also refers to "active imagining," or daydreaming, and says that she consciously works with imagination and active imagining together ("Preface: Gestures of the Body" 5). She says that imagination and naguala are "aspects of the same process, of creativity"; la naguala serves as a conduit to accessing imagination ("Preface: Gestures of the Body" 4). Because Anzaldúa claims to "talk *with* images/stories" and not "*about* them," writing to her was a "creative and spiritual" process with "ritualistic aspects" ("Preface: Gestures of the Body" 5).

8. I intentionally keep the term "white" as a racial category in lowercase letters as a rhetorical gesture to destabilize its meanings associated with dominance.

9. Europeans invented the term "shamanism," discussed more in chapter 2, to refer to a set of Indigenous beliefs and practices that they saw as consistent, albeit with some variation, from Eurasia to the Americas. Anzaldúa uses the term frequently and refers to herself as a "poet-shaman" and to writing as a shamanic journey, so I engage with the concept here, as well. In their broadest sense, shamans are believed to communicate with spirits, leave the body in a spiritual sense and travel across the cosmos in search of knowledge, and relieve suffering and provide healing when they return. See Thomas A. DuBois, *An Introduction to Shamanism,* and Margaret Stutley, *Shamanism.*

10. "Puddles" was published a decade later in Charles M. Tatum's *New Chicana/Chicano Writing 1.*

11. Anzaldúa refers to the nagual in her 1996 interview with Andrea Lunsford as "the part of the author that's the dreamer, the unconscious watcher, the soul or nagual, that which is not you but was born with you, that keeps vigil, that guides

you, in internal companion or nagual" ("Toward a Mestiza Rhetoric" 272). This interview is primarily about the writing process, and Anzaldúa's discussion here is consistent with the process she develops in "Putting Coyolxauhqui Together," published three years later. Anzaldúa also mentions her nagual in her 1998–1999 interview with AnaLouise Keating, calling it her "totem animal," her "other body" as jaguar, serpent, or eagle, and also a "visionary experience" ("Last Words? Spirit Journeys" 284).

12. As Keating mentions in the *Gloria Anzaldúa Reader*, a version of "Speaking Across the Divide" was published in the Fall–Winter 2003 issue of "Studies in American Indian Literatures." The interview took place in 2002.

13. Anzaldúa also discusses this idea in "Metaphors in the Tradition of the Shaman."

14. Anzaldúa's expansion of her theories of la naguala and conocimiento seems to develop simultaneously, each concept likely inspiring the development of the other. At the end of the chapter I suggest, with evidence from her early writing notes, that la naguala initiated her earliest theorizing on the seven stages of conocimiento.

15. Coyolxauhqui is Coatlicue's oldest daughter. Coyolxauhqui, who led her brothers and sisters to kill Coatlicue after Coatlicue was impregnated by a ball of feathers, was killed by her brother Huitzilopochtli when he emerged fully grown from the wound as the attack ensued. Huitzilopochtli then threw Coyolxauhqui's head into the sky, where it became the Earth's moon.

16. In the introduction to *In-Between: Latina Feminist Phenomenology, Multiplicity, and the Self*, Mariana Ortega describes the development of what she calls Latina feminist phenomenology. She outlines features in the theorizing of Anzaldúa, Lugones, and others that are in line with phenomenological thought, such as attention to lived experience, but offers new and important contributions to the movement, such as tending to the particularities—stories and struggles—of the body, that tended to be left out of the theorizing of such founding figures as Maurice Merleau-Ponty. Ortega identifies six characteristics of Latina feminist phenomenology, summarized as follows: consideration of the lived experience of Latinas/os in the United States, a focus on "concrete, embodied, *everyday* experience," consideration of intersectionality or "intermeshness" in Lugones's terms, attention to how Latina/o experience is obscured in philosophical discourse, attention to the heterogeneity of Latinas/os, and the use of "experiential knowledge" to resist or rethink conventional constructions of Latinas/os (10). Since the publication of Ortega's text, the terms "Latina/x" and "Latinx" have been more widely circulated; Ortega now uses "Latina/x" to describe the former Latina Feminism Roundtable; therefore, I use this language in the book.

17. For secondary scholarship that links Anzaldúa with posthumanism, see Suzanne Bost, "Life: The Gloria E. Anzaldúa Papers and Other-Than-Humanist Ontologies," and "Diabetes, Culture, and Food: Posthumanist Nutrition in the Gloria Anzaldúa Archive"; Betsy Dahms, "Formalizing Fluidity: Queer Second-Person

Narration in Anzaldúa's 'Putting Coyolxauhqui Together' and 'now let us shift . . . the path of conocimiento . . . inner works, public acts'"; and Pedro Javier DiPietro, "Ni Humanos, Ni Animales, Ni Monstruos: La Decolonización del Cueropo Transgénero" (this piece also works with Indigenous knowledges and trans studies and is taken up in chapter 2); Robyn Henderson-Espinosa, "The Borderlands of Subjectivity; the Subjectivity of the Borderlands: Nomadism, Mestizaje, and Bodies"; Tom Joeri Idema, "Beyond Representationalism: Deleuze and Guattari, Feminist Posthumanism, and Gloria Anzaldúa's Borderlands"; AnaLouise Keating, "Gloria Anzaldúa's Posthumanist Mythos"; AnaLouise Keating and Kimberly C. Merenda, "Decentring the Human? Toward a Post-Anthropocentric Standpoint Theory"; and Felicity Amaya Schaeffer, "Spirit Matters: Gloria Anzaldúa's Cosmic Becoming Across Human/Nonhuman Borderlands."

18. Haraway, however, did not use the term "posthuman" and even took issue with it. She clarifies this stance in her 2016 *Staying with the Trouble: Making Kin in the Chthulucene:* "I am a compostist, not a posthumanist. Critters—human and not—become-with each other, compose and decompose each other, in every scale and register of times and stuff in sympoietic tangling, in ecological evolutionary developmental earthly worlding and unworlding" (97). Despite her rejection of the term, her work influenced and continues to inspire those who identify as posthumanist feminist thinkers.

19. "Let Us Be the Healing of the Wound" was Anzaldúa's last published essay, which, as Keating explains, was written specifically for "a cross-border exploration of 9/11" book project, *One Wound for Another / Una Herida por Otra: Testimonios de Latin@s in the U.S. Through Cyberspace (11 Septiembre 2001–11 Marzo 2002)*, edited by Clare Lomas and Claire Joysmith. (*Gloria Anzaldúa Reader* 303). The essay is also published in the *Anzaldúa Reader* and *Light in the Dark: Luz en lo Oscuro* (the *Reader* version is cited in this note). In the first few paragraphs of the piece, Anzaldúa describes her intense personal reaction to watching the Twin Towers fall on television and the sadness she felt in the following weeks as she mourned the dead. Although much of the rest of the essay is a serious critique of the US government's handling of the response to the event, some might read her opening and comments, such as, "We are a nation in trauma, yes," as having the potential for reigniting or even reifying post–9/11 US nationalist identity and attitudes (304). Certainly, this is not what Anzaldúa intended to do; her critique of the George W. Bush administration is scathing, as she calls the attack on Afghanistan "barbarism," and she points a finger at US nationalism for the many other problems that intensified after 9/11, including racial profiling and violence against those who are or look Arab (305). The tone of the essay is, indeed, angry and oppositional, a harsh and sometimes raw and sweeping critique of US politicians and media. In the last pages of the essay, however, the content and tone become more poetic, elevated, and post-oppositional, as she explores potential for collective ("as world citizens") healing, calling on the images of Coyolxauhqui, Yoruba ocean goddess Yemayá, and nepantla states to aid in forward movement

(314). Keating reveals that Anzaldúa wanted to pull the essay and continue to revise it, but the editors and her friends convinced her to move forward with the publication (303). Although the essay is not as polished as most of her others, it does follow a conocimiento- or shamanic-like pattern consistent with her late works, which is discussed in chapter 4.

20. Testimonio in Latin American literature refers to a testimonial narrative of living under conditions of oppression.

21. According to Rick Dolphijn and Iris van der Tuin, Manuel DeLanda and Rosi Braidotti conceived (separately from each other) the term "new materialism" in the late 1990s (48). For book-length reading on new materialism and feminism, see, for example, Stacy Alaimo and Susan Hekman, *Material Feminisms*; Diana Coole and Samantha Frost, *New Materialisms: Ontology, Agency, and Politics*; and Dolphijn and van der Tuin, *New Materialism: Interviews and Cartographies*.

22. Indigenous feminist scholars Maile Arvin, Eve Tuck, and Angie Morrill employ the term "Native feminist theories" to emphasis that the field is "intellectually wide-reaching and ambitious," explaining that using this term instead of "identity-derived" terms like "Native feminist(s)" and "Native feminism(s)" leaves room for contributions to the field by those who do not identify as Native and by Natives who do not use the label "feminist" (11–12). Arvin, Tuck, and Morrill argue that Indigenous feminists are "central in leading and advancing" Indigenous feminist theories but also see the benefits of Native feminist theorizing having a "much wider audience and active engagement" than Indigenous feminists alone. These three authors contend that Native feminist theories point out the inextricable relationship between settler colonialism and heteropatriarchy and seek to center settler colonialism in women's and gender studies.

23. Maffie's definition of "teotl" stems from the work of several nineteenth-, twentieth-, and twenty-first-century scholars, including Elizabeth Boone, David Carrasco, R. H. Codrington, Arild Hvidtfeldt, Jorge Klor de Alva, Kay Read, and Richard Townsend.

24. Tuhiwai Smith recognizes that Christianity "attempted to destroy, then to appropriate, and then to claim" Indigenous spiritual concepts and points out that resisting this appropriation is critical to Indigenous struggles (78).

25. Soren C. Larsen and Jay T. Johnson offer practical examples of a concept similar to Watt's "Place-Thought" in their description of "the call of place" present in three different contemporary Indigenous communities and their activism to preserve landscapes from rivers to wetlands and ancestral villages to cemeteries. Larsen and Johnson's fieldwork includes the Cheslatta Carrier traditional territory in British Columbia, the Wakarusa Wetlands in northeastern Kansas, and the Waitangi Treaty Grounds in Aotearoa/New Zealand. See *Being Together in Place: Indigenous Coexistence in a More Than Human World*.

26. Maffie uses the term "Aztec" in place of the more accurate "Nahua" because of its "greater name recognition" and clarifies that the views of the Aztec, which refers specifically to the Nahuatl-speaking people who lived in Tenochtitlan at the

time of the conquest, were varied (2). Nahua philosophy and ritual are not specific to the Aztecs or the conquest period but more broadly refer to the worldview and practices of the largest Indigenous group in Mexico, the Nahua, a people of varied ethnicities. I make substantial reference to Maffie, an academic philosopher, in this section and throughout the text because his is the most exhaustive collection on Aztec/Nahua metaphysics to date, relying on numerous interdisciplinary sources across centuries. His interpretations draw on linguistic, literary, and graphic evidence and include full sections on objections and replies.

27. See Lucille N. Kaplan, "*Tonal* and *Nagual* in Coastal Oaxaca, Mexico." Also see Lisa Sousa, *The Woman Who Turned into a Jaguar and Other Narratives of Native Women in Archives of Colonial Mexico* (25–26).

28. Interpretations of the concept of tonal/tonalli vary, but all relate to a coessence or animal-soul, or pulse or inner heat (see Maffie 270–271), that has the potential to connect a person, in dream states, for example, to the sacred or sacred knowledges. See discussions in Alfredo López Austin, *Human Body and Ideology: Concepts of the Ancient Nahua*, and Saúl Millán, "The Domestication of Souls: A Comparative Approach to Mesoamerican Shamanism." In her explanation of the concept as an "irradiating vital force or internal sun," Patrisia Gonzales relies on Franciscan friar Bernardino de Sahagún's mentions of tonal/tonally (202). (Sahagún is discussed in chapter 2.)

29. See, for example, León-Portilla's comments on the *Manuscript of 1558* (108–110). His interpretations were gleaned from codices and narratives (written after the Conquest), including those of Nahua myths. His argument that the Aztecs were philosophers was initially met with resistance; however, his work ultimately established Aztec literature and thought as an academic discipline. In his 1956 *Aztec Thought and Culture* (translated into English in 1963), León-Portilla asserts that the Aztecs were dualists and, therefore, determines that they believed the divine was unknowable and "imperceptible" (102). Maffie, over a half-century later, carefully disputes this assertion. Anzaldúa also mentions in her notes on the nagual that she was influenced by the works of twentieth-century Mexican medical doctor, historian, and applied anthropologist Gonzalo Aguirre Beltrán, who focused on the history and concerns of African and Indigenous Mexicans (see "Notes from 1994").

30. The naguala can also take the self on other types of journeys that are isolating but ultimately productive, as in crossings into el cenote or even death, as described in chapter 4.

31. Because Anzaldúa doesn't provide an explanation for "ego" here, I interpret "ego" to mean the aspect of self that is absorbed in meeting its own individual needs and desires. Because Anzaldúa read psychoanalytic writers, especially Carl Jung, she could have also meant "ego" in this sense: the self-regulator, or that which adapts our desires to fit socially acceptable norms.

32. Scholarly discussions of Anzaldúa's use of the Nahuatl term "nepantla," meaning "middle" or "in between," are vast. Marcos de R. Antuna is critical of Anzaldúa's

use of the term and suggests that her definitions, which he pulls strictly from "now let us shift," are in conflict with recent interpretations (Maffie's, specifically) of Aztec worldview. Antuna and Maffie argue that nepantla is erroneously understood, back as far as León-Portilla's explanation, in terms of the Western concept, of liminality, coined by Arnold van Gennep and expanded on by Victor Turner. Maffie's study associates the term "nepantla" with other Nahuatl terms affiliated with the motion of weaving, including tlaxinepanoa ("to weave something"), tlaxinepanoliztli ("the act of weaving"), xinepanoa ("to weave something, like mats, fences, or something similar"), and tlaxinepanolli ("something woven") and sees nepantla as more of a well-ordered back-and-forth than an in-between—the creative process of teotl, the larger energy-in-motion of which everything is a part (359–360). Antuna doesn't completely reject Anzaldúa's definitions of nepantla as an "in-between" and "always-in-transition space" but says the term needs to be better grounded in Aztec philosophy as a result and process of teotl ("now let us shift" 544). In other words, transitional motions—nepantla—are a constant, not a temporary state, and we are always already in nepantla. Although I agree with Antuna that it is important to look at Anzaldúa's concept in relationship to its Indigenous foundations, I think a more thorough look at Anzaldúa's use of "nepantla" reveals consistencies with Maffie's. For example, in "Putting Coyolxauhqui Together," Anzaldúa refers to nepantla as an "interlacing" and "weaving" and "interweaving" motion (*Light in the Dark / Luz en lo Oscuro* 108). She is, indeed, mostly referring to thinking and writing here but also refers to symbols and metaphors becoming part of "sentient worlds" and "nepantla interlac[ing] those worlds into a coherent whole" (*Light in the Dark / Luz en lo Oscuro* 108). So, some ways in which Anzaldúa discusses nepantla seem not to be consistent with Maffie's interpretation, but in other ways they are. Scholars read Anzaldúa's interpretation of nepantla as similar to Maffie's, like Nancy Tuana and Charles Scott, who say, "We understand the in-between not as a static, unvarying state but as a situation of constant change, a dynamic weave of imporing, mutating, infusing process" ("Border *Arte* Philosophy" 75).

33. I thank Mariana Ortega, who encouraged my thinking in greater depth about the metaphysics of la naguala.

34. When Anzaldúa was first developing her theory of conocimiento, she used the metaphor of a train and "way stations" along the track to describe the journey of selfhood in relation and transformation. Way stations, in her usage, are periods of stability or stagnation. See her interview with Keating, "Making Choices," in Anzaldúa, *Interviews / Entrevistas* (167).

Chapter 2. "An Artist in the Sense of a Shaman"

The epigraph is from Anzaldúa's interview with Linda Smuckler in *Interviews / Entrevistas* (19).

1. Scholars who have sought to bring attention to the shamanism in Anzaldúa's work include David Carrasco and Robert Lint Sagarena in "The Religious Vision

of Gloria Anzaldúa: *Borderlands / La Frontera* as a Shamanic Space," Betsy Dahms in "Shamanic Urgency and Two-Way Movement as Writing Style in the Works of Gloria Anzaldúa," George Hartley in "The Curandera of Conquest: Gloria Anzaldúa's Decolonial Remedy" (addresses more specifically curanderismo), Leisa Kauffman in "'[A]nother set of teeth': Nahua Myth and the Authorizing of Writing in *Borderlands / La Frontera*," AnaLouise Keating in "Speculative Realism, Visionary Pragmatism, and Poet-Shamanic Aesthetics in Gloria Anzaldúa and Beyond," Sarah Ohmer in "Gloria E. Anzaldúa's Decolonizing Ritual de Conocimiento," and Felicity Schaeffer in "Spirit Matters: Gloria Anzaldúa's Cosmic Becoming Across Human/Nonhuman Borderlands."

2. Scholars have not settled on the origin of the term "shamanism"; some say it derives from the Tungus term "*šaman*," and others point to the Pali term "*samana*" and the Chinese term "*sha-men*" (Stutley 3). Interpretations of each of these terms vary but generally relate to one who is in tune with and moved by nature and spirits.

3. Although there is no one definition of animism, broadly conceived, it refers to the attribution of sentience to a wide range of beings and objects, such as plants, animals, weather processes, and places. Graham Harvey, editor of *The Handbook of Contemporary Animism*, is arguably best known for work on the concept. Recently, scholars, such as Darryl Wilkinson, are offering a critique of what's been called "new animism," or a resurgence of an interest in animism in light of contemporary environmental crises, asserting that interpretations associated with Indigeneity are flawed because they are filtered through Western humanism. For a review of scholarship on Indigenous animism and recent critique. See Wilkinson, "Is There Such a Thing as Animism?"

4. Social anthropologist Stephen Hugh-Jones makes the distinction between horizontal shamanism, affiliated with reciprocity and egalitarian relationships, and vertical shamanism, affiliated with hierarchical social structure. See "Shamans, Prophets, Priests, and Pastors."

5. See, for example Christian Roith, "Representations of Hands in the Florentine Codex by Bernardino de Sahagún (ca 1499–1590)."

6. Klein points to Donald Joralemon, "The Selling of the Shaman and the Problem of Informant Legitimacy" (1990); Alice B. Kehoe, "Eliade and Hultkrantz: The European Primitivism Tradition" (1996); and Jay Courtney Fikes, *Carlos Castaneda: Academic Opportunism and the Psychedelic Sixties* (1996), as important critiques of the academy's treatment of shamanism.

7. Furst's and others' rebuttals follow Klein et al.'s article "The Role of Shamanism in Mesoamerican Art: A Reassessment."

8. DiPietro explains that Abya Yala means "land of full maturity" in the language of the Kuna people and is used instead of the term "Latin American" by decolonial theorists and activists as an oppositional stance against settler colonialism and colonial histories (255). DiPietro explores what they call movilidades carnales, or carnal mobilities, which do not rely on trans identities (278). They

refer to three forms of bodily mobility: trans-monster, community of vitalities/ dekunafication, and *así* (278). The English translations of language from DiPietro's *Eidos* article, which is in Spanish, are based for the most part on an earlier unpublished English version of the piece the author shared with me. Since the early version does not line up precisely with the published version, some of the translations are mine.

9. DiPietro works with Anzaldúa's description in *Borderlands / La Frontera* of gazing into a mirror and seeing many faces, including "a stranger's face" in the "black obsidian mirror of the Nahuas" (Anzaldúa, *Borderlands / La Frontera* 66). DiPietro sees this passage as demonstrating the ongoing transitioning of decolonial subjectivity in ontological pluralism.

10. Peruvian sociologist Anibal Quijano coined the concept of "coloniality," more specifically, the "coloniality of power," to trace the relationship among capitalism, labor, and race rooted in the Spanish and Portuguese colonial periods of Latin America in which control over dominated groups includes control over personal, productive, and reproductive life, including ways of knowing and self-concept ("Coloniality of Power" 216). María Lugones later applied the concept of coloniality of power to the construction of gender as well.

Ohmer connects Mignolo's concept of colonial difference with the evolution of Anzaldúa's theorizing in "Gloria E. Anzaldúa's Decolonizing Ritual de Conocimiento." Mignolo speaks of being influenced by Anzaldúa in his theorizing of the colonial difference and border thinking. See his interview with Alvina Hoffman in "Interview with Walter Mignolo: Activism, Trajectory, and Key Concepts," *Critical Legal Thinking: Law and the Political*, January 23, 2017, criticallegalthinking.com.

11. I follow Édouard Glissant's sense of imaginary here, which refers to the ways in which a culture understands, constructs, and expresses its ideas of the world and reality.

12. Domino Perez's close reading here is of a section of Anzaldúa's 2001 interview with Irene Lara published in *EntreMundos / AmongWorlds: New Perspectives on Gloria Anzaldúa*. The full paragraph from Anzaldúa, from which the orange-tree metaphor is taken, is as follows: "New tribalism is a kind of mestizaje. Instead of somebody making you a hybrid without your control, you can choose. You can choose a little Buddhism, a little assertiveness, individuality, some Mexican views of the spirit world, something from blacks, something from Asians. I use the image of an orange tree, like an árbol de la vida, to illustrate. Some kinds have a very strong root and trunk system but don't put out as much of the fruit, so you graft them together to get a variety with better oranges" (42).

13. For an important critique of readings of mestizaje in *Borderlands / La Frontera* and the problematics of narratives of mestizaje in Chicano/a nationalism, see Nicole M. Guidotti-Hernández, *Unspeakable Violence: Remapping U.S. and Mexican National Imaginaries*.

14. María Lugones also uses the language of weaving and "worlds of sense" in

her influential essay "Playfulness, 'World'-Traveling, and Loving Perception," first published in 1987 in *Hypatia* and expanded on in her 2003 book, *Pilgrimages/Peregrinajes: Theorizing Coalition Against Multiple Oppressions*. Lugones's worlds of sense relate to intelligibility. A person can be different in different worlds, different in how they are seen within and how they experience a world, and visible, intelligible, and at ease in some and not in others. These overlapping worlds, or constructions of reality, that we travel in and out of and in between, are all part of the same society, but each has a different sociality. Importantly, Lugones's theorizing reveals the relationship between dominant and nondominate worlds of sense, where dominant ones render others illegible and powerless, while nondominate worlds can lend themselves to coalition and resistance. (Lugones gives credit to Audre Lorde for the term "nondominant," as chapter 3 discusses.) While Tuana and Scott use worlds of sense to refer specifically to worlds of "sensibilities," as they define it, their concern with how some "lifeways" are "rendered nonsense through dominant sense-making" and interest in "different ways of seeing or bodying forward . . . [and] new ways of thinking that resist and transform oppression," contain echoes of Lugones's work (78).

15. Translations are mine.

16. Translations are mine.

17. Ohmer is referring to Mignolo's *Local Histories / Global Design*, in which he describes how "the subaltern point of view" is the only one that recognizes the colonial difference and can prevent local histories and cultures from becoming part of the global design of coloniality.

18. Although she doesn't mention the name specifically, Anzaldúa is likely giving a nod here to Quetzalcoatl, or the feathered serpent deity, god of blowing winds and bringer of rain, as she also mentions a mirror in this passage, which is part of Quetzalcoatl's myth. In the myth, the smoking mirror represents fear of unknowns or death, what Wilson Harris refers to as "those veils that lay between oneself and the creator" (12). Quetzalcoatl transgresses the sky and earth, upper and lower worlds, and is "involved in bringing forth and begetting something new and it is thus involved in emergence and transformation" (Maffie 285). Anzaldúa's serpent that looks in the mirror is not feathered but recognizes the binary between the serpent and the eagle and seeks to subvert it: "Not many jump at the chance to confront the Shadow-Beast in the mirror without flinching at her lidless serpent eyes, her cold clammy moist hand dragging us underground, fangs bared and hissing. . . . How does one put feathers on this particular serpent?" (*Borderlands / La Frontera* 42). She closes that section, "But a few of us have been lucky—on the face of the Shadow-Beast we have seen not lust but tenderness; on its face we have uncovered the lie" (*Borderlands / La Frontera* 42). Anzaldúa invokes the feathered serpent and the clearing of the smoking mirror, in this section on homophobia, as an image for resisting traditional expectations of gender and desire and the taboos that surround queer desire.

Chapter 3. Connections with Arab American Feminism

The epigraphs are from Joanna Kadi [Joe Kadi], "Five Steps to Creating Culture," *Food for Our Grandmothers: Writings by Arab-American and Arab-Canadian Feminists* (233), and Gloria Anzaldúa, "Gestures of the Body," *Light in the Dark / Luz en lo Oscuro* (5), respectively.

1. Anzaldúa is speaking specifically here on behalf of the editors and authors of *this bridge we call home* about their project, but my reading of this comment is that this goal extends into her thinking about collective social-justice efforts overall.

2. I use the term "women" here as a social location and to engage with the body of writing that identifies itself as Arab American and/or Arab Canadian women's writing.

3. See Rabab Abdulhadi, Evelyn Alsultany, and Nadine Naber, *Arab and Arab American Feminisms: Gender, Violence, and Belonging.*

4. Joe Kadi was known as Joanna Kadi during the writing and publication of *Food.* Kadi now uses he/him/his pronouns but did not at the time of the writings to which I refer.

5. Carol Fadda-Conrey is exploring Diana Abu-Jaber's *Crescent: A Novel* in making these claims. She expands on this argument in *Contemporary Arab-American Literature.*

6. *This Bridge Called My Back* (2015), however, does include the new preface by Moraga in recognition of Arab women's experience and political contexts involving US involvement in the Middle East that have arisen since the original book was published in 1981.

7. The terms "Orientalist" and "Orientalism" as used in this chapter to refer to Edward Said's sense of the concept described in his foundational 1978 text by that name. In it he articulates how Western culture has created a hostile and inferior image of the East, a form of Eurocentric othering, one in which the West projects negative characteristics it denies exist among its own people onto the East.

8. For more on María Lugones's discussion of the logic of fusions and intersectionality, see "Radical Multiculturalism and Women of Color Feminisms." Recently, Emma D. Velez, in her critique of Lugones's discussion of intersectionality, says that Lugones "unwittingly distances herself from theories of intersectionality and, in so doing, also the intellectual labor of Black feminists" (392). Velez says that Lugones underplays how intersectionality and fusions work together simultaneously. As Lugones herself says, "We inhabit *both* the reality constructed categorically *and* the reality of fusion" (qtd. in Velez 396). Velez emphasizes that "it is only through space opened up by intersectionality that asking the question of coloniality of gender [referring to Lugones's theorizing] becomes possible" (399). I appreciate Velez's critique here. For this reason, I do not assert in my own

discussion of the concepts that the logic of fusions is a better tool of analysis than intersectionality. Both are crucial mechanisms.

9. Lugones borrows the term "nondominant" from Audre Lorde, who in "The Master's Tools Will Never Dismantle the Master's House" uses "nondominant" to link the experiences of groups of oppressed people while also recognizing that those experiences vary. Lorde says, "Within the interdependence of mutual (nondominant) differences lies that security which enables us to descend into the chaos of knowledge and return with true visions of our future, along with the concomitant power to effect those changes which can bring that future into being" ("Master's Tools" 111–112). I use this term later, following Lugones.

10. For a review of the history of Arab and Arab American feminisms, see Christina Najla LaRose, "Counter Fictions and Imaginary Topographies." In her history, LaRose traces the lack of attention to and stereotyping of Arab women in mainstream US feminisms. Also see the introduction to Abdulhadi, Alsultany, and Naber, *Arab and Arab American Feminisms*.

11. For an overview of the history of Arabs in in the United States and of Arab American literature and criticism, see Fadda-Conrey, *Contemporary Arab-American Literature: Transnational Reconfigurations of Citizenship and Belonging*. Steven Salaita in *Modern Arab American Fiction: A Reader's Guide* offers a review of Arab American fiction, specifically.

12. Scheherazade is also spelled Shahrazad.

13. In "The Generation of Postmemory," Marianna Hirsch raises German researcher Aleida Assman's distinction between intergenerational memory, which is passed down through families, and transgenerational memory, which is passed down through history and culture. My interest, like Al-Samman's, is in this broad, cultural phenomenon of transculture memory and subsequent trauma.

Al-Samman also points out how the tropes of the pre-Islamic (3500–3000 BCE) practice of wa'd al-banat (female infant burial) and al-maw'udah (the buried infant or wa'd al-banat's victim) function in contemporary diasporic Arab women's writing to preserve lost voices and communicate what she calls "anxiety of erasure."

14. Mai Al-Nakib brings Arab American experience into conversation with Gilles Deleuze and Baruch Spinoza and the concept of passive and active affects in "Disjunctive Synthesis: Deleuze and Arab Feminism." She identifies that scholarship in Arab feminism tends to fall under three approaches: Islamic (Muslim feminists claiming authority within Islam), status of women rights–based approaches, or those using Foucauldian lenses. She notes in this 2013 article that studies on sexuality and desire were on the rise but mostly overlooked at that point.

15. For more on second- and third-generation Arab Americans' complex treatment of gender roles, see Fadda-Conrey's chapter "Reimagining the Ancestral Arab Homeland" in *Contemporary Arab-American Literature*.

16. Karen Barad's term "intra-action" is briefly mentioned in chapter 1. In her theory of agential realism, Barad explains that individual entities or agents, human

and nonhuman, exist only in their process of relating to each other, blurring the familiar Western subject-object dichotomy. See *Meeting the Universe Halfway*.

17. Employing Mikhail Bakhtin's concept of the "chronotope," or writing that "materialize(s) time and space in literature," Carolina Núñez-Puente asserts that Anzaldúa contemplates three chronotopes or time-spaces in the poem, including domesticity, countryside, and borderland (144).

18. For more on differential consciousness, see Chela Sandoval, *Methodology of the Oppressed*. For Sandoval, differential consciousness is "self-consciously mobilized," as Jarmakani is doing here, and requires a fluid, expansive understanding of subjectivity and of categories of groups (Sandoval 58.8). Differential consciousness might take up binary-oppositional approaches, but it does so strategically. In this way, differential consciousness functions within and outside traditional, oppositional politics (such as, as she notes, separatism and supremacism).

19. Although one might argue that Shakir is romanticizing a Western image of Arab women here and is, therefore, inappropriately perpetuating a stereotype, one can also consider the use of this metaphor as an honoring of an Arab tradition and the variety of meanings found in it. In other words, the image itself, cupped hands moving in and out, though appropriated, symbolizes ambiguity of identity, not the essentializing of it. The metaphor shows up in the context of Shakir opening her mind to what her students had to teach her and to the nuances in their readings of texts and situations. Arab women's dance might be approached in this same way: as a text to be read and understood with respect to the culture in which it emerges. The cupped hands and their movement speak to a small detail that Western observers might overlook in a sweeping impression of the activity. Shakir demonstrates that she is willing to reserve judgment, even her expert one as a literature professor, in order to see what she has been missing: richness of meaning in Arab cultural contexts. Another way to read the metaphor is as satire, that Shakir's use of a Western image of Arab women is in a sense self-reflexive; she realizes and is admitting her shortcomings as an American and is mocking her own limited views. Shakir's use of self-reflexivity and intellectual humility is at the base of her approach to the memoir, so the latter reading is certainly a viable one.

Chapter 4. "Reaching Through the Wound to Connect"

The chapter subhead, "Reaching Through the Wound to Connect," is from "now let us shift" (571).

The epigraphs are from Gloria Anzaldúa, "Geographies of Selves," *Light in the Dark / Luz en lo Oscuro* (88); Ghada Samman, qtd. in Paula De Capua, *Al-Tamarrud wa-al-Iltizam fi Adab Ghada al Samman* (10) (I borrow this reference from Hanadi Al-Samman, *Anxiety of Erasure: Trauma, Authorship, and the Diaspora in Arab Women's Writings*); and adrienne maree brown, *Emergent Strategy: Shaping Strategy, Changing Worlds* (126), respectively.

1. Hirsch defines "postmemory" as "the experience of those who grow up dominated by narratives that preceded their birth, whose own belated stories are evacuated by the stories of the previous generation shaped by traumatic events that can be neither understood nor recreated" (*Family Frames* 22).

2. The concept of blood memory or cellular memory, also associated with some Native American cultures, takes the idea of extended trauma further by suggesting that there is knowledge of memories and experiences passed on genetically. The term "blood memory" was coined by Kiowa writer N. Scott Momaday in his novel *House Made of Dawn*. Within the last decade, scientists have found evidence for transgenerational epigenetic inheritance, including the evidence for the inheritance of the effects of trauma.

3. For more on decolonial coalition work, see, for example, the special issue Indigenous Art, Aesthetics, and Decolonial Struggle of *Decolonization: Indigeneity, Education, and Society*, vol. 3, no. 1, 2014, coedited with guest editor Jarrett Martineau, for essays and interviews on the relationship between Indigenous art and decoloniality.

4. See Cassie Premo Steele, *We Heal from Memory*, particularly her discussion "Toward a Definition of Collective Trauma" (42–44). Premo Steele examines in *Borderlands / La Frontera* Anzaldúa's concept of the border as a literal and figurative site of trauma and identifies a textual pattern of departures—deaths, losses, leavings—and returns—to origins, memory, to sites of trauma—that are consistent with the traumatic history of precolonial and colonial Mexico. According to Premo Steele, in returning to the past textually, Anzaldúa gains a sense of collective traumas faced and establishes a sense of "we" that allows the collective to move forward toward healing.

5. The concept of "aestheSis" is taken from Walter Mignolo and Rolando Vazquez's 2012 to 2014 work that is part of a larger project on modernity, coloniality, and decoloniality that began with conversations among South American and Caribbean scholars and intellectuals in 1998. The collective sees modern aestheTics as a part of coloniality that regulates, in the creating of canons and other forms of normativism, what is sensed as beautiful and tasteful. In other words, the aesthetic standards that were set in eighteenth-century Europe, particularly with Immanuel Kant's connecting of philosophy to aesthetics in *Observations on the Feeling of the Beautiful and Sublime* (1764) and *Critique of Judgment* (1790), were extended across the world, therefore colonizing the senses and perception. Mignolo and Vasquez take up the term "aesthesis," "an unelaborated elementary awareness of stimulation" to confront modern colonial aesthetics and to liberate or decolonize the senses ("Decolonial AestheSis"). AestheTics and AestheSis are stylized to emphasize their distinction and to assert that aestheSis seeks not to regulate the senses but to recognize the many ways of the senses and sensibilities that have been silenced.

6. Mignolo calls for a "locus of enunciation," or condition of expression that is outside coloniality and universalistic understandings of identity and experience.

Mignolo has been using the language of "enunciation" since the early 1990s. In a 1993 publication, he does so in reference to Anzaldúa's work: "Chicano writer Gloria Anzaldúa, for instance, has articulated a powerful alternative aesthetic and political hermeneutic by placing herself at the cross-road of three traditions (Spanish-American, Nahuatl, and Anglo-American) and by creating a locus of enunciation where different ways of knowing and individual and collective expression mingle" ("Colonial and Postcolonial Discourse" 129–130).

7. Drawing his definition of nepantla from multiple sources, including Diego Durán, Alonso de Molina, Frances Karttunen, and R. Joe Campbell, Maffie makes a distinction between nepantla and liminality in the vein of Victor Turner; to Maffie, nepantla is not "temporary nor exceptional" but is "the permanent condition of the cosmos, human existence, and indeed reality itself (teotl)" (363). In other words, the nepantla process is always in the making, always becoming, never static. To argue whether Anzaldúa's idea of nepantla is in line with Maffie's interpretations is beyond the scope and point of this chapter and text. Some aspects of Anzaldúa's theories of nepantla, especially with relationship to conocimiento, might seem to conflict with Maffie's point here, as conocimiento occurs in stages, and nepantla does, indeed, seem to be a temporary state or place in the grand process of knowing and transformation; however, Anzaldúa also makes it clear that all stages of conocimiento "occur concurrently" and "[y]ou're never only in one space," suggesting that her experiences and interpretations of nepantla and other Nahua concepts related to process metaphysics are consistent with much of the research findings and interpretations laid out by Maffie ("now let us shift" 545).

8. See Michael Winkelman's chapter 2 of *Shamanism: The Neural Ecology of Consciousness and Healing*, in which he reviews studies on the initiatory crisis for shamans (78–83). Also see Holger Kalweit's chapter on sickness and self-healing in *Dreamtime and Inner Space: The World of the Shaman*, and Patrisia Gonzales, "Ceremony of Return," in *Red Medicine: Traditional Indigenous Rites of Birthing and Healing*.

9. For example, in "Putting Coyolxauhqui Together," Anzaldúa describes listening to rain and staring at a painting of her naguala so that "la bruja naguala takes over" as she writes (250).

10. Despite this manuscript's title, "Esperando la Serpiente con Plumas," Anzaldúa makes reference to la serpiente only one time in the document and not at all to la serpiente con plumas (the feathered serpent or Quetzalcoatl), although the characteristics of Quetzalcoatl, such as its associations with the wind, malinalli (sweeping) motion-change, renewal and regeneration, are present. Anzaldúa says in the section "En Carne Viva," which AnaLouise Keating notes is part of "Dream of the Double-Faced Woman" in *La Serpiente*: "That hurricane inside her raging raging raging [*sic*] Gathering force in the inner terrain. She was afraid if it got out of control it would mow people down, would lay them flat. They might never get up from the floor. Her huge reservoir of anger. She could kill people with it. It is bursting at the seams—this dam. Shakti, the power of the female. The shadow her

'priestess' that black serpent, sexuality. La serpiente, the spirit in the body. That black thing, that bright thing. The thing that would save her, that would liberate her. Coatl" (25; [*sic*] in original). A discussion of Anzaldúa's references to the snake, serpent, feathered serpent, or víbora follow later in this chapter.

11. The trauma and healing of the trashed womb shows up in "La Prieta" as well, when Anzaldúa recounts her hysterectomy as "La Chingada ripped open, raped with the white man's wand," her "soul in one corner of the hospital ceiling" telling her to let go of "the fears and garbage from the past." With "La Muerte's scythe" she "cuts the umbilical cord" tying her to the past (203). This imagery in "La Prieta" recasts the excision of the womb as a cleansing, as limpia, as well.

12. Dahms acknowledges that Anzaldúa relies not only on shamanism but other Western sources in her understanding of "the wounded healer," mostly notably Carl Jung and James Hillman. Jung invokes the Chiron the Wounded Healer myth in Greek mythology in his own belief that healers must examine their own psychological ailments and heal and draw from them in their capacity to heal others.

13. Dahms's use of shaman as shapeshifter is consistent with Nahua/Aztec's ontological monism.

14. Garcia Lopez makes a distinction between "spirit" and "soul," saying that "spirit suggests the animating force of interconnection between all forms of existence," and "soul signifies the unique essence of a person, place, or thing" (2). I see her using "spirit" as something similar to "teotl." Anzaldúa seems to use the terms "spirit" and "soul" interchangeably. I don't see that she necessarily made a distinction between them.

15. I use the terms "serpent," "snake," and "víbora" interchangeably, as Anzaldúa does.

16. "El nagual in my house" is a subtitle in "Flights of the Imagination" (27).

17. Anzaldúa makes reference in "Flights of the Imagination" to James Hillman, working with his ideas in *The Dream and the Underworld* (1979).

18. In "Putting Coyolxauhqui Together" Anzaldúa explains that the Maya in Chichén Itzá put their valued belongings into el cenote for the god of rain (el dios de la lluvia), an offering for information about the year to come (244).

Conclusion

The epigraphs at the beginning of the chapter are from Pérez, *Eros Ideologies: Writings on Art, Spirituality, and the Decolonial* (2); and Anzaldúa, "Flights of the Imagination," *Light in the Dark/Luz en lo Oscuro* (44), respectively. The later epigraph is from Patrisse Khan-Cullors and Asha Bandele, *When They Call You a Terrorist* (253).

1. We know we can transform this world.

2. Clare uses the term "body-mind" to emphasize that he sees body and mind as one entity (xvi).

Works Cited

Abdelrazek, Amal Talaat. *Contemporary Arab American Women Writers: Hyphenated Identities and Border Crossings*. Cambria, 2007.

Abdulhadi, Rabab, Evelyn Alsultany, and Nadine Naber, editors. *Arab and Arab American Feminisms: Gender, Violence, and Belonging*. Syracuse UP, 2011.

Abu-Jaber, Diana. *Crescent: A Novel*. Norton, 2004.

———. *Life Without a Recipe: A Memoir*. Norton, 2016.

Ahmed, Sara. "Some Preliminary Remarks on the Founding Gestures of the 'New Materialism.'" *European Journal of Women's Studies*, vol. 15, no. 1, 2008, 23–39.

Alaimo, Stacy, and Susan Hekman, editors. *Material Feminisms*. Indiana UP, 2009.

Alarcón, Francisco X. *Snake Poems: An Aztec Invocation (Camino del Sol)*. U of Arizona P, 2019.

Alcoff, Linda. "The Unassimilated Theorist." *PMLA*, vol. 121, no. 1, 2006, 255–259.

Alessandri, Mariana. "Gloria Anzaldúa as Philosopher: The Early Years (1962–1987)." *Philosophy Compass*, 2020. https://doi.org/10.1111/phc3.12687.

———. "'Leave Out Kierquegard': Reading Gloria Anzaldúa Reading Kierkegaard." *El Mundo Zurdo 7: Selected Works from the 2018 Meeting of the Society for the Study of Gloria Anzaldúa*, edited by Sara A. Ramírez, Larissa M. Mercado-Lopez, and Sonia Saldívar-Hull. Aunt Lute, 2019, 21–27.

———. "Three Existentialist Readings of Gloria Anzaldúa's *Borderlands / La Frontera*." *Cuadernos de ALDEEU*, vol. 34, 2019, 117–135.

Alexander, M. Jaqui. *Pedagogies of Crossing: Meditations on Feminism, Sexual Politics, Memory, and the Sacred*. Duke UP, 2006.

Al-Nakib, Mai. "Disjunctive Synthesis: Deleuze and Arab Feminism." *Signs: Journal of Women in Culture and Society*, vol. 38, no. 2, 2013, 459–482.

Al-Samman, Hanadi. *Anxiety of Erasure: Trauma, Authorship, and the Diaspora in Arab Women's Writings*. Syracuse UP, 2015.

Anderson, Arthur J. O. "Sahagún in His Times." *Sixteenth-Century Mexico: The*

Work of Sahagún, edited by Munro S. Edmundson. U of New Mexico P, 1974. 17–25.

Antuna, Marcos de R. "What We Talk About When We Talk About Nepantla: Gloria Anzaldúa and the Queer Fruit of Aztec Philosophy." *Journal of Latinos and Education*, vol. 17, no. 2, 2018, 159–163.

Anzaldúa, Gloria. Anzaldúa, Gloria Evangelina, Papers, 1942–2004. Benson Latin American Collection, University of Texas at Austin.

——. Appendix 3. Anzaldúa, *Light in the Dark / Luz en lo Oscuro*, 176–179.

——. "Border Arte: Nepantla, el Lugar de la Frontera." Anzaldúa, *Gloria Anzaldúa Reader*, 176–186. (Citations are to the *Light in the Dark / Luz en lo Oscuro* edition.)

——. "Border Arte: Nepantla, el Lugar de la Frontera." Anzaldúa, *Light in the Dark / Luz en lo Oscuro*, 47–64. (Citations are to this edition.)

——. "Border Arte: Nepantla, el Lugar de la Frontera." *La Frontera / The Border: Art about the Mexico / United States Border Experience*. Museum of Contemporary Art, San Diego, 1993. 107–203. (Citations are to the *Light in the Dark / Luz en lo Oscuro* edition.)

——. *Borderlands / La Frontera: The New Mestiza*. 4th ed. Aunt Lute, 2012.

——. "Bridge, Drawbridge, Sandbar, or Island." Anzaldúa, *Gloria Anzaldúa Reader*, 140–156.

——. "El paisano is a bird of good omen." Anzaldúa, *Gloria Anzaldúa Reader*, 51–69.

——. "First draft, Esperando la Serpiente con Pluma / Waiting for the Feathered Serpent, 1981 July–1982 September." Folder 9. box 78, Nonfiction. Anzaldúa Papers.

——. "Flights of the Imagination." Anzaldúa, *Light in the Dark / Luz en lo Oscuro*, 23–46.

——. "Geographies of Selves." Anzaldúa, *Light in the Dark / Luz en lo Oscuro*, 65–94.

——. *The Gloria Anzaldúa Reader*, edited by AnaLouise Keating. Duke UP, 2009.

——. "Immaculate, Inviolate: *Como Ella*." Anzaldúa, *Borderlands / La Frontera*, 130–133.

——. *Interviews / Entrevistas*, edited by AnaLouise Keating. Routledge, 2000.

——. "La Prieta." Anzaldúa, *This Bridge Called My Back*, 198–209.

——. "Last Words? Spirit Journeys: An Interview with AnaLouise Keating (1998–1999)." Anzaldúa, *Interviews / Entrevistas*, 281–291.

——. "Lechuza. Dedicated to Alonso M. Perales." Folder 19, box 72. Anzaldúa Papers.

——. "Let Us Be the Healing of the Wound." Anzaldúa, *Light in the Dark / Luz en lo Oscuro*, 9–22. (Citations are to this edition.)

——. "Let Us Be the Healing of the Wound: The Coyolxauhqui Imperative—la Sombra y el Sueño." *One Wound for Another / Una Herda por Otra: Testimonios de Latin@s in the U.S. through Cyberspace (11 Septiembre 2001–11 Marzo 2002)*, edited by Clara Lomas and Claire Joysmith. Centro de Investigaciones Sobre América del Norte (CISAN), Universidad Nacional Autónoma de México (UNAM), 2003, 92–103. (Citations are to the *Light in the Dark / Luz en lo Oscuro*, edition.)

———. *Light in the Dark / Luz en lo Oscuro: Rewriting Identity, Spirituality, Reality*, edited by AnaLouise Keating. Duke UP, 2015.

———. "Making Choices: Writing, Spirituality, Sexuality, and the Political. An Interview with AnaLouise Keating (1991)." Anzaldúa, *Interviews / Entrevistas*, 151–176.

———. "Metaphors in the Tradition of the Shaman." Anzaldúa, *Gloria Anzaldúa Reader*, 121–123.

———. "My Nagual." "Suicide," manuscript draft, undated. Folder 11, box 73. Anzaldúa Papers.

———. "The New Mestiza Nation: A Multicultural Movement." Anzaldúa, *Gloria Anzaldúa Reader*, 203–216.

———. "Nopalitos." Anzaldúa, *Borderlands / La Frontera*, 134–135.

———. "Notes from 1994." Folder 6, box 107, Writing Notes, Series 3 Written Works. Anzaldúa Papers.

———. "now let us shift . . . the path to conocimiento . . . inner works, public acts." Anzaldúa, *Light in the Dark / Luz en lo Oscuro*, 117–159. (Citations are to *this bridge we call home* edition.)

———. "now let us shift . . . the path to conocimiento . . . inner works, public acts." Anzaldúa, *this bridge we call home*, 540–578. (Citations are to this edition.)

———. "'now let us shift,' writing notes, manuscript." Folder 3, box 49, Writing Notes, Series 3: Written Works. Anzaldúa Papers.

———. "Preface: Gestures of the Body—Escríbiendo para idear." Anzaldúa, *Light in the Dark / Luz en lo Oscuro*, 1–8.

———. "[Preface]: (Un)natural bridges, (Un)safe spaces." Anzaldúa, *Gloria Anzaldúa Reader*, 243–248.

———. "Preface: (Un)natural bridges, (Un)safe spaces." Anzaldúa, *this bridge we call home*, 1–5. (Citations are to this edition.)

———. *Prietita and the Ghost Woman / Prietita y la Llorona*. Children's Book, 2001.

———. "Puddles." *New Chicana/Chicano Writing*, edited by Charles Tatus. U of Arizona P, 1992. 1:43–45.

———. "Putting Coyolxauhqui Together: A Creative Process." Anzaldúa, *Light in the Dark / Luz en lo Oscuro*, 95–116. (Citations are to the 1999 edition.)

———. "Putting Coyolxauhqui Together: A Creative Process." *How We Work*, edited by Marla Morris, Mary Aswell Doll, and William F. Pinar. Lang, 1999. 241–261. (Citations are to this edition.)

———. "Quincentennial: From Victimhood to Active Resistance with Inés Hernández-Ávila y Gloria Anzaldúa (1991)." Anzaldúa, *Interviews / Entrevistas*, 177–194.

———. "Reading LP." Anzaldúa, *Gloria Anzaldúa Reader*, 250–273.

———. "Sleepwalkers." Folder 6, box 81, Fiction. Anzaldúa Papers.

———. "Speaking Across the Divide." Anzaldúa, *Gloria Anzaldúa Reader*, 282–294. Originally published in slightly different form in *Studies in American Indian Literatures*, Fall–Winter 2003.

———. "Speaking in Tongues: A Letter to Third World Women Writers." Anzaldúa, *Gloria Anzaldúa Reader*, 26–35.

———. *This Bridge Called My Back: Writings by Radical Women of Color*, edited by Cherríe Moraga and Gloria Anzaldúa. 4th ed. State U of New York P, 2015.

———. *this bridge we call home: radical vision for transformation*, edited by Gloria Anzaldúa and AnaLouise Keating. Routledge, 2002.

———. "Tlilli, Tlapalli / The Path of Red and Black Ink." Anzaldúa, *Borderlands / La Frontera*, 87–97.

———. "Toward a New Mestiza Rhetoric: Gloria Anzaldúa on Composition, Postcoloniality, and the Spiritual. An Interview with Andrea Lunsford (1996)." Anzaldúa, *Interviews / Entrevistas*, 251–280.

———. "Turning Points: An Interview with Linda Smucker (1982)." Anzaldúa, *Interviews / Entrevistas*, 17–70.

———. "Werejaguar." Folder 1, box 82, Fiction. Anzaldúa Papers.

———. "When I Write I Hover." Anzaldúa, *Gloria Anzaldúa Reader*, 238.

———. "Within the Crossroads: Lesbian/Feminist/Spiritual Development An Interview with Christine Weiland (1983)." Anzaldúa, *Interviews / Entrevistas*, 71–127.

Arvin, Maile, Eve Tuck, and Angie Morrill. "Decolonizing Feminism: Challenging Connections Between Settler Colonialism and Heteropatriarchy." *Feminist Formations*, vol. 25, no. 1, Spring 2013, 8–34.

Austin, Alfredo López. *Human Body and Ideology: Concepts of the Ancient Nahua*. U of Utah P, 1988.

Barad, Karen. *Meeting the Universe Halfway: Quantum Physics and the Entanglement of Matter and Meaning*. Duke UP, 2007.

———. "Meeting the Universe Half Way: Realism and Social Constructivism Without Contradiction." *Feminism, Science, and the Philosophy of Science*, edited by L. H. Nelson and J. Nelson. Kluwer, 1996, 161–194.

———. "Posthumanist Performativity: Toward an Understanding of How Matter Comes to Matter." *Signs*, vol. 28, no. 3, 2003, 801–831.

Bardenstein, Carol. "Beyond Univocal Baklava: Deconstructing Food as Ethnicity and the Ideology of Homeland in Diana Abu Jaber's *The Language of Baklava*." *Journal of Arabic Literature*, vol. 41, 2010, 160–179.

Bayardo, Sergio Javier Villaseñor. "El Nagualismo." *Revista Universidad de Guadalajara*, vol. 30, 2003–2004. http://www.cge.udg.mx/revistaudg/rug30/babel 30nagualismo.html. Accessed 17 Feb. 2020. Web address is no longer valid.

Bennett, Jane. *Vibrant Matter: A Political Ecology of Things*. Duke UP, 2010.

Bost, Suzanne. "Diabetes, Culture, and Food: Posthumanist Nutrition in the Gloria Anzaldúa Archive." *Rethinking Chicana/o Literature Through Food: Postnational*

Appetites, edited by Nieves Pascual Soler and Meredith E. Abarca. Palgrave Macmillan, 2013, 27–43.

——. *Encarnación: Illness and Body Politics in Chicana Feminist Literature*. Fordham UP, 2010.

——. "Life: The Gloria E. Anzaldúa Papers and Other-Than-Humanist Ontologies." *Shared Selves: Latinx Memoir and Ethical Alternatives to Humanism*. U of Illinois P, 2019, 102–138.

Braidotti, Rosi. *The Posthuman*. Polity, 2010.

Brinton, Daniel. *Nagualism: A Study in Native American Folk-Lore and History*. The Project Gutenberg EBook of Nagualism. Case Western Reserve University Preservation Department Digital Library, *Project Gutenberg*, 24 Aug. 2008. https://www.gutenberg.org/ebooks/26426. Accessed 20 Jan. 2020.

brown, adrienne maree. *Emergent Strategy: Shaping Change, Changing Worlds*. AK Press, 2017.

Caputi, Jane. "Shifting the Shapes of Things to Come: The Presence of the Future in the Philosophy of Gloria Anzaldúa." *EntreMundos / AmongWorlds: New Perspectives on Gloria E. Anzaldúa*, edited by AnaLouise Keating. Palgrave Macmillan, 2005, 183–193.

Carrasco, Davíd, and Roberto Lint Sagarena. "The Religious Vision of Gloria Anzaldúa: *Borderlands / La Frontera* as a Shamanic Space." *Mexican American Religions: Spirituality, Activism, and Culture*, edited by Gastón Espinosa and Mario T. García. Duke UP, 2008, 223–241.

Castaneda, Carlos. *Tales of Power*. Simon and Schuster, 1974.

Castillo, Debra A. "Anzaldúa and Transnational American Studies." *PMLA*, vol. 121, no. 1, 2006, 260–265.

Chávez-Eakle, Rosa Aurora. "The Relevance of Creativity in Education." *New Horizons*, Spring 2010. Web. Accessed 16 Oct. 2014.

Cisneros, Natalie. "Embodied Genealogies: Anzaldúa, Nietzsche, and Diverse Epistemic Practice." *Theories of the Flesh: Latinx and Latin American Feminisms, Transformation, and Resistance*, edited by Andrea J. Pitts, Mariana Ortega, and José Medina. Oxford UP, 2020, 199–215.

Clare, Eli. *Brilliant Imperfections: Grappling with Cure*. Duke UP, 2017.

Contreras, Shiela. "Literary Primitivism and 'the New Mestiza.'" *Interdisciplinary Literary Studies*, vol. 8, no. 1, Fall 2006, 49–71.

Coole, Diana, and Samantha Frost, editors. *New Materialisms: Ontology, Agency, and Politics*. Duke UP, 2010.

Dahms, Betsy. "Formalizing Fluidity: Queer Second Person Narration in Anzaldúa's 'Putting Coyolxauhqui Together' and 'now let us shift . . . the path of conocimiento . . . inner works, public acts.'" The Society for the Study of Gloria Anzaldúa, El Mundo Zurdo Conference, University of Texas San Antonio, 15 Nov. 2013.

——. "Shamanic Urgency and Two-Way Movement as Writing Style in the Works of Gloria Anzaldúa." *Letras Femeninas*, vol. 38, no. 2, 2012, 9–27.

Darraj, Susan Muaddi. "Third World, Third Wave Feminism(s): The Evolution of Arab American Feminism." *Catching a Wave: Reclaiming Feminism for the 21st Century*, edited by Rory Dicker and Alison Piepmeier. Northeastern UP, 2003, 188–205.

Darwich, Lynn, and Sirene Harb. "Violent Intersectionalities and Experiences of Marked Arabness in Randa Jarrar's *A Map of Home*." *Arab Studies Quarterly*, vol. 40, no. 4, Fall 2018, 300–318.

De Capua, Paula. *Al-Tamarrud wa-al-Iltizam fi Adab Ghada al Samman*. Translated by Nura al-Samman-Winkel. Dar al-Tali'ah, 1992.

Delgadillo, Theresa. *Spiritual Mestizaje: Religion, Gender, Race, and Nation in Contemporary Chicana Narrative*. Duke UP, 2011.

De Line, Sebastian. "All My/Our Relations: Can Posthumanism Be Decolonized?" *Open! Platform for Art, Culture, and the Public Domain*, 7 July 2016. https://onlineopen.org/all-my-our-relations. Accessed 1 Jan. 2021.

Deloria, Vine, Jr. "If You Think About It, You Will See That It Is True." *Spirit and Reason: The Vine Deloria Jr. Reader*, edited by Barbara Deloria, Kristen Foehner, and Sam Scinta. Fulcrum, 1999, 40–60.

DiPietro, Pedro Javier [PJ]. "Ni Humanos, Ni Animales, Ni Monstruos: La Decolonización del Cuerpo Transgénero." *Eidos*, vol. 34, 2020, 254–291.

Dolphijn, Rick, and Iris van der Tuin. *New Materialism: Interviews and Cartographies*. Open Humanities, 2012.

DuBois, Thomas A. *An Introduction to Shamanism*. Cambridge UP, 2009.

Elia, Nada. "The Burden of Representation: When Palestinians Speak Out." *Arab and Arab American Feminisms: Gender, Violence, and Belonging*, edited by Rabab Abdulhadi, Evelyn Alsultany, and Nadine Naber. Syracuse UP, 2011, 141–158.

Fadda-Conrey, Carol. "Arab American Literature in Ethnic Borderland: Cultural Intersections in Diana Abu-Jaber's *Crescent*." *MELUS* vol. 31, no. 4, 2006, 187–205.

———. *Contemporary Arab-American Literature: Transnational Reconfigurations of Citizenship and Belonging*. New York UP, 2014.

Ferrera-Balanquet, Raul Moarquech, and Miguel Rojas-Sotelo. "Decolonial AestheSis at the 11th Havana Biennial." "Decolonial AestheSis," "Periscope," *Social Text Online*, 15 July 2013. https://socialtextjournal.org/periscope.

Franklin, Sarah. "Rethinking Nature-Culture: An Anthropology and the New Genetics." *Anthropological Theory*, vol. 3, no. 1, 2003, 65–85.

Garcia Lopez, Christina. *Calling the Soul Back: Embodied Spirituality in Chicanx Narrative*. U of Arizona P, 2019.

Gaztambide-Fernández, Rubén. "Decolonial Options and Artistic/AestheSic Entanglements: An Interview with Walter Mignolo." *Decolonization: Indigeneity, Education and Society*, vol. 3, no. 1, 2014, 196–212.

Gonzales, Patrisia. *Red Medicine: Traditional Indigenous Rites of Birthing and Healing*. U of Arizona P, 2012.

Guidotti-Hernández, Nicole M. *Unspeakable Violence: Remapping U.S. and Mexican National Imaginaries*. Duke UP, 2011.

Gutierrez-Perez, Robert. "A Return to El Mundo Zurdo: Anzaldúan Approaches to Queer of Color Worldmaking and the Violence of Intersectional Heteronormativity." *Women's Studies in Communication*, vol. 43, no. 4, 2020, 384–399. https://doi.org/10.1080/07491409.2020.1824504.

Halaby, Laila. "Browner Shades of White." *Food for Our Grandmothers: Writings by Arab-American and Arab-Canadian Feminists*, edited by Joanna Kadi. South End, 1994, 204–205.

Haraway, Donna J. "A Cyborg Manifesto: Science, Technology, and Socialist Feminism in the Late Twentieth Century." *Simians, Cyborgs, and Women: The Reinvention of Nature*. Routledge, 1991, 149–156.

———. *Primate Visions: Gender, Race, and Nature in the World of Modern Science*. Routledge, 1989.

———. *Staying with the Trouble: Making Kin in the Chthulucene*. Duke UP, 2016.

Harris, Wilson. "Quetzalcoatl and the Smoking Mirror: Reflections on Originality and Tradition." *Review of Contemporary Fiction*, vol. 17, 1997, 12–23.

Hartley, George. "The Curandera of Conquest: Gloria Anzaldúa's Decolonial Remedy." *Aztlán: A Journal of Chicano Studies*, vol. 35, no. 1, Spring 2010, 135–161.

———. "'Matriz sin tumba': The Trash Goddess and the Healing Matrix of Gloria Anzaldúa's Reclaimed Womb." *MELUS*, vol. 35, no. 3, Fall 2010, 41–61.

Hartsock, Nancy. *The Feminist Standpoint Revisited and Other Essays*. Westview, 1998.

Henderson-Espinoza, Robyn. "The Borderlands of Subjectivity; The Subjectivity of the Borderlands: Nomadism, Mestizaje, and Bodies." The Society for the Study of Gloria Anzaldúa El Mundo Zurdo Conference, University of Texas, San Antonio, 15 Nov. 2013.

Hirsch, Marianne. *Family Frames: Photography, Narrative, and Postmemory*. Harvard UP, 1997.

———. "The Generation of Postmemory." *Poetics Today*, vol. 29, no. 1, Spring 2008, 103–128.

Hugh-Jones, Stephen. "Shamans, Prophets, Priests, and Pastors." *Shamanism, History, and the State*, edited by Nicholas Thomas and Caroline Humphreys. U of Michigan P, 1996, 32–75.

Idema, Tom Joeri. "Beyond Representationalism: Deleuze and Guattari, Feminist Posthumanism, and Gloria Anzaldúa's *Borderlands*." Master's thesis, Universiteit Utrecht, Netherlands, 2007. Open Access Theses and Dissertations, https://dspace.library.uu.nl/handle/1874/24999. Accessed 28 Oct. 2013.

Jarmakani, Amira. "Arab American Feminisms: Mobilizing the Politics of Invisibility." *Arab and Arab American Feminisms: Gender, Violence, and Belonging*, edited by Rabab Abdulhadi, Evelyn Alsultany, and Nadine Naber. Syracuse UP, 2011, 227–241.

———. *Imagining Arab Womanhood: The Cultural Mythology of Veils, Harems, and Belly Dancers in the U.S.* Palgrave Macmillan, 2008.

Kadi, Joanna [Joe Kadi]. "Five Steps to Creating Culture." Kadi, *Food for Our Grandmothers*, 231–237.

———, editor. *Food for Our Grandmothers: Writings by Arab-American and Arab-Canadian Feminists.* South End Press, 1994.

———. Introduction. Kadi, *Food for Our Grandmothers*, xiii–xx.

Kahf, Mohja. "My Grandmother Washes Her Feet in the Sink of the Bathroom at Sears." *E-mails from Scheherazad.* U of Florida P, 2003, 26–28.

Kalweit, Holger. *Dreamtime and Inner Space: The World of the Shaman.* Shambhala, 1984.

Kaplan, Lucille N. "*Tonal* and *Nagual* in Coastal Oaxaca, Mexico." *Journal of American Folklore*, vol. 69, no. 274, Oct.–Dec. 1956, 363–368.

Kauffman, Leisa. "'[A]nother set of teeth': Nahua Myth and the Authorizing of Writing in *Borderlands / La Frontera*." *MELUS*, vol. 38, no. 2, 2013, 57–70.

Keating, AnaLouise. "Editor's Introduction: Re-envisioning Coyolxauhqui, Decolonizing Reality: Anzaldúa's Twenty-First-Century Imperative." Anzaldúa, *Light in the Dark / Luz en lo Oscuro*, ix–xxxvii.

———, editor. *The Gloria Anzaldúa Reader.* Duke UP, 2009.

———. "Gloria Anzaldúa's Posthumanist Mythos." The Society for the Study of Gloria Anzaldúa, El Mundo Zurdo Conference, University of Texas San Antonio, 15 Nov. 2013.

———. "Introduction: Reading Gloria Anzaldúa, Reading Ourselves . . . Complex Intimacies, Intricate Connections." Anzaldúa, *Gloria Anzaldúa Reader*, 1–15.

———. "Mesoamerican Mythmaking as Queer(ed) Visionary Hermeneutics." *The Cambridge History of Gay and Lesbian Literature*, edited by E. L. McCallum and Mikko Tuhkanen. Cambridge UP, 2014, 529–547.

———. "Risking the Personal: An Introduction." Anzaldúa, *Interviews / Entrevistas*, 1–15.

———. "Speculative Realism, Visionary Pragmatism, and Poet-Shamanic Aesthetics in Gloria Anzaldúa and Beyond." *WSQ: Women's Studies Quarterly* vol. 40, nos. 3–4, 2012, 51–69.

———. *Transformation Now! Toward a Post-Oppositional Politics of Change.* U of Illinois P, 2013.

Keating, AnaLouise, and Kimberly Merenda. "Decentring the Human? Towards a Post-Anthropocentric Standpoint Theory." *Theoretical Practice (Prakyka Teoretyczna)*, vol. 10, 2013, 65–86.

Khan-Cullors, Patrisse, and asha bandele. *When They Call You a Terrorist: A Black Lives Matter Memoir.* St. Martin's, 2018.

Klein, Cecelia F., Eulogio Guzmán, Elisa C. Mandell, and Maya Stanfield-Mazzi. "The Role of Shamanism in Mesoamerican Art: A Reassessment." *Current Anthropology*, vol. 43, no. 3, June 2002, 383–419.

Koegeler-Abdi, Martina. "Shifting Subjectivities: Mestizas, Nepantleras, and Gloria Anzaldúa's Legacy." *MELUS*, vol. 38, no. 2, 2013, 71–88.

Lara, Irene. "Daughter of Coatlicue: An Interview with Gloria Anzaldúa." *EntreMundos / AmongWorlds: New Perspectives on Gloria Anzaldúa*, edited by AnaLouise Keating. Palgrave Macmillan, 2005, 41–56.

LaRose, Christina Najla. "Counter Fictions and Imaginary Topographies: Auto/ Biographical Methodologies, and the Construction of Group Knowledge in Evelyn Shakir's *Bint Arab: Arab and Arab American Women in the United States.*" *Journal of Women of the Middle East and the Islamic World*, vol. 12, 2014, 237–267.

Larsen, Soren C., and Jay T. Johnson. *Being Together in Place: Indigenous Coexistence in a More Than Human World*. U of Minnesota P, 2017.

Lavie, Smadar. "Staying Put: Crossing the Israel-Palestine Border with Gloria Anzaldúa." *Anthropology and Humanism*, vol. 36, no. 1, 2011, 101–121.

Lee, Jongsoo. *The Allure of Nezahualcoyotl: Pre-Hispanic History, Religion, and Nahua Poetics*. U of New Mexico P, 2008.

———. "Nezahualcoyotl and the Notion of Individual Authorship in Nahuatl Poetry." *Confluencia*, vol. 20, no. 1, Fall 2004, 73–84.

León-Portilla, Miguel. *Aztec Thought and Culture: A Study of the Ancient Nahuatl Mind*. 1956. Translated by Jack Emory Davis. U of Oklahoma P, 1963.

López, Tiffany Ana. "Reading Trauma and Violence in U.S. Latina/o Children's Literature." *Ethnic Literary Traditions in American Children's Literature*, edited by Michelle Pagni Stewart and Yvonne Atkinson. Palgrave Macmillan, 2009, 203–226.

Lorde, Audre. "The Master's Tools Will Never Dismantle the Master's House." *Sister Outsider: Essays and Speeches*. Crossing, 1984, 110–113.

Lugones, María. "On *Borderlands / La Frontera*: An Interpretative Essay." *Hypatia*, vol. 7, no. 4, 1992, 31–37.

———. "On Complex Communication." *Hypatia*, vol. 21, no. 3, Summer 2006, 75–85.

———. "Playfulness, 'World'-Traveling, and Loving Perception." *Hypatia*, vol. 2, no. 2, Summer 1987, 3–19.

———. "Radical Multiculturalism and Women of Color Feminisms." *Journal for Cultural and Religious Theory*, vol. 13, no. 1, 2014, 68–80.

Maffie, James. *Aztec Philosophy: Understanding a World in Motion*. UP of Colorado Boulder, 2014.

Martineau, Jarrett, and Eric Ritskes. "Fugitive Indigeneity: Reclaiming the Terrain of Decolonial Struggle Through Indigenous Art." *Decolonization: Indigeneity, Education, and Society*, vol. 3, no. 1, 2014, i–xii.

Martinez-Cruz, Paloma. *Women and Knowledge in Mesoamerica: From East L.A. to Anahuac*. U of Arizona P, 2011.

McMahon-Coleman, Kimberley, and Roslyn Weaver. *Werewolves and Other*

Works Cited   159

Shapeshifters in Popular Culture: A Thematic Analysis of Recent Depictions. McFarland, 2012.

Mignolo, Walter. "Colonial and Postcolonial Discourse: Cultural Critique or Academic Colonialism." *Latin American Research Review*, vol. 28, no. 3, 1994, 120–134.

———. *Local Histories / Global Designs: Coloniality, Subaltern Knowledges, and Border Thinking.* Princeton UP, 2000.

Mignolo, Walter D., and Catherine E. Walsh. *On Decoloniality: Concepts, Analytics, Praxis.* Duke UP, 2018.

Mignolo, Walter, and Rolando Vazquez. "Decolonial AestheSis: Colonial Wounds / Decolonial Healings." "Decolonial AestheSis," "Periscope," *Social Text Online*, 15 July 2013, https://socialtextjournal.org/periscope.

Millán, Saúl. "The Domestication of Souls: A Comparative Approach to Mesoamerican Shamanism." *Social Analysis*, vol. 63, no. 1, Spring 2019, 64–82.

Momaday, N. Scott. *House Made of Dawn.* Harper and Rowe, 1968.

Moraga, Cherríe. "La Journada: Preface, 1981." Anzaldúa, *This Bridge Called My Back*, xxxv–xlvii.

Moraga, Cherríe, and Gloria Anzaldúa, editors. Anzaldúa, *This Bridge Called My Back.*

Naber, Nadine. "Class Equality, Gender Justice, and Living in Harmony with Mother Earth: An Interview with Joe Kadi." *Arab and Arab American Feminisms: Gender, Violence, and Belonging*, edited by Rabab Abdulhadi, Evelyn Alsultany, and Nadine Naber. Syracuse UP, 2011, 242–247.

Núñez-Puente, Carolina. "Dialoguing with Anzaldúa's Poetry: 'Nopalitos' as a Poetic Reflection of Time-Space." *Geographies of Identity: Mapping, Crossing, and Transgressing Urban and Human Boundaries*, edited by Esther Álvarez López. Universidad de Alcalá, 2016, 143–151.

Ohmer, Sarah Soanirina. "Gloria E. Anzaldúa's Decolonizing Ritual de Conocimiento." *Confluencia*, vol. 26. no. 1, Fall 2010, 141–153.

———. *Re-membering Trauma in the Flesh: Literary and Performative Representations of Race and Gender in the Americas.* PhD dissertation. University of Pittsburgh. 2012. d-scholarship.pitt.edu.

Ortega, Mariana. *In-Between: Latina Feminist Phenomenology, Multiplicity, and the Self.* State U of New York P, 2016.

———. "Latina Feminism, Experience, and the Self." *Philosophy Compass*, vol. 10, no. 4, 2015, 244–254.

———. "Wounds of Self: Experience, Work, Image, and Identity." *Speculative Philosophy*, vol. 22, no. 4, 2008, 235–247.

Paccacerqua, Cynthia. "Gloria Anzaldúa's Affective Logic of Volverse Una." *Hypatia*, vol. 31, no. 2, 2016, 334–351.

Perez, Domino. "New Tribalism and Chicana/o Indigeneity in the Work of Gloria Anzaldúa." *The Oxford Handbook of Indigenous American Literature*, edited by James H. Cox and Daniel Heath Justice. Oxford UP, 2014, 489–502.

————. "Words, Worlds in Our Heads: Reclaiming La Llorona's Aztecan Antecedents in Gloria Anzaldúa's 'My Black Angelos.'" *Studies in American Indian Literatures*, series 2, vol. 15, nos. 3–4, Fall 2003 and Winter 2004, 51–63.

Pérez, Emma. "The Imaginary as Will to Feel: Beyond the Decolonial Turn in Chicanx/Latinx Feminism." *Aztlán: A Journal of Chicano Studies*, vol. 45, no. 1, Spring 2020, 243–256.

Pérez, Laura E. *Eros Ideologies: Writings on Art, Spirituality, and the Decolonial.* Duke UP, 2019.

Pitts, Andrea. "Gloria E. Anzaldúa's Autohistoria-teoría as an Epistemology of Self-Knowledge/Ignorance." *Hypatia*, vol. 31, no. 2, 2016, 352–369.

————. "Toward an Aesthetics of Race: Bridging the Writings of Gloria Anzaldúa and José Vasconcelos." *Inter-American Journal of Philosophy*, vol. 5, no. 1, 2014, 80–100.

Pitts Taylor, Victoria, editor. *Mattering: Feminism, Science, and Materialism.* New York UP, 2016.

Quijano, Aníbal. "Coloniality of Power and Eurocentrism in Latin America." *International Sociology*, vol. 15, no. 2, 2000, 215–232.

Rieff, David. "Professional Aztecs in Popular Culture." *New Perspectives Quarterly: NPQ*, vol. 8, no. 1, 1991, 42–46.

Roith, Christian. "Representations of Hands in the Florentine Codex by Bernardino de Sahagún (ca 1499–1590)." *Paedagogica Historica: International Journal of the History of Education*, vol. 54, nos. 1–2, Feb.–April 2018, 114–133.

Rose, Jacqueline. "On the 'Universality' of Madness: Bessie Head's *A Question of Power.*" *Critical Inquiry*, vol. 20, 1994, 401–418.

Rosiek, Jerry Lee, Jimmy Snyder, and Scott L. Pratt. "The New Materialisms and Indigenous Theories of Non-Human Agency: Making the Case for Respectful Anti-Colonial Engagement." *Qualitative Inquiry*, 2019, 1–16.

Saenz, Benjamin Alire. "In the Borderlands of Chicano Identity." *Border Theory: The Limits of Cultural Politics*, edited by Scott Michaelson and David E. Johnson. U of Minnesota P, 1997, 68–96.

"Sahagún, Bernardino de." *Oxford Encyclopedia of Mesoamerican Cultures: The Civilizations of Mexico and Central America*. Carrasco, Davíd, editor in chief. Oxford UP, 2006. Web. 1 Apr. 2020.

Said, Edward. *Orientalism*. Pantheon, 1978.

Salaita, Steven. *Modern Arab American Fiction: A Reader's Guide.* Syracuse UP, 2011.

Saliba, Therese. "Sittee (or Phantom Appearances of a Lebanese Grandmother)." Kadi, *Food for Our Grandmothers*, 7–17.

Sandoval, Chela. *Methodology of the Oppressed: Theory Out of Bounds.* U of Minnesota P, 2000.

Schaeffer, Felicity Amaya. "Spirit Matters: Gloria Anzaldúa's Cosmic Becoming Across Human/Nonhuman Borderlands." *Signs: Journal of Women in Culture and Society*, vol. 43, no. 4, 2018, 1005–1029. https://doi.org/10.1086/696630.

Schutte, Ofelia. "Crossroads and In-Between Spaces: A Meditation on Anzaldúa and Beyond." *Theories of the Flesh: Latinx and Latin American Feminisms, Transformation, and Resistance*, edited by Andrea J. Pitts, Mariana Ortega, and José Medina. Oxford UP, 2020, 131–142.

Shakir, Evelyn. *Bint Arab: Arab and Arab American Women in the United States*. Praeger, 1997.

———. *Teaching Arabs, Writing Self: Memoirs of an Arab-American Woman*. Olive Branch, 2014.

Sirvent, Roberto. "Interview with María Lugones." *American Philosophical Association Newsletter*, vol. 15, no. 2, Spring 2016, 3–4.

Sousa, Lisa. *The Woman Who Turned into a Jaguar and Other Narratives of Native Women in Archives of Colonial Mexico*. Stanford UP, 2017.

Steele, Cassie Premo. *We Heal from Memory: Sexton, Lorde, Anzaldúa, and the Poetry of Witness*. Palgrave Macmillan, 2001.

Sterling, Colin. "Critical Heritage and the Posthumanities: Problems and Prospects." *International Heritage Studies*, vol. 26, no. 11, 2020, 1029–1046.

Stutley, Margaret. *Shamanism: A Concise Introduction*. Routledge, 2003.

Tabuenca Córdoba, María-Socorro. "Viewing the Border: Perspectives from 'The Open Wound.'" *Discourse*, vol. 18, nos. 1–2, 1995–1996, 146–168.

Tatum, Charles M., editor. *New Chicana/Chicano Writing 1*. U of Arizona P, 1992.

Todd, Zoe. "An Indigenous Feminist's Take on the Ontological Turn: 'Ontology' Is Just Another Word for Colonialism." *Journal of Historical Sociology*, vol. 29, no. 1, 2016, 4–22.

Tuana, Nancy, and Charles Scott. "Border *Arte* Philosophy: Altogether Beyond Philosophy." *Journal of Speculative Philosophy*, vol. 32, no. 1, 2018, 70–91.

Tuhiwai Smith, Linda. *Decolonizing Methodologies: Research and Indigenous Peoples*. 2nd ed. Zed, 2012.

Velez, Emma D. "Decolonial Feminism at the Intersection: A Critical Reflection on the Relationship Between Decolonial Feminism and Intersectionality." *Journal of Speculative Philosophy*, vol. 33, no. 3, 2019, 390–406.

Vila, Pablo. "The Limits of American Border Theory." *Ethnography at the Border*, edited by Pablo Vila. U of Minnesota P, 2003, 306–341.

Watts, Vanessa. "Indigenous Place-Thought and Agency Amongst Humans and Non-Humans (First Woman and Sky Woman Go on a European World Tour!)." *Decolonization: Indigeneity, Education, and Society*, vol. 2, no. 1, 2013, 20–34.

Weasel, Lisa H. "Embodying Intersectionality: The Promise (and Peril) of Epigenetics for Feminist Science Studies." *Mattering: Feminism, Science, and Materialism*, edited by Victoria Pitts Taylor. New York UP, 2016, 104–121.

Wilkinson, Darryl. "Is There Such Thing As Animism?" *Journal of the American Academy of Religion*, vol. 85, no. 2, June 2017, 289–311.

Winkelman, Michael. *Shamanism: The Neural Ecology of Consciousness and Healing*. Bergin and Garvey, 2000.

Wolfe, Carey. *What Is Posthumanism?* U of Minnesota P, 2010.

Yamada, Mitsuye. "Asian Pacific American Women Feminism." Anzaldúa, *This Bridge Called My Back*, 68–73.

Zaytoun, Kelli. "A Focus on the 'I' in the 'I→We': Considering the Lived Experience of Self-in-Coalition in Active Subjectivity." *Speaking Face to Face: The Visionary Philosophy of María Lugones*, edited by Pedro DiPietro, Jennifer McWeeny, and Shireen Roshanravan. State U of New York P, 2019, 47–64.

———. "New Pathways Toward Understanding Self-in-Relation: Anzaldúan (Re)Visions for Developmental Psychology." *EntreMundos / AmongWorlds: New Perspectives on Gloria Anzaldúa*, edited by AnaLouise Keating. Palgrave Macmillan, 2005, 147–159.

———. "'Now Let Us Shift' the Subject: Tracing the Path and Posthumanist Implications of la Naguala/the Shapeshifter in the Works of Gloria Anzaldúa." *MELUS*, vol. 40, no. 4, Winter 2015, 69–88.

Subject Index

Abdelrazak, Amal Talaat, 72, 85–86
Abdulhadi, Rabab, 67
Abu-Jaber, Diana, 72, 80–84
Abya Yala, 47–48, 141–42n8
agency: in Arab American experience, 74, 77; in Indigenous / Nahua worldview, 20, 28–30, 36, 117; subjective and decolonial, 96, 97; in the writing process, 115, 117, 122. *See also* self / selfhood
Ahmed, Sara, 25–27
Alarcón, Francisco X., v
Alcoff, Linda Martín, 49–50
Alessandri, Mariana, 16–17, 28
Alexander, M. Jacqui, 3
Alsultany, Evelyn, 67
animism / new animism, 43, 141n3
Antuna, Marcos de R., 139–40n32
Anzaldúa, Gloria: as border artist, xiii–xiv, 9–10 (*see also* border arte); conocimiento theory and, 5, 63, 107–8, 136n14, 140n34; critiques of, xv, 5–6, 41, 49–53, 57–58; Indigeneity and mestizaje heritage, 9, 41–42, 51, 59–60, 109–10, 133–34n1; as "la Prieta," 59, 101–2, 104–5, 107, 109, 149n11; Mesoamerican mythology and, 4–5, 30–31, 41–42, 62; la naguala (shapeshifter) theory and, 6, 9–16, 57–59, 106, 135–36n11; new tribalism and, 49–53; as poet-shaman, 8, 26–27, 105–7, 127, 135n9, 140–41n1; racial and queer identity of, 53, 77–78, 101–2, 107, 147–48n6; second-person plural and, 115–16, 123; as shapeshifter, 35–37; spiritual activism / social justice work and, 1, 13–15, 47, 65–66, 108, 116, 118–19, 122; use of Nahua concepts, stories, and traditions, 57–59
Arab American / Arab Canadian feminist writers, 4, 65–94; Diana Abu-Jaber, 72, 80–84; Arab American literary scholarship and, 72–75; Carol Fadda-Conrey, 67, 68, 74, 80, 81; Amira Jarmakani, 73, 74, 87–88; Joe / Joanna Kadi, 6, 65–68, 70–72, 76–80, 86, 144n4; Mohja Kahf, 85–86; Therese Saliba, 79–80; Evelyn Shakir, 6, 68, 70, 72, 78–79, 91–92
el arrebato (rupture or fragmentation), 6, 16, 63–64, 96–97, 99
Aztecs. *See* Nahua people; Nahua philosophy; Nahuatl language

Bakhtin, Mikhail, 83, 146n17
Barad, Karen, 26–27, 145–46n16
Bardenstein, Carol, 80–81
Barthes, Roland, punctum and, 105–6
Bennett, Jane, 23, 24
Berlant, Lauren, 115
Bhabhai, Homi K., 72
blood memory / cellular memory, 115, 147n2
body-mind (Clare), 125–26, 149n2

border arte: concept of, 4, 5–6, 9–10, 31, 48, 122–23; as decolonial project, 53–61, 108–19, 124–29; shapeshifting subject and, 61–64; text as example of, 60–61
Bost, Suzanne, 21, 51–52
Braidotti, Rosi, 23, 24, 27
brown, adrienne maree, 7–8, 95–96, 127–28, 146
Butler, Octavia, 7–8, 128

Castaneda, Carlos, 31–32, 33–34
Castillo, Debra, 60
el cenote (unconscious reservoir of meaning), 7, 24, 63, 111–13, 118–19, 123–24, 139n30, 149n18
chamanería, 23–24, 30, 111
La Chingada / Malinche, 57–58, 74, 149n11
chronotopes (Bakhtin), 83, 146n17
Cihuacoatl ("Snake Woman"), 47, 124
Clare, Eli, 7–8, 124–29, 149n2
Coatlalopeuh / La Virgen de Guadalupe, 74, 124
Coatlicue (Serpent Skirt), 16, 57–60, 99, 102–3, 136n15
coloniality / coloniality of power, 3–4, 8, 70–71, 117–18, 142n10
conocimiento (path of inner work, public acts): as decolonizing mechanism, 61; la naguala in, 15, 41–42, 61, 63, 136n14, 140n34; as shamanic exercise, 41–42; stages of, 15–16, 37–39, 63–64; text as example of, 63–64
Contreras, Sheila, 57–58
Coyolxauhqui (Nahua moon goddess and Coatlicue's oldest daughter), 16, 59–60, 99, 136n15
creativity: motivated by wound or rupture, 96–111; la naguala (shapeshifter) as aspect of, xiii–xiv, 5, 135n7; in Nahua metaphysics, 135n6
critical witnessing (López), 116–17
curandera (healer), Anzaldúa as, 47, 102–3, 140–41n1
curanderismo (blending of Indigenous Mexican spiritual traditions and Catholicism developed in colonial Mexico), 47, 108

Dahms, Betsy, 35, 106–7
Darraj, Susan Muaddi, 74

Darwich, Lynn, 73–74
decoloniality: Anzaldúa and, 47–48, 52–61, 108–19; border arte as decolonial project, 53–61, 108–19, 124–29; decolonial aestheSis (Mignolo and Vazquez), 7, 96–97, 118, 147n5; defined, 134n2
Delgadillo, Theresa, 17
De Line, Sebastian, 20
desconocimiento (excessive dwelling on wounds), 39, 105, 108
differential / nonbinary form of oppositional consciousness (Sandoval), 87–88, 146n18
DiPietro, PJ, 47–48, 141–42nn8–9
DuBois, Thomas A., 43, 44–45

eagle / eagle symbolism, 62, 111–12, 135–36n11, 143n18
Elia, Nadia, 89–90
Eliade, Mircea, 45, 107
Enlightenment-based humanism: "connectionist" view of la naguala vs., 16, 36, 37, 80, 92–93; subjectivity of, 2–3, 26, 134–35n5
ensueños (fantasies/daydreams), 24, 77, 110, 125–26
Espino, Andy "Feo," xviii–xix

la facultad, 2, 18–19, 77, 132–33n4
Fadda-Conrey, Carol, 67, 68, 74, 80, 81
Franklin, Sarah, 25–26

Garcia Lopez, Christina, 108, 110
"generation after" trauma / postmemory (Hirsch), 7, 96, 145n13, 147n1
Gibran, Gibran Kahlil, 73
Gonzales, Patrisia, 7, 24–25, 28, 96, 99, 108, 139n28
Gutierrez-Perez, Robert, 107–8

Haddad Carol, 71–72
Halaby, Laila, 70
Haraway, Donna J., 21, 25–26, 137n18
Harb, Sirene, 73–74
Hartley, George, 47, 102–3, 108, 140–41n1
Hartsock, Nancy, 68
Heraclitus of Ephesus, 131n3
Hernández-Ávila, Inés ("Speaking Across the Divide," interview with Anzaldúa), 14–15, 49, 52, 58–59, 133–34n1, 136n12
Hirsch, Marianne, 7, 96, 145n13, 147n1

Hugh-Jones, Stephen, 141n4
Huitzilopochitli, 62, 136n15

Indigenismo, 52, 59

jaguar / jaguar symbolism, 13, 33, 39, 104, 111, 122, 135–36n11
Jarmakani, Amira, 73, 74, 87–88
Jarrar, Randa, 73–74

Kadi, Joanna (Joe Kadi), 6, 65–68, 70–72, 76–80, 86, 144n4
Kahf, Mohja, 85–86
Kauffman, Leisa, 42, 46–47, 52
Keating, AnaLouise, ix–xi; "Decen-tring the Human?" (with Merenda), 36–37; *The Gloria Anzaldúa Reader* (ed.), 51–52, 65–66, 89, 108; "Gloria Anzaldúa's Posthumanist Mythos," 22–23; *Light in the Dark* (ed.) (*see separate index of Anzaldúa works*); "Mesoamerican Mythmaking as Queer(ed) Visionary Hermeneutics," 31; on metaphysics of interconnected-ness, 14, 29–30; "Risking the Personal: An Introduction, *Interviews / Ent-revistas* (Anzaldúa), 14; "Speculative Realism, Visionary Pragmatism, and Poet-Shamanic Aesthetics in Gloria Anzaldúa and Beyond," 26–27, 31; *this bridge we call home: radical vision for transformation* (Anzaldúa and Keat-ing, eds.), 65–66, 89–90; on threshold theorizing, 2; *Transformation Now! Toward a Post-Oppositional Politics of Change*, 2–3, 69, 71, 84–94. *See also* post-oppositional consciousness (Keating)
Klein, Cecelia, 43–46
Koegeler-Abdi, Martina, 37–38

Lara, Irene, 142n12
LaRose, Christina Najla, 68, 78
Latina/x feminist phenomenology: la naguala in, 16–20; nature and charac-teristics of, 136n14
la lechuza (owl), 13, 39, 111, 122, 131
León-Portilla, Miguel, 34, 45, 139n29, 139–40n32
limpia / levantando la sombra / raising the shadow (cleansing ceremony), 102–3, 108, 110

La Llorona (Serpent Woman), 24, 47, 52, 95, 99, 113, 124
locus of enunciation (Mignolo), 113–14, 147–48n6
Lopez, Tiffany Ana, 116–17
Lorde, Audre, 91, 142–43n14, 145n9
Lugones, María, 9; language of weaving and worlds of sense, 142–43n14; logic of fusions and intersectionality, 70–71, 136n16, 144–45n8; logic of narrow identity, 93–94; logic of oppression, 71; "nondominant," as term and, 142–43n14, 145n9; "On Complex Commu-nication," 86, 93–94; "world-traveling" and, 18, 142–43n14

Maffie, James: masks in shamanic tradi-tions and, 33; nepantla and, 32–33, 98, 139–40n32, 148n7; review of Aztec philosophy, 32–34, 46, 48, 138–39n26, 139–40n32; teotl (self-generating life force or energy) and, 28, 32–33, 36, 138n23
Malinche / La Chingada, 57–58, 74, 149n11
Martineau, Jarrett, 117
Martinez-Cruz, Paloma, 24–25, 44
"Matriz sin tumba o 'el baño de la basura ajena'" ("Womb Without Tomb" or "The Bath of Other People's Trash," Anzaldúa), 102–3
Matus, Juan, 31–32, 33–34
McMahon-Cohen, Kimberley, 11–12
Merenda, Kimberly, 36–37
Mignolo, Walter: decolonial aestheSis (with Vazquez), 7, 96–97, 118, 147n5; on enunciation, 113–14, 147–48n6
Morales, Rosario, 88–89
El Mundo Zurdo (the left-handed world), 59–60, 102, 107

Naber, Nadine, 67
la naguala (shapeshifter): as aspect of conocimiento, 15, 41–42, 61, 63, 136n14, 140n34; border arte and, 61–64 (*see also* border arte); compassion in triggering transformation, 36–38, 86, 91, 103–4; "connectionist" view of, 36, 37, 80, 92–93; as creative process and practice, xiii–xiv, 5, 135n7; as decolonial writing practice, 111–19; as imaginal consciousness / dreaming

naguala, 15, 24, 76–77, 93–94, 110–12; and Indigenous metaphysics and practice, 28–37, 138n22; as nahual / nahualli (transformation / changing form), 134n3; nature of, 1–2, 4, 10–11, 134n2; new materialisms and, 10–11, 17, 25–27; in popular culture, 11–12; posthumanism and, 10–12, 20–25; shamanism and (see nagualismo / chamaneria; shamanism); storytelling as a shapeshifting activity, 7–8, 110–11, 123–29 (see also storytelling); as subjective practice, 5, 10–11, 37–40; in texts of Anzaldúa, 5, 9–16, 57–59, 86, 135–36n11; theoretical considerations in academic feminism, 16–30; as vehicle to el cenote, 7, 59, 63, 111–13, 118–19, 123–24; "writing from the wound" and, 7, 97–111, 113–19

nagualismo / chamaneria: conocimiento and, 15, 41–42, 61, 63, 136n14, 140n34 (see also conocimiento); as theory of subjectivity, 1, 132n2 (see also la naguala (shapeshifter)); "writing from the wound" as a shamanic act, 7, 97–111. See also shamanism

Nahua people: as "Aztec" people, 50–52, 138–39n26; defined, 133n5

Nahua philosophy: agency in Nahua worldview, 20, 28–30, 36, 117; Anzaldúa and, 50–52, 97–111; constitutional vs. materialist monism and, 32, 33, 48; creativity in, 135n6; León-Portilla on, 34, 45, 139–40n32, 139n29; Maffie on, 32–34, 46, 48, 138–39n26, 139–40n32; la naguala in, 19–20, 31–37, 62–63 (see also la naguala (shapeshifter)); nepantla in (see nepantla); pantheism, 32, 41, 58; process vs. substance metaphysics and, 32, 119

Nahuatl language, 10, 28, 45, 53

Native feminist theories, 28–30, 138n22

nepantla: Anzaldúa and, 2, 5, 37–38, 52–61, 92–93, 98, 139–40n32; creative process and, 98; defined, 16, 32–33, 132–33n4; liminality vs., 139–40n32, 148n7; Maffie and, 32–33, 98, 139–40n32, 148n7; in stage 2 of conocimiento, 16, 38–39; varying uses of term, 37–38, 139–40n32

new materialisms, 4, 10–11, 17–18, 25–27, 28, 46, 47–48, 138n21. See also posthumanism

new tribalism, 49–53

"nondominant," as term, 88, 142–43n14, 145n9

nos / otras (we / others): Anzaldúa and, 82, 91; concept of "Other," 43–46; defined, 132–33n4; Pitts and, 131–32n7

Nuñez-Puente, Carolina, 83

Ohmer, Sarah Soanirina, 41–42, 60–61, 105

Olmecs, 10, 44, 63, 105, 131n3

Orientalist / Orientalism (Said), 4, 67, 70–72, 74–75, 144n7

Ortega, Mariana: In-Between, 17–19, 76–77, 106, 136n16; Latina feminist phenomenology, 18, 136n16; "Wounds of Self," 105–6, 115

patalache / queer (woman-loving woman), 107

Perez, Domino, 50–52

Pérez, Emma, 114–15, 131n5

Pérez, Laura E., 17, 121

Pitts, Andrea J., 131–32n7

Place-Thought (Watts), 30, 138n25

politics of invisibility (Jarmakani), 87–88

posthumanism, 2–3, 4, 10–12; of Anzaldúa, 3, 5, 20–25, 47–48, 136–37n17; transhumanism vs., 21

postmemory / "generation after" trauma (Hirsch), 7, 96, 145n13, 147n1

post-oppositional consciousness (Keating), 3, 69–72, 84–94; Arab American feminist writers and, 65–66, 69, 71–72, 84–94; "Bridge" lessons overview and, 6, 69, 84–85; nature of, ix–x, 3; oppositional perspective and, 3, 87, 89–94; origins of "post-oppositionality," as term, 84

poststructuralism, 26–27

Pratt, Scott L., 20, 28, 30, 117

punctum, concept of (Barthes), 105–6

Quetzalcoatl (feathered serpent deity), 143n18, 148–49n10

Rieff, David, 49

Rihani, Ameen, 73

Ritskes, Eric, 117

Rosiek, Jerry Lee, 20, 28, 30, 117

Sahagún, Bernardino de, 45, 139n28
Said, Edward, 70–72, 74
Saliba, Therese, 79–80
Samman, Ghada, 95, 146
Sandoval, Chela, 87–88, 146n18
Schaeffer, Felicity Amaya, 17–18, 47,
   77–78, 122
Scheherazade trope, 74–75, 87
Scott, Charles, 55–56
self / selfhood: Enlightenment humanism and, 26; Ortega and, 17–19, 105–6,
   115; as terms, 1–2, 4–5, 132n3
serpent / snake symbolism: el cenote
   and, 105; Cihuacoatl ("Snake Woman"), 47, 124; Coatlicue, 16, 57–60,
   102–3, 136n15; "Entering into the Serpent" (Anzaldúa), 62–63, 105, 123–24,
   131n1; "Esperando la Serpiente con
   Pluma / Waiting for the Feathered
   Serpent" (Anzaldúa), 99–100, 109–11,
   148–49n10; female sexuality and,
   112–13; La Llorona (Serpent Woman),
   24, 47, 52, 95, 99, 113, 124; Quetzalcoatl
   (feathered serpent deity), 143n18, 148–
   49n10; la víbora (the nagual snake), 7,
   62–64, 100, 110–13, 124, 149n15
Shakir, Evelyn, 6, 68, 70, 72, 78–79, 91–92
shamanism: Anzaldúa as poet-shaman,
   8, 26–27, 105–7, 127, 135n9, 140–41n1;
   Castaneda and, 31–32, 33–34; conocimiento as shamanic exercise, 41–42;
   horizontal / vertical (Hugh-Jones), 44,
   141n4; importance to Anzaldúa, 42,
   46–48; Indigenous Studies and, 31–37,
   131n3, 133n6; Mesoamerican, 42–48;
   "Other" and, 43–46; primitivism and,
   43–46; shaman as "wounded healer,"
   105–7, 149n12; as term, 43, 135n9,
   141n2
shapeshifting: Anzaldúa as shapeshifter,
   35–37; as aspect of creativity, xiii–xiv,
   5, 135n7; border arte and, 61–64; in
   popular culture, 11–12; storytelling as,
   7–8, 110–11, 123–29; trauma and healing as (see trauma and healing). See
   also la naguala (shapeshifter)
Smith, Andrea, 102
Smith, Linda Tuhiwai, 29, 133n6
Smuckler, Linda, 13, 21–22, 34, 41, 140–41
Snyder, Jimmy, 20, 28, 30, 117
Sterling, Colin, 20

storytelling: as shapeshifting, 7–8, 110–11,
   123–29; in sharing interconnections,
   66–69
subjectivity: Anzaldúa and, 1–2, 4–5;
   conocimiento (path of inner work,
   public acts), 5, 37–38, 136n14, 140n34;
   of humanisms based in Enlightenment principles, 2–3, 26, 134–35n5; la
   naguala (shapeshifter) as subjective
   practice, 5, 10–11, 37–40; as term, 1–2,
   132n3. See also self / selfhood
susto / susto pasado (trauma / past trauma), 7, 63–64, 96

Taylor, Victoria Pitts, 26
teotl (self-generating life force or energy), 5, 97–98, 100; Maffie and, 28,
   32–33, 36, 138n23; nepantla, 32–33;
   text as participation in, 7
threshold theorizing (Keating), 2
Tlazolteotl (earth goddess of trash or
   filth), 57–58, 102–3
Todd, Zoe, 20
Toltec people, 59, 133n5
tonal / tonalli (tonally), 33–34, 139n28
trauma and healing, 95–119; Anzaldúa
   and creative praxis motivated by a
   "wound" or rupture, 96–111; el arrebato stage of conocimiento, 6, 16,
   63–64, 96–97, 99; ceremony of return
   (Gonzales), 99, 100, 108, 110; Coatlicue
   and (see Coatlicue (Serpent Skirt));
   connection between love and wounds,
   103–5; Coyolxauhqui and, 16, 59–60,
   99, 136n15; decolonial aestheSis (Mignolo and Vazquez) and the colonial
   wound, 7, 96–97, 118, 147n5; decolonial potential of trauma and writing,
   113–19; "generation after" trauma /
   postmemory (Hirsch), 7, 96, 145n13,
   147n1; la herida abierta, 47, 102; impact
   of the cure and, 124–27; limpia, 102–3,
   108, 110; El Mundo Zurdo (the left-
   handed world) and, 59–60, 102, 107;
   nepantla and (see nepantla); shaman
   as "wounded healer," 105–7, 149n12;
   susto / susto pasado (trauma / past
   trauma), 7, 63–64, 96; Tlazolteotl
   and, 57–58, 102–3; transgenerational
   epigenetic inheritance of trauma,
   4, 145n13, 147n2; "writing from the

wound" as a shamanic / decolonial act, 7, 108–10, 113–19. *See also* wounding
Tuana, Nancy, 55–56

vagina dentata (devouring mouth), 47, 123–24
Vazquez, Rolando, decolonial aestheSis (with Mignolo), 7, 96–97, 118, 147n5
la víbora (the nagual snake), 7, 62–64, 100, 110–13, 124, 149n15
La Virgen de Guadalupe / Coatlalopueh, 74, 124

Watts, Vanessa, 30, 138n25
Weasel, Lisa H., 26
Weaver, Roslyn, 11–12
weaving, language of, 32–33, 98, 139–40n32, 142–43n14

Weiland, Christine, 13, 23, 34, 36, 112–13
werejaguar, 13, 104, 122
Wolfe, Carey, 21
women-of-colors, as term, 132n1
wounding: Anzaldúa's creative practice and, 96–111; el arrebato, 6, 16, 63–64, 96–97, 99; blood imagery, 100–102; desconocimiento, 39, 105, 108; la herida abierta, 47, 102; shaman as "wounded healer," 105–7, 149n12; "writing from the wound" as a shamanic / decolonial act, 7, 108–10, 113–19. *See also* trauma and healing

Yamada, Mitsuye, 88
Yemayá, 137–38n19

Gloria Anzaldúa Works Index

"Border Arte: Nepantla, el Lugar de la Frontera," 52–61, 112

Borderlands / La Frontera: The New Mestiza: border as literal and figurative site of trauma, 147n4; critique of, 57–58; la facultad and, 18–19; la herida abierta ("open wound") of the US-Mexican border and, 47, 102; new tribalism and concept of mestizaje, 41–42, 51–52; psychological / sexual / spiritual borders and, xiv, 13–14; shapeshifting subject in, 61–64; spiritual mestizaje and, 17–18

"Bridge, Drawbridge, Sandbar, or Island," 13–14

"La Conciencia de la Mestiza," 64, 132

"Entering into the Serpent," 62–63, 105, 123–24, 131n1

"Esperando la Serpiente con Pluma / Waiting for the Feathered Serpent" (unpublished autobiography), 99–100, 109–11, 148–49n10

"Flights of the Imagination," 7, 23–24, 50, 55, 63, 111–13, 125–26, 135n7

Friends from the Other Side / Amigos del Otro Lado (children's book), 116

"Geographies of Selves," 36, 82, 146

Gloria Anzaldúa Reader, The (Keating, ed.), 51–52, 108; Preface: "(Un)natural bridges, (Un)safe spaces," 65–66, 89

"La Herencia de Coatlicue / The Coatlicue State," 46–47, 63

"How to Tame a Wild Tongue," 64

"Immaculate, Inviolate: *Como Ella*," 77–78, 80

"Last Words? Spirit Journeys: An Interview with AnaLouise Keating," 111, 135–36n11

"Lechuza, Dedicated to Alonso M. Perales," 13, 131, xiii

"Let Us Be the Healing of the Wound: The Coyolxauhqui Imperative," 22–23, 110, 137–38n19

Light in the Dark / Luz en lo Oscuro (edited by Keating), 7, 12, 29, 51–52, 107, 108, 125–26; "Editor's Introduction: Re-envisioning Coyolxauhqui, Decolonizing Reality," 14, 22, 24, 25, 31–32; "Preface: Gestures of the Body-Escríbiendo para idear," 65, 98, 110–11, 119, 122, 135n7, 144

"Making Choices: Writing, Spirituality, Sexuality, and the Political" (interview with AnaLouise Keating), 140n34

Making Face, Making Soul / Haciendo Caras (ed.), 72

"Metaphors in the Tradition of the Shaman," 54–55, 59, 127, 136n13
"My Black Angelos," 52
"My Nagual." "Suicide," 13

"The New Mestiza Nation: A Multicultural Movement," 12, 14
"Nopalitos," 83–84
"Notes from 1994," 139n29
"now let us shift . . . the path to conocimiento . . . inner works, public acts," 10, 12–16, 33–36, 37–40, 60–61, 99, 123, 124; language of "shifting" in, 4; nagualismo and, 1

"El paisano is a bird of good omen," 107
"La Prieta" (autohistoria / self history), 101–2, 104–5, 107, 109, 149n11
Prietita and the Ghost Woman / Prietita y la Llorona (children's book), 47
"Puddles," 13, 107
"Putting Coyolxauhqui Together: A Creative Process," 15, 107, 118–19, 134n4, 135–36n11, 139–40n32, 148n9, 149n18

"Quincentennial: From Victimhood to Active Resistance with Inés Hernández-Ávila y Gloria Anzaldúa," 15

"Reading LP," 29, 30

"Sleepwalkers," 104, 105, 107, 114
"Speaking Across the Divide," 14–15, 49, 52, 58–59, 133–34n1, 136n12

"Speaking in Tongues: A Letter to Third World Women Writers," 107, 115–16, 129

This Bridge Called My Back: Writings by Radical Women of Color (Moraga and Anzaldúa, eds.), 129, 144n6; and post-oppositionality among Arab American feminist writers, 65–66, 69, 71–72, 84–94; "La Prieta" (autohistoria / self-history), 101–2, 104–5, 107, 109, 149n11
this bridge we call home: radical vision for transformation (Anzaldúa and Keating, eds.), 65–66, 89–90
"Tlilli, Tlapali / The Path of Red and Black Ink," 64, 100, 102–3, 128
"Toward a New Mestiza Rhetoric: Gloria Anzaldúa on Composition, Poscoloniality, and the Spiritual. An Interview with Andrea Lunsford," 135–36n11
"Turning Points: An Interview with Linda Smuckler," 13, 21–22, 34, 41, 140–41

"Vigil of the Lizard," 13

"Werejaguar," 13, 104
"When I Write I Hover," 129
"Within the Crossroads: Lesbian/Feminist/Spiritual Development. An Interview with Christine Weiland," 13, 23, 34, 36, 112–13

KELLI D. ZAYTOUN is a professor and director of
graduate studies in the Department of English
Language and Literatures at Wright State University.

Transformations: Womanist, Feminist,
and Indigenous Studies

Teaching with Tenderness: Toward an Embodied Practice   *Becky Thompson*
Building Womanist Coalitions: Writing and Teaching in the Spirit of Love
    Edited by Gary L. Lemons
Hungry Translations: Relearning the World through Radical Vulnerability
    *Richa Nagar, in journeys with Sangtin Kisan Mazdoor Sangathan and
    Parakh Theatre*
Shared Selves: Latinx Memoir and Ethical Alternatives to Humanism
    Suzanne Bost
Shapeshifting Subjects: Gloria Anzaldúa's Naguala and Border Arte
    Kelli D. Zaytoun

The University of Illinois Press
is a founding member of the
Association of University Presses.

University of Illinois Press
1325 South Oak Street
Champaign, IL 61820-6903
www.press.uillinois.edu